FOUNDATIONS OF SECONDARY EDUCATION-HISTORICAL, COMPARATIVE, AND CURRICULAR

by

Donald F. Popham
California State College
Long Beach, California

426 South Sixth Street • Minneapolis, Minn. 55415

Copyright © 1969 by Burgess Publishing Company
All rights reserved. Printed in the United States of America.
Library of Congress Catalog Card Number 77-81940
Standard Book Number 8087-1626-3

PREFACE

This text is written for the course in Secondary Education or Principles and Curriculum of Secondary Education usually required in the preparation of teachers for American secondary schools. It presents the subjects of the history and philosophy of secondary education, comparative European secondary school systems, and the curriculum of American secondary schools. These are areas of subject matter often taught and/or referred to in such courses. This book is also designed as a source of information and ideas for all those who are interested in or who plan to work in secondary schools.

The first four chapters of the text present a history of Western secondary education from primitive and ancient times through the nineteenth century. The purpose in preparing these chapters is based on a belief that an institution may be defined as its career in time. While an institution unlike an organism has no exact moment of birth nor instant of death it does span a period of time. Understanding what an institution is may be assisted by inquiry into what it has been. Institutions, like people, are creatures of their past. The secondary school is one of the oldest formal institutions of Western civilization. It predates the nation-state system. Only the Christian church is older. Only when one appreciates the role played by the secondary school in the social order can one begin to formulate an answer to the question: What is secondary education?

American educators have become increasingly interested in educational developments in other nations. One cannot appreciate the uniqueness of the American secondary school until he knows what secondary schools are like elsewhere. Most systems of secondary education in the Western world and many in the Eastern world as well are based on the national systems developed by Great Britain, France, Germany, and Russia since the beginning of the nineteenth century. Accordingly, chapters five and six deal with the current systems of secondary education in these four European countries.

Chapters seven through twelve explore the growth and development of the secondary school in the American social order. It is only through a more complete understanding of the evolution of the comprehensive high school that the prospective teacher can acquire the perspective necessary to understand the achievements and shortcomings of American secondary education. These chapters also describe and explain the decentralized and democratic character of the administration of public education in the United States. The responsibilities of each level of government—federal, state, and local—are carefully delineated.

The curriculum of the American secondary school is discussed in chapters thirteen through nineteen. These chapters survey the several branches of knowledge taught in the secondary school. The history of each subject area, the content of each subject area, and the trends in each of these subject areas are described.

The final chapter is a look into the future. Here the author discusses the possible curricular routes the American secondary school may follow in the twenty-first century. He points out the social and educational reasons for each, and then presents his ideas as to what he thinks should be the course for the secondary school in the third millenium A.D.

The author is indebted to many publishers for permission to extract statements from their copyrighted publications. In each case where materials have been quoted, acknowledgement is made. It is more difficult to acknowledge the influence that has come by absorption through the reading and rereading of others' writings, and through personal contact.

The author is also indebted to many people for their help to him in preparing this book. Particularly, he would like to express his gratitude to his father, Harold E. Popham, Esq. of Denver, Colorado for his careful reading of the contents and helpful suggestions. Professor Vincent C. Di Pasquale of Moorhead State College, Moorhead, Minnesota made a detailed review of the manuscript, and his suggestions, sometimes critical though always helpful, are gratefully acknowledged and appreciated. Miss R. Monteen Manning and Mr. Sidney B. Simms of the Education and Curriculum Library of California State College at Long Beach were especially helpful in the preparation of the manuscript. The author wishes to express a very deep appreciation to Mrs. Eva Miner, formerly of Washington, D. C., for her diligent labors at the typewriter in typing and retyping the manuscript. Finally, a word of thanks is due to the many colleagues and friends of the author who have followed closely the preparation of this text. Their encouragement and understanding will never be forgotten.

Donald F. Popham

February, 1969

TABLE OF CONTENTS

                                                                                Page

PREFACE i

CHAPTER

   I.   EDUCATION IN THE ANCIENT WORLD 1
          Education in Primitive Societies 1
          Conclusion 2
          Education Among the Greeks 3
          Hellenistic Education 11
          Conclusion 14
          Education Among the Romans 14
          Conclusion 20

   II.   EDUCATION IN THE MIDDLE AGES 24
          Education in the Early Medieval Period 24
          Education in the Late Middle Ages 29
          Conclusion 34

   III. EDUCATION DURING THE RENAISSANCE
        AND REFORMATION 37
          Education During the Renaissance 37
          Education During the Reformation 43
          Education During the Counter-Reformation 49
          Conclusion 52

   IV. EDUCATION FROM THE REFORMATION
        THROUGH THE NINETEENTH CENTURY 55
          Development of Educational Philosophy 55
          Development of National Systems of Education ... 66
          Conclusion 75

CHAPTER		Page

V.	COMPARATIVE EUROPEAN SECONDARY SCHOOL SYSTEMS: GREAT BRITAIN AND FRANCE	79
	England and Wales	79
	France	91
	Conclusion	100

VI.	COMPARATIVE EUROPEAN SECONDARY SCHOOL SYSTEMS: GERMANY AND THE SOVIET UNION	104
	West Germany	104
	Soviet Union	112
	Conclusion	118

VII.	AMERICAN SECONDARY SCHOOLS: BEGINNINGS	123
	Introduction: The European Heritage	123
	The Grammar School in America	124
	Colonial Legislation in New England	125
	Educational Developments Outside New England	126
	Period of the Academies	127
	Early American Educational Reformers	129
	Conclusion	133

VIII.	THE MOVEMENT TO ESTABLISH HIGH SCHOOLS	136
	Introduction	136
	The Boston English Classical High School	136
	Massachusetts Law of 1827	137
	First Compulsory School Law	138
	Kalamazoo Case and Decision	139
	Nature of, Curriculum, and Practices of the Early American High School	140
	Committee of Ten	141
	Committee on College Entrance Requirements	143
	Educational Reformers of the Nineteenth and Early Twentieth Centuries	143
	Conclusion	148

CHAPTER		Page
IX.	TWENTIETH CENTURY DEVELOPMENTS IN AMERICAN SECONDARY EDUCATION	151
	The Junior High School	151
	The Junior College	152
	Commission on the Reorganization of Secondary Education	154
	Smith-Hughes Act	156
	The Eight-Year Study	157
	Educational Policies Commission	158
	Commission on Life Adjustment Education	160
	School Desegregation Decision	161
	White House Conference on Education, 1955	164
	National Defense Education Act, 1958	165
	The Public Prayer Decision of 1962	165
	White House Conference on Education, 1965	166
	The 1965 Elementary-Secondary Education Act	167
	Conclusion	167
X.	THE STRUCTURE OF SECONDARY EDUCATION IN THE UNITED STATES	171
	The Graded System	171
	Development of the Junior High School	172
	The Six-Year High School	174
	The Eight-Year Secondary School Program	175
	Associations of Colleges and Secondary Schools	175
	The Conant Reports on the High School	178
	Conclusion	181
XI.	ADMINISTRATION OF SECONDARY EDUCATION: ROLE OF THE FEDERAL GOVERNMENT	184
	Growth of Federal Aid to Education	184
	Major Programs of Federal Aid Since World War II	187
	The 1965 Elementary-Secondary and Higher Education Acts	191
	The United States Office of Education	193
	Federal Operation of Educational Institutions	195
	Education and Constitutional Rights	195
	Conclusion	198

CHAPTER	Page

- XII. ADMINISTRATION OF SECONDARY EDUCATION: ROLE OF THE STATES AND LOCAL COMMUNITIES 201
  - Role of the States 201
  - Role of the Local School Districts 206
  - Role of the Counties........................210
  - Public School Systems of the United States (Statistics) 211
  - Conclusion 212

- XIII. DEVELOPMENT OF THE SECONDARY SCHOOL CURRICULUM 215
  - Origin of the Curriculum 215
  - Evolution of the Humanities 216
  - The Progress of Science in the Curriculum 217
  - Introduction of Modern Languages and History into the Curriculum 218
  - Reappearance of Physical Education in the Curriculum 218
  - Introduction of Vocational Education into the Curriculum 219
  - Role of the Fine Arts in the Curriculum 220
  - Building the Modern Curriculum 220
  - Organization of the Modern Curriculum 221
  - Conclusion 223

- XIV. THE PLACE OF THE HUMANITIES IN THE SECONDARY SCHOOL CURRICULUM 225
  - The English Language Arts 225
  - The Foreign Language Arts 230
  - Speech and Journalism 233
  - Conclusion 235

- XV. THE PLACE OF HISTORY AND THE SOCIAL SCIENCES IN THE SECONDARY SCHOOL CURRICULUM 238
  - Introduction: The Social Sciences and the Social Studies 238
  - History and the Social Studies Curriculum 239
  - Anthropology in the Social Studies Curriculum ...242
  - Geography and the Social Studies Curriculum 243

CHAPTER		Page
	Economics in the Social Studies Curriculum	245
	Political Science and the Social Studies Curriculum	249
	Sociology in the Social Studies Curriculum	252
	Conclusion	253
XVI.	THE PLACE OF MATHEMATICS AND SCIENCE IN THE SECONDARY SCHOOL CURRICULUM	257
	Mathematics	257
	The Biological and Physical Sciences	260
	Conclusion	267
XVII.	THE PLACE OF THE FINE ARTS AND THE DRAMATIC ARTS IN THE SECONDARY SCHOOL CURRICULUM	269
	The Fine Arts	269
	Dramatic Arts	273
	Conclusion	274
XVIII.	THE PLACE OF PHYSICAL EDUCATION AND HEALTH AND SAFETY EDUCATION IN THE SECONDARY SCHOOL CURRICULUM	275
	Physical Education	275
	Health and Safety Education	277
	Conclusion	279
XIX.	THE PLACE OF VOCATIONAL TRAINING AND THE PRACTICAL ARTS IN THE SECONDARY SCHOOL CURRICULUM	281
	Introduction: Definition of Terms	281
	Vocational Training	282
	The Practical Arts	288
	Conclusion	293
XX.	THE FUTURE OF SECONDARY EDUCATION	295
	The Modern Industrial State and Education	295
	Liberal Education Versus Vocational Education	298
	Trends in Secondary Education	303
	Conclusion	307
NAME INDEX		311
SUBJECT INDEX		314

Chapter I
EDUCATION IN THE ANCIENT WORLD
Education in Primitive Societies

Introduction

Formal education is often thought to be a characteristic of civilized or advanced societies, but education, both formal and informal, is as old as man himself. Educational practices of so-called primitive societies have been uncovered through research by anthropologists. A primitive society is the earliest state of human social development. Primitive peoples are pre-literate, stone-age men. Primitive peoples inhabited the continent of Europe some 25,000 years ago. The North American Indian was a primitive at the time of the discovery of the New World. Today primitive groups still can be found in the jungles of central Africa, the interior forest lands of South America, and on the island groups in the far South Pacific Ocean area, as well as in the hinterlands of the Australian continent. Life in primitive societies is relatively simple, and social organization is tribal rather than political. Primitive arts are not highly specialized, and the sciences are nonexistent. Life in general is governed by superstition and custom.

Educational Aims

Education in primitive societies has both practical and theoretical aspects. Practical educational goals include the following: (1) those practices that enable the individual to satisfy his immediate wants for food, shelter, and protection; (2) those practices that enable the individual to live peaceably with his fellow tribal members; and (3) those practices that enable him to give expression to his artistic and other creative impulses. Theoretical education is concerned with the speculative and religious aspects of life. The primitive lives in a world he believes to be inhabited by demons, spirits, and other supernatural powers. Religious education consists largely of ceremonies, dances, processions, and even sacrifices aimed at a propitiation or conciliation of those powers thought to be superior to man and that direct and control the course of nature and human life. The aims of theoretical and religious education, then, are to enable the individual to cope successfully with the supernatural and to make him feel at home in the world of nature. The prime educational objective of primitive man is to inculcate the unchanging practices of his culture that have proved successful.

Educational Methods

In many primitive societies formal education is, in part, carried out in the form of initiation ceremonies of adolescents by special classes of people that may be elders, priests, wizards, or shamans. Among the aborigines of Australia and the primitives of New Guinea puberty rites often include harsh and cruel tests of physical endurance, obedience, and self-control. An essential initiatory rite among some of these tribes when the boy reaches puberty is the painful act of circumcision. After its removal from the penis of the lad, the foreskin may be thrown into a river, buried in the ground, hidden within some object, or even eaten, according to the custom of the particular tribe.[1] It is not unusual for novices to go into a period of seclusion lasting from ten to thirty days following the rite of circumcision. During this time the young men are subjected to additional hardships that may include beatings, starvation, purification by emetics, and scrubbing with sand. Another initiatory rite is the practice of knocking out teeth of the adolescent lad.[2] The boy who fails to undergo these tests without complaining is not considered worthy of full tribal membership.

During adolescence there is a differentiation in the types of tasks performed by boys and girls. Among girls there is little specialization except in the case of those who will be trained in medicine and midwifery. The emphasis of education for girls is upon home and family duties. Pottery making, the gathering of fruits, vegetables, cereals, nuts, and the care of the very young constitute in part the work of the women of the tribe. Initiatory ceremonies are usually held as well for girls at adolescence.

Conclusion

In primitive societies which are relatively homogeneous, where there is little division of labor and a simple system of social stratification, education is largely a process by which the individual is inducted into his cultural inheritance. Yet even in such societies there is specialization and differentiation, and a period of training for the performance of certain specialized roles. A leader may be a priest who has mastered secret cults or he may be a person who has demonstrated proficiency in some craft.

About primitive societies it may be safe to generalize and say that there are no classes or groups which receive preferential treatment by virtue of birth or wealth; there are no special strata from which people are recruited to high positions.

Education Among the Greeks

Introduction

The study of education in ancient Greece has meaning and relevance for modern man. First, Greek history provides the oldest example of the evolution of a people from a semiprimitive and semifeudal culture to a highly developed and, in many respects, a democratic culture. Second, the Greeks are the intellectual ancestors of Western civilization, and were responsible for education as it is known in Europe and the United States.

Greek civilization represents the flowering of the spirit of the ancient world. The Greek genius was the result of a number of personal characteristics of the Greek people. First, the intense competitive spirit of the Greeks drove them to excel in everything they undertook. Second, their discriminating and highly developed senses made possible the extraordinary Grecian development of art, literature, and science. Third, Greek love of beauty and orderliness was expressed by the emphasis they placed on the harmonious development of both the mental and physical aspects of living. Fourth, Greek intelligence was reflected in their passion for clarity in ideas.

Homeric Period

Documentary evidence for the origins of Greek education in the period before the eighth century B.C. is supplied in the epic poems attributed by the Greeks to Homer. In the *Iliad* and the *Odyssey* is found the image of the mythical godlike leader of men—a Ulysses, a man of wisdom and an Achilles, the man of courage. Homer's archaic society was aristocratic. Education was largely informal and in the form of apprenticeship designed to equip the young man with skills and attitudes necessary for an aristocratic-warrior. Training was carried out in the family, clan, court, and army. Emphasis was upon the physical and the military, and method was largely participation.

The informal activities of the young hero-warrior were also in themselves educative. Sports, music, and participation in religious ceremonies, combined with training in the arts of war and speech, made up much of the education and ideals of the Homeric warrior.

The aristocratic ideal of Homeric times was influential in shaping subsequent Greek educational thought and hence Western European thought. The Homeric emphasis on military prowess and glory was developed into a way of life and a social system by the Greek city state of Sparta.

Spartan Education

Near the eighth century B.C. a Dorian tribe of Greeks pushed into a fertile plain known as Laconia in the southeastern part of Greece. Here they conquered the original inhabitants and set up a rigid monolithic state. Sparta was essentially a military state, and the aim of education was to develop individuals for military and public usefulness.

In Sparta, as soon as an infant was born, it had to be presented to a committee of elders. If it were not a well-formed and healthy child, it was not accepted. Sickly and deformed children were thrown in the dungpit. Up to the age of seven years the child was reared at home. At seven years of age he became state property, and he was taken to live in public barracks until he reached the age of twenty. Everything centered around military training. Athletics and sports were aimed at developing physical strength, and later the boy began real military training as well as gymnastics. When the lad was twenty, he took his oath of loyalty to Sparta. Between the ages of twenty and thirty he engaged in further military training and warfare. At the age of thirty citizenship was conferred, and the young man was required to marry and to engage in such public duties as jury and assembly service. Girls were also brought up to be Spartans. Their education was severe. Music and dancing were accorded less importance than gymnastics and sports. The first duty of the woman was to produce healthy babies for the state.

Spartan training was one of the most exacting forms of education ever devised. The Spartan aim—the training of citizen-soldiers—was a phenomenal success. Sparta conquered Athens in 404 B.C., but only at the cost of an inordinate effort that destroyed all her elasticity and exhausted her spiritual reserves. When Sparta became mistress of Greece, she was incapable of leadership. She was educated and built for war and could not lead in times of peace.

Athenian Education

In the history and philosophy of education during the ancient period, it is the Greek city-state of Athens that left the strongest impression on the development of Western civilization. The plan of Athenian education was to prepare youth for active Athenian citizenship that involved political as well as military services. The emphasis of training was on the development of the individual through his participation in social, religious, political, and military activities. The Athenian ideal was the young man who would combine within himself beauty of body with beauty of the soul. It is written in Book II of Plato's *Republic* that, "The love of wisdom, then, and high spirit and quickness and strength will be combined for us in the nature of him who is to be a good and true guardian of the state."[3]

Athenian schools up to the fourth century B.C. were private, and the status of ordinary teachers was low. Up to the age of six the child was trained in the home. The child was initiated into state ceremonials and taught how to behave toward men and gods. When the boys had learned their letters they were furnished with the works of poets. When the boy began his formal education, he was guarded by a slave called a paedagogus who excorted him to school and supervised his conduct. From the age of six to fourteen the Athenian lad attended elementary school. His elementary studies consisted of reading, arithmetic, and music. For physical training he went to a palaestra, a low building with a central courtyard in the interior covered with fine sand and rooms about it for undressing and washing. It was frequently the private property of the schoolmaster and was especially used by boys who were there taught the rules of wrestling.[4]

The Athenian youth attended high school between the ages of fourteen and eighteen. Secondary school studies consisted primarily of mathematics, rhetoric, and literature. At the age of eighteen the young man took the oath of loyalty to Athens and was inducted into two years of compulsory military training. At twenty he became a citizen. Higher education at Athens was supplied by wandering Sophists (pp. 6-7) and by schools of philosophy such as Plato's Academy and Aristotle's Lyceum. Around 200 B.C. a merging of the philosophical schools resulted in the creation of the University of Athens.

Athenian girls were trained to engage in domestic life. Their education was directed at beauty and grace. They were taught home management, sewing, cooking, and supervision of slaves. They received some instruction in reading, writing, singing, and playing the lyre. Their education strongly emphasized piety, religion, and manners.

The Sophists

Originally the term sophist referred to a wise man or one who was skilled at any particular activity. In time it came to mean a profession of itinerant teachers who went from city to city giving instruction for a fee. The subjects of instruction varied somewhat in content, but they always had a relation to the art of successful living, a certain attitude of mind which placed emphasis on material success and on the ability to argue any point of view irrespective of its merit.[5] The best known Sophists were Protagorus, Prodicus, Hippias, and Gorgias.

Protagorus. Protagorus was one of the earliest and best known of the Sophists. His birth is thought to have been around 485 B.C. He was highly respected, and his significance rests on his doctrine that 'Man is the measure of all things.' He claimed to teach virtue, which perhaps is better expressed as efficiency in the conduct of life.[6] Protagorus is reputed to have boasted that his pupils would make good citizens because they were trained to be successful in private affairs and efficient in public service.

Prodicus. Prodicus was the most prominent teacher in Athens after Protagorus. He received high fees for his courses of instruction. His teachings are described as being concerned with the right use of words and the subtle discriminations between the precise meanings of related terms. He was also employed by his native city of Ceos as a diplomat on occasion.[7]

Hippias. Hippias was a younger contemporary of Protagorus. He acquired great fame and wealth by traveling all over Greece as a teacher and orator, claiming competence in mathematics, astronomy, grammar, poetry, music, and history. He was also frequently employed by his native city of Elis on state business.[8]

Gorgias. Gorgias won renown at Athens by his eloquence. He wrote a philosophical treatise in which he despaired of attaining positive knowledge. The treatise is lost but is known to have maintained that—nothing exists; that if anything exists, it is unknowable; and that if anything can be known, the knowledge cannot be communicated by language. As the founder of artistic prose, he made the teaching of style an essential part of rhetoric.[9]

Socrates

The Sophists were pioneers who discovered and set in motion a whole series of educational tendencies. Their fundamental utilitarianism, however, prevented them from probing the depths of knowledge. Socrates, who was less commercially minded than they were, may have been the first person to apply serious critical and philosophical thought to questions of morality and the conduct of life.

Socrates, who is believed to have been born in Athens in 469 B.C., was a man reported to be physically strong and capable of great physical endurance. He was remarkable for his unflinching courage, both moral and physical, and his strong sense of duty. Together with these characteristics he is said to have possessed a genial and kindly temperament and a sharp sense of humor. He must obviously have been a man of phenomenal intellectual ability and insight.

He devoted himself to the work of inquiry into the right conduct of life, carried on by the familiar Socratic method of cross-questioning the people with whom he came in contact. Socrates believed that knowledge was virtue. To know the good was to do it, he claimed. A man who fully understood the consequences of his actions could only do the right thing. Man, he explained, only chose evil when he was ignorant of the consequences of such an act.

The subject of most significance to Socrates was the art of living. Reason, he found, was the element common to all men. He advocated the use of intelligence in the devising of a system of ethics. To Socrates the aim of education was wisdom, and the road to wisdom was rational thought.

In 399 B.C. Socrates was brought to trial before a popular jury on the charge of introducing strange gods and of corrupting youth. After a none-too-conciliatory speech in his own defense, he was sentenced to death. He refused to take advantage of a plan of escape made by some of his friends because he believed in obedience to law—and the law must be obeyed. A month from the time of his condemnation he drank the hemlock.

Plato

Plato was born about 429 B.C. and lived to 347. He had wealthy parents from the Athenian aristocracy and was given every cultural advantage. He was a pupil of Socrates, and in his writings he shows the enormous influence that Socrates had upon him both by his life and by his death. After the execution of Socrates, Plato fled Athens and traveled and studied abroad for a number of years. When he returned to Athens, he founded his school named the Academy.

The Academy was situated in the shade of the sacred wood dedicated to the hero Academos in a lonely and secluded spot in the northern environs of Athens. The chief object of the school was to train men for the service of the state, and a number of his pupils played a considerable part in the political life of their cities. Plato's method of training consisted of a thorough education in science and philosophy, and the school is best known for its contributions to these subjects.[10]

Plato's ideas on education are found in his treatises entitled the *Republic* and the *Laws.* Plato believed that the state should be responsible for the total education and development of the child. Each individual he thought should be placed by the state and prepared by education for the position for which he is best fitted. Education, he maintained, should be a monopoly and prime function of the state. Plato's definition of education was that it is a process of moral training where the older generation passes on to the next the good habits of living and wisdom gathered from their experience.

Plato devised a plan where both boys and girls would be required to attend school between the ages of six and eighteen. Two years of intensive military training would then follow for the young men. At the age of twenty the male youths would take a series of state examinations, and those who passed would continue their studies until the age of thirty. Those who failed the first examinations would be required to enter the ranks of the military or the workers. At the age of thirty the youths continuing their studies would again be tested, and those who passed would spend the next five years studying the higher subject areas of philosophy, sociology, psychology, politics, and education. The group that failed the examinations would be placed in positions within the bureaucracy of the state. At the age of thirty-five, upon completion of their studies, the remaining scholars would be placed in the high offices of the state, and there they would remain in these positions until they reached the age of fifty.

Plato's curriculum was based on the theory that concentrated study over a period of years would produce a mature personality. Three curricular areas stressed by Plato were music, gymnastics, and mathematics. He wrote:

> ... *education in music is more sovereign because more than anything rhythm and harmony find their way to the inmost soul and take strongest hold upon it...*
>
> ....
>
> *After music our youth are to be educated by gymnastics? Certainly... It would be a simple and flexible gymnastic, and especially so in the training for war... Surely; and yet what other study is left apart from music [and] gymnastics... Why, for example, this common thing that all arts and forms of thought and all sciences employ... I mean in sum, number and calculation...* [11]

The Greek intellectual spirit reached its zenith in the mind and philosophy of Plato. At a time when the Athenian state was being undermined by individualism, Plato wrote that the state was superior to the individual and education was to produce social unity. The purposes of education were to produce the good citizen—to awaken the rational faculty, stimulate love of the beautiful, and produce harmony within the individual and for the state.

Aristotle

Aristotle, who probably lived between the dates 384-322 B.C., was born into a family that had for generations produced physicians. He may have acquired his interest in physical science in his father's surgery. At the age of seventeen he entered Plato's school at Athens, and there he remained until Plato's death. Later, Philip of Macedon invited Aristotle to act as tutor to his son Alexander, and for four years he instructed the future world conqueror. In 335 B.C. he returned to Athens, and outside the city to the northeast in a grove sacred to Apollo and the Muses he rented some buildings and founded a school called the Lyceum.[12]

Aristotle's views on education are contained in his works the *Politics* and the *Nicomachean Ethics*. Aristotle believed education to be a state responsibility. He wrote: "It is clear . . . that there should be legislation about education, and that it should be conducted as a public system."[13] His plan for the education of youth involved four stages: infancy, elementary training, secondary education, and higher education.

The first stage of Aristotle's system covered the period in the child's life from birth to the age of seven years. The child was to be reared in the home, and the only educational recommendations he made were for play and physical exericse. He wrote:

> ... *up to the age of five [it] is not well to direct as yet... any study nor... compulsory labors... nevertheless [they] should be allowed*

> *enough movement to avoid bodily inactivity; and this exercise should be obtained by means of various pursuits, particularly play ... The Tutors must supervise the children's pastimes ... and up to seven years old, [then] must necessarily be reared at home.* [14]

Elementary schooling was to cover the years from the age of seven to puberty. The child was at this time to study the subjects of reading and writing, gymnastics, music, and drawing. He wrote:

> *But when the five years from two to seven have passed, the children must now become spectators at the lessons which they will themselves have to learn ...*
>
> ....
>
> *There are perhaps four customary subjects ... reading and writing, gymnastics, music, and fourth, ... drawing.* [15]

According to Aristotle's scheme, secondary instruction was to cover the years from puberty to the age of sixteen or seventeen. The secondary curriculum was to include mathematics, instrumental music, poetry, grammar, rhetoric, literature, and geography. Higher education was for men beyond the age of twenty-one years. The principal studies were to be psychology, politics, education, biology, physical sciences, and philosophy.

The ultimate aim of education as well as life, Aristotle believed, was happiness. He wrote, "Happiness, therefore, being found to be something final and self-sufficient is the End at which all actions aim."[16] Happiness, Aristotle thought, was to be attained through the development of a good moral character, the development of one's intellectual capacities, health, and the wise use of leisure.

The philosophy of Aristotle left little impact on the society of his own time. It was not until the Middle Ages when his writings were rediscovered that his ideas became a rich source of educational thought. The philosophy of Aristotle deeply influenced the medieval church scholars who formulated an intellectual system and theology based on Aristotelian logic. From the Middle Ages to the present day Aristotelian ideas have affected the course of intellectual history.

Schools of Philosophical Thought

The schools of philosophical thought that held the strongest interest for the Greeks and later for the Romans were: Hedonism, Epicureanism, and Stoicism.

Hedonism. The philosophy of hedonism was the outgrowth of the teachings of the Greek philosopher Aristippus. His birthdate is uncertain, but he was a companion of Socrates and was probably somewhat older than Plato. Aristippus taught that immediate pleasure was the only end of action. The goal of man's life, he insisted, is the avoidance of misery. This is combined with a theory of knowledge and the belief that the present moment is the only reality.

Epicureanism. Epicureanism was rooted in, and an outgrowth of, Hedonism. Epicurus (c.342-271) belonged to a family of ancient nobility. In 306 he went to Athens to compete with the great philosophical schools. There he bought a house and the famous garden he used as the place for his school. He lived a simple, remote, and hidden life with his pupils. He taught that man should seek the simple and quiet life and avoid the tensions and pressures of the world. Epicurus defines philosophy as the attempt to gain happiness by means of discussion and reasoning. He regards sense-perception as the one and only basis of knowledge. Everything is due, he believes, to the atoms and their movement. At death the atoms of the soul are dispersed and sensation ceases. At his death he bequeathed his property to his followers and stipulated monthly meetings be held by all the members of his sect. These sessions took the form of monthly dinner meetings, and today the term epicure is defined as one who has discriminating taste for foods and liquors.

Stoicism. Stoicism is the philosophy that pain and death is indifferent. This school of thought was founded by Zeno (335-263) who was probably of Phoenician descent. He came to Athens in 313, attended lectures at the Academy, and later created a complete philosophical system consisting of logic, physics, and ethics. He taught in the Stoa Poikile, a public hall in Athens, from which the name of his school is derived. According to his doctrine, the only real good is virtue, the only real evil, moral weakness; everything else, including poverty, pain and death, is of no consequence. Since nobody can deprive the wise man of his virtue, he is always in possession of the only real good, and therefore happy.

Hellenistic Education

Background

Athens was defeated by Philip of Macedon at the battle of Chaeronea in 338 B.C. and became part of the Macedonian empire. In 146 B.C. the city came under the control of Rome. Hellenes was the national name of the Greeks, and the term Hellenistic Education actually refers to the classical education of Greece which was spread throughout the whole Mediterranean world following the conquests of Alexander the Great, and which lasted into the Roman era. Roman education, which will be discussed later, was only an adaptation of Hellenistic education to the Latin experience.

In its most developed form, Hellenistic education consisted of a complicated course of studies which began when the pupil was seven and continued on until he was about twenty. Gymnastics was the most characteristic part of the curriculum. The Greeks believed physical training was as important as mental training. Children of secondary school age were given instruction in sports. Girls as well as boys engaged in physical education activities.

Music was at least as important as gymnastics. Young Greeks learned to play the lyre and the aulos (which may be best translated as an oboe). They also learned to sing, and choral singing was stressed. Choirs were required for many religious ceremonies and at times of state festivals and certain feasts. Dancing was closely associated with the study of music, and the Greeks had a large repertoire of dances that were performed to music.

Elementary Education

Formal education did not begin until the child was seven. Among the people who helped to train the child was the pedagogue — the family servant or slave whose job it was to take the boy to school and bring him home again. The schoolmaster was held in low esteem in ancient societies. Teaching was a badly paid job, and it required no special qualifications.

The aim of the primary school was to teach the three R's— reading, writing and counting. Reading began by memorizing the alphabet, then syllables were learned, followed by words. The time then came when pupils were allowed to read continuous passages and certain amounts of selected poetry. Writing was taught by having the child draw the letters one by one. After the letters came syllables, and then came short sentences. Exercises in grammar and composition, however, were reserved for the secondary school. The Greek child, after learning numbers, studied fractions; but addition, subtraction, multiplication, and division were not taught in the primary school.

Secondary Education

The secondary education curriculum heavily stressed literary studies and was taught by the grammarian. Literature included the epic poets such as Homer and Hesiod, the lyric poets–Alcman, Sappho, and Pindar; and finally there were the plays of Aeschylus, Sophocles, and Euripides. Prose writers studied were mainly the historians Herodotus, Xenophon, and Thucydides.

The Hellenistic Greeks placed the mathematical sciences on the same level with language and literature. Geometry was the foremost Greek science. Greek arithmetic was the science of whole numbers. The third mathematical science was music, which consisted of the numerical laws governing intervals and rhythm. Astronomy was the fourth Greek mathematical science, and Greek advances in this field were notable.

Higher Education

Higher education consisted of two different forms–*i.e.*, the study of rhetoric, or the study of philosophy. Rhetoric was the queen of studies. The study of rhetoric began with classifications and definitions of speech. Theory was then balanced by the study of models, and finally, after the imitation of good models, came applied exercises.

Philosophy was the second route to higher education. There were three main forms for the teaching of philosophy. First, there were the schools organized originally by one master whose teaching was carried on by duly appointed successors. Plato chose his nephew Speusippus to succeed him, and Aristotle left the Lyceum to Theophrastus. Second, there were the isolated teachers working on their own in some city where they had established themselves. Epictetus, for example, left Rome and settled in Nicopolis in Epirus where he opened a school. Finally, there were the wandering philosophers who preached at street corners or in the market places. The Cynics and many Stoics were specialists at this type of activity.

The research institution of the Hellenistic period was the museum. Originally the term meant a place connected with the Muses or the arts inspired by them. By far the most famous museum was the one founded at Alexandria by Ptolemy Soter, c. 280 B.C. Lectures were secondary to research, and the museum at Alexandria housed about 100 research scholars drawn from all parts of the Mediterranean.[17]

Greek medicine made great progress and played an important part in Hellenistic life. Besides private physicians, there were public physicians maintained by the city or the kingdom. Many schools of medicine were set up throughout the Greek world. The writings of Hippocrates and Galen show the Greek genius for the teaching and practice of this ancient and honorable profession.

Conclusion

Hellenistic education spread through space as well as time. As shall be seen, what is called Roman education was, on the whole, an extension of Hellenistic education to the Latin-speaking regions in the West. Furthermore, Hellenistic education had significance that extended beyond antiquity. What is called classical culture in Western Europe and America is the culture of the Hellenistic era and is present and living at the heart of modern-day thought.

Education Among the Romans

Introduction

Latin education remained in some ways different from classical Greek education in spite of the fact that it was greatly influenced by it. Roman culture itself profoundly affected the development of Western civilization. Some of its more notable contributions have been: (1) Roman law, which is the basis for the legal systems of Western nations; (2) Roman institutions such as the Roman Catholic Church; (3) Latin, from which has been derived the romance languages of Italian, French, Spanish, Portuguese, Rumanian, and no less than fifty per cent of the English vocabulary; (4) Latin literature, which in addition to many classics of antiquity, includes an enormous body of religious works; and (5) the Latin grammar school, from which has evolved the modern secondary school.

Education During the Roman Republic

Family Education. The basis and backbone of Roman education was the family. In the eyes of the Romans the obvious place in which children should grow up and be educated was the family. In the Roman family the father had absolute authority over the household. The son's vocation was largely determined by the standing and birth of his parents. It was the father who taught the son and prepared him for life as an adult. Law played a great part in Roman education and the *Law of the Twelve Tables* was learned by heart by the Roman child.

When the boy was about sixteen, his home education came to an end, and he was inducted into a year's preparation for military service (<u>tirocinium</u>). During this time he practiced physical exercises and riding, paraded at great festivals, and participated in games.[18]

The first year of military service was spent in the ranks, and if one were a young aristocrat he would soon be promoted to the officer class.

Thus, in the beginning Rome had her own tradition of teaching. Soon, however, Latin education took a different course, and the eternal city found herself captivated by the forms and methods of Hellenistic education.

Early Schools. The general principles, the syllabus, and the methods used in Roman schools were copied from their Hellenistic prototypes. In Rome, as in Greek-speaking countries, there were three successive stages in education and usually three corresponding kinds of schools run by three different specialists. Children went to the primary school when they reached the age of seven, then on to the grammaticus when they were eleven, and when they were fifteen—to the rhetor. This last stage lasted till they were about twenty.

The Romans adopted the Greek custom of providing the child with a slave-companion who was called, as also by his Greek name, paedagogus. The pedagogue took his young master to primary school—the ludus litterarius as it was called—where he was responsible for the conduct of his young charge. In the school of the elementary teacher the three R's were taught, and prominence was especially given to the study of arithmetic. In the school of the grammaticus pupils read texts aloud, with careful attention to pronunciation and enunciation, and learned passages by heart. The school-master added commentary on literary or philosophical points.

The rhetor, in the educational hierarchy, had a distinctly higher place than either of his colleagues in the two lower stages. In Rome, as in Greece, rhetoric belonged to the sphere of higher education. In the school of the rhetor the students' tasks consisted of speeches on a given theme advocating a course of action, or else debates. These speeches were often marred by artificiality, a tendency that was increased by the 'cult of the epigram'.[19]

Greek Teachers. Since the Roman aristocracy adopted Greek education for its sons, among the great number of slaves that conquest had provided, some were picked as teachers. The oldest known example of the slave-teacher was Livius Andronicus, a Greek from Tarentum who was taken to Rome as a slave after his city had been captured and later freed by his master after bringing up his children. Not all teachers began as slaves, however. For instance, Ennius was born in the Roman allied city of Rudiae in Calabria. Educated in Greek culture, he learned to speak Greek and Latin and was brought by Cato, the great Roman statesman, to Rome where he lived frugally first by teaching Greek. But soon he was writing poetry, and he has since become known as the 'father of Roman poetry.'[20]

Education During the Empire

Introduction. The Roman Empire did not bring any linguistic unification to correspond to the dual movement of political and cultural unification—one coming from Rome, the other from Greece—that had welded the two halves of the Mediterranean world into a powerful unity. That world remained divided into zones based on its two cultural languages. Greek culture had made such an impact on Romans that the Roman State never made any serious attempt to impose Latin on its Eastern subjects; but Latin, which was the national language, was used by magistrates and other imperial administrators throughout the empire in all their work. The following Romans were Latin scholars who helped adapt Hellenistic education to the Latin experience.

Roman Educators. MARCUS TULLIUS CICERO (106-43 B.C.). Cicero was one of Rome's leading orators and men of letters who moulded the Latin language into an incomparably clear and effective vehicle of thought. He was for a Roman unusually witty and skilled in repartee, and as an orator he was supreme in the courts for years. He also wrote extensively in the fields of politics, philosophy, and education. His thoughts on education are contained in his treatise, *De Oratore*.

Cicero believed the professional training of the orator should include a well-rounded education in the liberal arts as well as wide experience in living. Style, he maintained, was only secondary in importance. Cicero's life bridges the transition of Rome from a republic to an empire, and he was virtually the last of the old republican orators and statesmen. When Renaissance educators rediscovered his works more than a millenium later, Ciceronian ideas and style became vogue in humanist schools of the time.

MARCUS TERENTIUS VARRO (116-27 B.C.). Varro was a Roman scholar who contributed greatly to the form, use, and spread of Latin grammar and rhetoric. Fifty-five of his works have been preserved in fragments and only two substantially: *De lingua Latina libri* and *Rerum rusticarum libri*. He wrote on a variety of subjects including languages, religion, law, customs, political institutions, philosophy, and geography.

POLLIO VITRUVIUS. Vitruvius was a Roman architect and military engineer who lived in the first century of the Christian era. His fame rests chiefly on his treatise *De architectura*, on architecture and engineering compiled partly from his own experience, and partly from the works of other noted architects. His influence was strongly felt among Christian and medieval architects. His outlook is essentially Hellenistic, and he insisted that architects be liberally and broadly educated as well as trained as skilled craftsmen.

PLUTARCH (c. A.D. 46- c. 120). Plutarch was a Greek biographer and educator who traveled widely and taught at Rome. In his later years he composed biographies of soldiers and statesmen, mainly in pairs—first a Greek, then a Roman, then a comparison. The *Lives* include much peripatetic detail but provide the reader with examples of political and moral virtues. His basic work on education is called the *Moralia*. Plutarch thought education ought to be many-sided, including both training of the mind and of the body. Of the education of children, he wrote, in the *Moralia*:

> *Two elements in Man's nature are supreme over all—mind and reason... For the corresponding tool of education is the use of books, and by their means it has come to pass that we are able to study knowledge at its source.*
>
> *It is not proper to overlook the exercise of the body... But the amount of bodily exercise should be so limited as not to be a drain in the children and make them too tired to study...* [21]

Plutarch believed the educated man was the aristocratic gentleman who possessed all human characteristics, but in moderation. He wrote:

> *Let us consider what may be said of the education of the free-born children and what advantages they should enjoy to give them a sound character when they grow up.*
>
> *It is perhaps better to begin with their parentage first; and I should advise those desirous of becoming fathers of notable offspring to abstain from random cohabitation with... such women as courtesans and concubines. For those who are not well-born, whether on the father's or the mother's side, have an indelible disgrace in their low birth, which accompanies them throughout their lives...* [22]

Plutarch was one of the great classical authors who profoundly influenced the humanist scholars of the Renaissance. He was to them the model of the genteel, learned, and well-rounded person they themselves would like to be.

MARCUS FABIUS QUINTILIAN. Quintilian was born probably between A.D. 35 and 40 and died shortly before A.D. 100.

Born in Spain and educated at Rome, he became the greatest exponent of the training of the orator during the first century of the Christian era. He became famous as a teacher and was appointed Professor of Rhetoric by the emperor Vespasian, and upon his retirement he devoted his time to writing. His best known work is the *Institutio Oratoria.* In this treatise Quintilian covers the education of an orator from his cradle almost to his grave. He counseled that the education of the future orator's earliest years is critical because early impressions are most important to the subsequent development of the learner. He wrote:

> *I would ... have a father conceive the highest hopes of his son from the moment of birth. If he does so, he will be more careful about the groundwork of his education ... you will find that most are quick to reason and ready to learn ...*
>
> *Above all see that the child's nurse speaks correctly. The ideal ... would be that she should be a philosopher ... It is the nurse that the child first hears, and her words that he will first attempt to imitate.*[23]

Quintilian believed the boy should study several subjects at a time because he thought there was little danger in pushing learning too rapidly. He also thought that children could receive a better education from public schools than from private tutors, and that the bright child would learn more when he was given a varied curriculum. He strongly disapproved of corporal punishment. He warned:

> *I disapprove of flogging ... when children are beaten, pain or fear frequently have results ... which are likely subsequently to be a source of shame which unnerves and depresses the mind and leads the child to shun the light.*[24]

The educational theories of Quintilian exerted strong influence upon the ideas of humanist educators at the time of the Renaissance, and in his *Institutes* he stated many of the principles that have shaped educational thought since the period of the Renaissance.

Establishment of State Control of Education. As long as the Republic lasted, the Roman state had no scholastic policy. Education was left to the initiative and activity of its citizens. Public subsidies to education were begun by the emperor Vespasian (69-79 A.D.), and he decreed also that all teachers of secondary school standard and above were to be exempt from payment of municipal taxes. The emperor Trajan (98-117) reserved scholarships for poor but deserving youths. Hadrian (117-138), who succeeded Trajan, established a pension retirement system for teachers. Antoninus (138-161) granted further tax relief for teachers in the higher schools and, furthermore, exempted them from military service. Julian (360-363) decided that no one should be allowed to teach until he had been approved by the municipal council and had this properly confirmed by the emperor. Gratian (375-383) established a salary scale for teachers throughout the Empire. Finally, the emperor Theodosius (383-392) established a state monopoly of education.

The School Curriculum. Under the emperors the curriculum of the Roman elementary school stressed correct speech, writing, reading, and Latin grammar. The grammar school, in addition to correct speaking, literature, and literary criticism, also taught the subjects of astronomy, philosophy, geometry and music. The school of rhetoric emphasized literary subjects, history, composition, rhetoric, and ethics.

Rise of Professional Schools. The coming of Empire and the consequent loss of political liberty from the time of Augustus onwards caused Roman culture to model itself more and more on Hellenistic culture; and aesthetic eloquence, not political eloquence, became the aim of the schools of rhetoric. Training in philosophy and medicine also had its strong Greek imprint. However, the Romans did create their own original type of professional education with their law schools. It is, however, correct to state that the institutionalization of higher and professional education occurred during the time of the Roman empire. Schools of rhetoric, law, medicine, and philosophy were established throughout the empire.

RHETORIC. The schools of rhetoric, as above described, while emphasizing literary subjects seem to have been necessary preparation leading directly to the Bar. Cicero tried to persuade his followers of the need to make a thorough study of the law, and Quintilian made it clear that his purpose was to produce, mainly, the advocate.

LAW. Law is the greatest achievement Rome bequeathed the Western world. In Rome there was developed a science of law, and over a long period of time a body of legal principles emerged that became the basis of future legal codes. The emperor Theodosius was responsible for a codification of Roman law that bears his name. An even more important compilation was made by Justinian (527-565). The law school at Beirut in the East became the most flourishing center for the study of law, and Justinian, called the 'law-giver,' decreed that law was only to be taught at Rome, Constantinople, and Beirut.

MEDICINE. Medicine was originally a Greek science, and the Romans took an interest in it. It was Caesar who gave the medical profession official sanction, and Augustus, his successor, who granted its practitioners tax exemption. At first Greek physicians taught Roman youths by apprenticeship methods, but later schools were established for teaching medical knowledge. The *De Re Medicina* of Hippocrates (469 B.C.-399), contemporary of Socrates and most famous Greek physician, is the oldest surviving classic in the field. The best-educated and most distinguished doctor in Rome was the second century A.D. Greek physician Galen (129?-199). He wrote extensively on medicine, and his works were for centuries accepted as authoritative in Greek, Roman, and Arabic medical practice.

PHILOSOPHY. Greek philosophy early became popular during the days of the Republic, and the subject was cultivated both by literary and public figures. No ancient peoples ever practiced greater tolerance or allowed wider freedom for opinion and religious and philosophical expression than the Romans. The schools of philosophical thought that held strongest interest for the Romans were the following: Hedonism, Epicureanism, and Stoicism.

Hedonism is the philosophy, or doctrine, that pleasure or happiness is the highest good. Epicureanism is the philosophical system of Epicurus which emphasized that the external world resulted from a fortuitous concourse of atoms, and that the highest good is pleasure, which consists in freedom from disturbance or pain. Stoicism is based on the philosophical system of the Stoics who held that it is man's duty to conform to natural law, and that virtue is the highest good, and also that the wise man should be free from passion and equally undisturbed by joy or grief.

Developments During the Fourth and Fifth Centuries A.D. During the fourth and fifth centuries of the Christian era, Roman power and influence were in serious decline. Elementary and rhetorical schools almost ceased to exist. During this time some schools of practical subjects began to appear. As the machinery of empire broke down and Roman culture waned, the schools of Gaul in Western Europe did much to preserve the classical learning and wisdom of the ancient world.

Conclusion

In primitive cultures education was found to be largely a process of socialization and imitation. In the Western tradition formal education emerged as a distinct cultural characteristic in classical Greece. The curriculum favored by the Greeks survived the Romans to pass through countless centuries into the Middle Ages where it became the seven liberal arts, and from which it evolved, altered and enlarged, into modern times. The arrangement of the Roman educational system into lower, middle, and higher schools has, of course, come down to the present day. As Rome plummeted from her zenith to her nadir, and the Teutons poured over the borders of the Empire from all directions, the peoples of Europe passed into a long period of confusion, but the supreme fact amid Europe's time of travail was the growing force of Christianity. Chapter Two discusses education during the Middle Ages.

Chapter I

Footnotes

[1] Sir James G. Fraser, *The Golden Bough — The Magic Art*, Vol. I (London: Macmillan and Company, Ltd., 1955), pp. 95-96.

[2] *Ibid.*, p. 97.

[3] Plato, *The Republic*, Book II, as quoted by Robert Ulich, *Three Thousand Years of Educational Wisdom* (Cambridge, Massachusetts: Harvard University Press, 1959), p. 31.

[4] Frederick Adam Wright, "Palaestra," *The Oxford Classical Dictionary* (1964), p. 638.

[5] Guy Cromwell Field, "Sophists," *The Oxford Classical Dictionary* (1964), p. 848.

[6] Field, "Protagorus," *op. cit.*, pp. 740-741.

[7] Field, "Prodicus," *op. cit.*, p. 733.

[8] Percy Neville Ure, "Hippias," *The Oxford Classical Dictionary* (1964), p. 429.

[9] John William Hey Atkins, "Gorgias," *The Oxford Classical Dictionary* (1964), p. 391.

[10] Field, "Academy," *op. cit.*, p. 1.

[11] Plato, *op. cit.*, pp. 36-51.

[12] William David Ross, "Aristotle," *The Oxford Classical Dictionary* (1964), p. 94.

[13] Aristotle, *Politics*, Book VIII as quoted by Ulich, *op. cit.*, p. 65.

[14] *Ibid.*, p. 63.

[15] *Ibid.*, p. 66.

[16] *Ibid.*, p. 74.

[17] Theodore Johannes Haarhoff, "Museum," *The Oxford Classical Dictionary* (1964), p. 583.

[18] John Percy Balsdon, "Iuveness," *The Oxford Classical Dictionary* (1964), p. 465.

[19] Haarhoff, "Education," *op. cit.*, p. 306

[20] Edward James Wood, "Ennius," *The Oxford Classical Dictionary* (1964), p. 316.

[21] *The Education of Children,* Vol. I of Plutarch's *Moralia* as quoted by Ulich, *op. cit.*, pp. 93-95.

[22] *Ibid.*, p. 90.

[23] Quintilianus, *Institutes of Oratory,* Book I as quoted by Ulich, *op. cit.*, pp. 103-104.

[24] *Ibid.*, pp. 110-111.

Selected References

Beck, Robert Holmes. *A Social History of Education.* Englewood Cliffs, New Jersey: Prentice-Hall, Inc., 1965.

Butts, R. Freeman. *A Cultural History of Western Education.* New York: McGraw-Hill Book Company, 1955.

Cary, M. and others, eds. *The Oxford Classical Dictionary.* London: Oxford University Press, 1964.

Cole, Percival Richard. *A History of Educational Thought.* London: Oxford University Press, 1931.

Cubberley, Ellwood P. *Readings in the History of Education.* Boston: Houghton Mifflin Company, 1948.

Eby, Frederick and Charles Flinn Arrowood. *The History and Philosophy of Education — Ancient and Medieval.* Englewood Cliffs, New Jersey: Prentice-Hall, Inc., 1964.

Fraser, Sir James G. *The Golden Bough — The Magic Art,* Vol. I. London: Macmillan and Company, Ltd., 1955.

Good, H. G. *A History of Western Education.* New York: The Macmillan Company, 1960.

Kazamias, Andreas J. and Byron G. Massialas. *Tradition and Change in Education.* Englewood Cliffs, New Jersey: Prentice-Hall, Inc., 1965.

Marrou, H. I. *A History of Education in Antiquity.* New York: Mentor Book, 1964.

Monroe, Paul. *Source Book of the History of Education for the Greek and Roman Period.* New York: The Macmillan Company, 1901.

Mulhern, James. *A History of Education.* New York: The Ronald Press Company, 1959.

Nakosteen, Medhi. *The History and Philosophy of Education.* New York: The Ronald Press Company, 1965.

Price, Kingsley. *Education and Philosophical Thought.* Boston: Allyn and Bacon, Inc., 1965.

Rusk, Robert. *The Doctrines of the Great Educators.* London: Macmillan and Company, Ltd., 1954.

Ulich, Robert. *Three Thousand Years of Educational Wisdom.* Cambridge, Massachusetts: Harvard University Press, 1947.

Chapter II

EDUCATION IN THE MIDDLE AGES

Education in the Early Medieval Period

Background

The fifth and sixth centuries of the Christian era witnessed the downfall of the Roman Empire and the end of the classical or ancient period of European history. These two important centuries also saw the beginning of that period in European history known as the Middle Ages. During this transition period Roman institutions, thought and culture, though greatly modified, were transmitted to the new era under the aegis of the Roman Catholic Church.

Christianity has had a significant influence in Western education. The basis of moral behavior in the ancient world had been the preservation of the state, and patriotism was considered to be the highest virtue. Chirstianity brought a new spiritual basis for morality. Christians believed each human soul had a greater value than the whole material world. In the Gospel according to St. Mark, Christ is reported as saying, "For what shall it profit a man, if he shall gain the whole world and lose his own soul?"[1] The Christain religion gave people an individual, Jesus, who embodied all the characteristics of the highest and noblest nature. The ancient church advised civic obedience, but stressed loyalty to Christ over all others. St. Luke records Christ as advising, "Render unto Caesar the things which be Caesar's, and unto God the things which be God's."[2]

The Christian cultures which sprang up in the barbarian lands of northern and western Europe were simply an adaptation of Greek Christian culture to the local linguistic medium, itself already thoroughly permeated with classical elements. Because they were living in a classical world, the early Christians accepted the fundamental Hellenistic views of institutions and education. A man educated according to classical standards could become an orator or a philosopher, but with Christianity he was offered the additional choice of availing himself of heavenly grace and faith, receiving the sacrament of baptism, and becoming a Christian.

The following Romans were scholars whose ideas helped bridge the gap between the classical world and the Middle Ages, and whose ideas influenced the development of education in the early medieval period.

Educational Writers

MARTIANUS CAPELLA. Capella, a Latin writer, lived in the fifth century, A.D. He was probably born sometime between Alaric's sack of Rome in 410 and before the Vandal conquest of north Africa (429). He may have practiced law in Carthage. His chief work was a Latin allegory in prose and verse containing two books of allegory and seven books of exposition. In the two books of allegory, the god Mercury, desiring to marry, is introduced by Apollo to Philologia, who is raised to heaven while the Muses celebrate the marriage. The seven remaining books celebrate the bridesmaids: Grammar, Dialectic, Rhetoric (the later Trivium of the seven liberal arts), Geometry, Arithmetic, Astronomy, and Music (the later Quadrivium of the seven liberal arts). The work had amazing popularity for eight centuries, and hardly a monastic library during the Middle Ages lacked a copy.[3]

ANICIUS SEVERINUS BOETHIUS (480-524). Boethius was the son of a high Roman official and was himself an official of Theodoric (454?-526), Ostrogoth ruler of the western regions of the Roman Empire following 500 A.D. Boethius was involved in a charge of high treason and was thrown into prison and executed. While languishing in prison he wrote the *De Consolatione Philosophiae,* a dialogue between himself and a figure representing philosophy, in which he as a Christian employs arguments of pagan philosophy.[4] He was a prolific writer, and his works on music, arithmetic, and his translations and commentaries were used widely in the schools during the medieval period.

FLAVIUS MAGNUS AURELIUS CASSIODORUS (c. 480 - c. 575). Except for Boethius, Cassiodorus was the most important writer of the sixth century. He was also a Roman official under Theodoric and his successor Athalaric (516-534). After serving in public positions for forty years, he retired to the monastery of Vivarium, which he founded in Bruttium, and there devoted himself to collecting a library and writing theological and encyclopedic works. His *Institutiones Divinarum et Saecularium* was written for the purpose of providing the equivalent of a classical education for his monks. This encyclopedic work was the first Christian treatise to use the phrase, "the seven liberal arts." He emphasized the value of both sacred and secular literature. Both, he thought, were important as a means of developing Christian character. The *Institutiones* was a widely used work in the Middle Ages.

ISIDORE OF SEVILLE (560-636). Isidore was a significant seventh century prelate and scholar, and one of the most important links between the learning of antiquity and the Middle Ages. He was Bishop of Seville in Spain for the last thirty-six years of his life. His monumental work (now divided into twenty books) is called the *Etymologiae* or *Origines,* and it was a widely used encyclopedia which deals not only with the seven liberal arts, but also with such subjects and topics as geography, agriculture, law, theology, medicine, natural history, prodigies, gems, foods, drinks, utensils, clothing, vocabulary, etc. He based his studies of the liberal arts, sciences, and nature on the works of earlier scholars, and his religious writings were derived from the works of the great Church fathers and decisions of Church councils.

FLACCUS ALCUIN (735-804). Alcuin was an English poet and scholar from York who was employed by the powerful Frankish emperor, known as Charlemagne (742-814), as master at the palace school of the emperor's court at Aachen. Charles the Great was vitally interested in educating priests who could read, monks who could understand theology, and bishops who could administer a diocese. He also wanted the Church to provide him with trained civil servants. In training future scholars Alcuin stressed the writing of correct Latin and the composition of elegant verse. Appreciation for the works of the classical authors, he felt, was a chief concern of the teacher-scholar. His various textbooks on the subjects of grammar, rhetoric, spelling, and dialectics were planned to serve the needs of beginners, and the Scriptures he reserved for the use of more advanced students. His students later became the foremost scholars, writers, and teachers of their time.

The Seven Liberal Arts

Reference has been made to the term the liberal arts. This expression refers to Graeco-Roman education preserved by the Church during the Middle Ages. The Seven Liberal Arts of Martianus Capella (see above) form the two parts of the medieval curriculum known as the *Trivium* and the *Quadrivium.* The *Trivium* consisted of Latin grammar (including literature), rhetoric, and dialectic (which ranged from bare logic to the combination of pagan and Christian philosophy). The *Quadrivium* included the classical and so-called mathematical arts of arithmetic, geometry, astronomy, and music. During the medieval period the liberal arts were the advanced studies offered in the monastic schools, the cathedral and collegiate schools, and the court schools. As late as the seventeenth century the exercises contained in the *Rhetores Graeci* were used in the schools of Europe.[5]

Early Medieval Schools

Early Christian Schools. CATECHUMENAL SCHOOLS: When Christianity was first seeking converts in the more spacious days before the collapse of the Roman Empire, the simple and unschooled folk attracted to the Gospel were in need of at least some rudimentary tutoring. The catechumenal school was set up to offer instruction for the convert in the leading postulates, moral mandates, and the fundamentals of worship of the Christian religion.

CATECHETICAL SCHOOLS: In 325, after the emperor Constantine (306-337) had sanctioned Christianity as the Empire's official religion, Church authorities had to establish an efficient ecclesiastical organization. A hierarchy was effected that extended from the parish priest to the bishop of the diocese, with the Bishop of Rome as the overall head. To episcopal duties was added the business of attracting promising young men into the Church and of providing them with the necessary instruction and learning. Catechetical schools were established in the respective dioceses of the Church to provide for the training of the clergy.

MONASTIC SCHOOLS: The first monks were probably hermits who, frightened by the temptations of everyday life, sought to save themselves by seeking refuge in the seclusion of some remote place. In years that followed, it is not inconceivable that these fugitives from evil would seek out each other and merge their common interest in collective endeavor. In this way was undoubtedly born the first monastery.

In the sixth century Benedict of Nursia (c. 480 - c. 543) founded his famous monastery at Monte Cassino in southern Italy in 528 that became the model for others. Life in the monasteries was rigidly prescribed, including certain periods for reading, physical labor, and meditation. Each monastery was self-sufficient, and the ruling abbot, generally, was elected by his own monks. Cassiodorus (see above), after founding several monasteries, established the practice of having monks gather and copy books. The writing room of the monastery was called the scriptorium and was the scene of the actual practice of the transcription of ancient manuscripts. In the years that followed Benedict and Cassiodorus, monasteries became important centers of medieval learning, and from the copy rooms there issued a steady flow of writing, both religious and secular.

The first monastic schools were established to insure that the monks had the necessary learning to carry out their literate activities. In these schools instruction was carried on in Latin, and the holy clerk began his reading by memorizing his letters as untold numbers of Roman schoolboys had done before him. The cornerstone of medieval learning was Latin and would remain so until the sixteenth century when Protestant reformers, suspicious of its Romish tinge, made an end of it in the elementary school.[6]

Weaker monastic schools taught only Latin reading, writing, psalmony, and calculation, but the stronger schools taught the seven liberal arts. Teaching methods in the monastic schools were strict. The question-and-answer procedure was generally used and supplemented by dictation by the teacher, and memorization. The schools were not only for those intending to become monks, but lay pupils also were admitted who could profit from an education. Teaching, however, was secondary to worship in the life of the monk.

CATHEDRAL AND COLLEGIATE SCHOOLS: Charlemagne by edict in 789 advocated the establishment of schools by the cathedrals as well as by the monasteries. The cathedral is the principal church of a diocese, and the diocese is the ecclesiastical district under the jurisdciton of a bishop. By the end of the tenth century there were a number of cathedral schools alongside their monastic counterparts. St. Peter's School in York, England, was founded in 627 and is the oldest grammar school in England. The great period of expansion for the cathedral schools was between 1050 and 1150. Teachers associated with the great cathedrals; and famous collegiate churches like St. Genêvieve in Paris gave instruction, not only in the elements of Latin, but also rhetoric and the subjects of the Quadrivium. The Quadrivium served as a preparation for the study of medicine, law, and also dialectic (medieval scholasticism). Libraries and archives were often maintained by important cathedrals, and a large part of the time of the students attending these schools was spent in copying ancient manuscripts.

COURT SCHOOLS: Other centers of intellectual life in the early medieval period were to be found at the courts of the secular princes and rulers. Charlemagne launched his educational reforms by overhauling and improving the school of the royal palace at Aachen that had been established to instruct the courtly young. To accomplish his purpose he brought the energetic English scholar Alcuin (see above) to the Frankish capital. After fourteen years of palace service, Alcuin was awarded with the abbacy of St. Martin of Tours. In the ages following, other princely rulers also established court schools that were seminaries of distinction and privilege. In German states these palace schools were called <u>Furstenschulen</u>. Their purpose was, according to Meyer, "to confect a full-fledged man, comfortable in the classics, but at the same time a person of high character, sturdy in body, and lofty in spirit, a man in short, ready to serve competently in the princely calling or, at all events in higher public service."[7] Scholars throughout Europe were attracted to these courts where they studied, taught, collected manuscripts, and wrote their own treatises.

Education in the Late Middle Ages

Characteristics

The eleventh and twelfth centuries represent the flowering of medieval culture. Among the achievements of these centuries were: (1) the beginnings of constitutional monarchy and parliamentary government; (2) the evolution of the Church as an institution independent of secular control; (3) the formulations of systems of law, philosophy, and theology; (4) the perfection of the Gothic style of architecture; (5) the development of vernacular languages and literatures; and (6) the founding of universities.

Education for Chivalry

During the Dark Ages that followed the collapse of the Roman Empire in the West, the feudal system provided a social, economic, and political pattern of life in which loyalty to superiors was exacted and which aimed at service to overlord, king, God, and country. Chivalry is the term used to designate the way of life of the feudal noble classes during the Middle Ages. Nobles were landed aristocrats who devoted their time to the management of their estates and to the profession of arms. Chivalry is also the term used to identify the medieval system of education for knighthood. Knights were mounted troops who held estates as fiefs or gifts from their overlords. Chivalry began in the ninth century, reached its peak during the Crusades, and disappeared in the sixteenth century.

To be received into the fraternity of knighthood the youth had to submit to a long term of training. His education was begun at the age of seven when, as a page, he was inducted into service in a castle. The boy was taught hunting, swimming, wrestling, riding, and jousting. His intellectual fare, by contrast, was light and consisted of a little reading and writing and perhaps a bit of Latin. The lady of the castle had charge of the intellectual subjects that also included some poetry, singing, dancing, and chess. As a page of the castle the boy executed his lord's errands, served him at the table, prepared his bedchamber, and other amenities.[8]

At the age of fourteen the page became a squire. As squire he was the personal valet and bodyguard of his lord. His training at this time consisted almost wholly of military instruction. He simulated combat and applied himself to the mastery of his weapons. Around the age of twenty he selected a lady love who might be older or even wed, and to whom he pledged his everlasting service and devotion.

When the young squire reached the age of twenty-one, he was ready to be knighted. The religious ceremony of knighthood was indeed impressive. The investiture was consummated in a cathedral in the presence of the noble, both lay and ecclesiastical. In his vows the knight-candidate solemnly pledged to defend the Church, protect the poor and weak, fight against treachery, serve unstintingly his overlord, and keep the peace in his own province. The chivalric ideal has been forever immortalized in the English tales of King Arthur and his Roundtable, and the French legends of Roland.

Rise of the Universities

Characteristics. The purpose of the medieval university was to train men for high positions in civil and ecclesiastical government, and for the practice of the professions of medicine, law, and theology. The seven liberal arts formed the basis of all university studies. Higher education was modest in its beginnings. There were no cathedral-like buildings, no campus, very little equipment, and only a handful of students eager to learn and a few professors, who for a modest fee were willing to instruct them.

In the thirteenth century, the higher academic establishment had become sufficiently large for its participants to give consideration to organization. In Italy students formed guilds that sought to control the selection of the professorial staff, and to fine, boycott, or even dismiss incompetent teachers.[9] In turn, professors formed associations of their own. The professorial guild which developed at Paris grew in time into the four faculties of the liberal arts: canon law, civil law, medicine, and theology, each headed by a dean elected by the teaching masters—a practice which still prevails in many European universities.[10]

As the years passed, the professors' and students' guilds coalesced, and from their fusion emerged a corporation that over a long period of time gained certain liberties, privileges, and immunities by sanctions of custom, or charter from some acknowledged authority, civil or ecclesiastical. The most famous of early universities were established at Bologna and Salerno in Italy, and Paris, France.

Bologna (1189). Bologna became the great medieval center for the study and teaching of law. The Roman laws which had survived in the West through the Dark Ages had done so at the cost of considerable distortion. They did not harmonize well with the later additions from Teutonic or Christian sources. As litigation grew more common, cases were constantly coming up which lawyers could not settle because the law they knew did not give them sufficient guidance. The northern Italian city of Bologna became a center of the struggle between the church, municipal, and feudal authorities, each of whom sought recourse to Roman law to support its claims; also, the revival of Italian commerce in and around Bologna brought about a demand for lawyers. In 1189 Pope Clement III issued an official pronouncement that recognized and sanctioned the existence of the university at Bologna.

Paris (1208). Paris became the famed university center for theology, dialectic, and philosophical learning in general. The university evolved out of the ecclesiastical character of such schools in Paris as: (1) the Cathedral School of Notre Dame, (2) the school of the collegiate church of Sainte Genevieve, and (3) the school conducted by the canons of Saint Victor. Students and masters in these schools were almost without exception men preparing for, or in, holy orders. The education they offered was primarily vocational in the sense that theology, especially the philosophical theology of twelfth century Canon Law, and the technicalities of ecclesiastical administration can be regarded as serving professional interests. Many famous scholars of ecclesiastical argumentation as, for example, Peter Abelard (1079-1142), were attracted to Paris. In 1208 the French king Louis VII officially recognized the University of Paris.

Salerno (1230). The university center for the study and teaching of medicine developed at the southern Italian city of Salerno. Medicine was further advanced in Italy than in the north. Italians were better placed to obtain the information they needed because of their contacts with the Arab world. The earliest medieval translator of medical knowledge was a figure named Constantine who died in 1087. He was an African by birth and traveled widely in the East before settling in Salerno, where he acquired fame by producing Latin translations of Arabic and Greek medical writings, including works of Hippocrates. At Salerno, Greek, Graeco-Arabic, and Roman streams of medical knowledge merged.

In time a voluntary association of physicians, students, and teachers of the liberal arts evolved at Salerno. In 1230 the German emperor Frederick II, who at the time was ruler of the area, gave the masters at Salerno the right to examine those who wished to practice and to teach medicine. In order to be licensed, students were required to complete three years study in the liberal arts and spend five years studying medical knowledge.

Instructional Methods and Practices. The first universities drew their students from many lands. The one requirement for admission was that the prospective student understand Latin, inasmuch as all lectures, books, and discussions were in that language. Once enrolled, the student then studied the subjects of the Trivium—grammar, rhetoric, and dialectic—for about four or five years to qualify for the bachelor of arts degree. For a master's degree in arts he put in another three to four years, completing the seven liberal arts. To earn a doctor's degree in one of the professions, he assiduously studied the works and commentaries of his specialty.[11]

If there were no special building, classes gathered in cathedral cloisters, or in houses in the neighborhood, or even in a room rented by the professor. Classes usually began soon after sunrise. The professor lectured, limiting himself to one or more of the following procedures: (a) reading of the text, (b) giving an exposition of the text, (c) commenting on matters of special concern, or (d) raising problems for discussion. The usually bookless student attempted to copy the lecturer's utterance, writing after the ancient fashion on a waxen tablet. Some student guilds even attempted to regulate the speed at which the professor could speak.[12]

Reviews of lectures were held by students in the fashion of discussions held at the close of the day or on the week ends. An important formal method of medieval learning was the disputation, a medium of argumentation that took two forms. In one form the student would present arguments for and against a particular thesis or topic and then indicate which side he thought had the weightiest evidence. In the second form the disputation consisted of a formal debate between opponents of an important question. The doctoral candidate was required to make an oral and public defense of his thesis. The examination was begun early in the morning, was carried on by a succession of questioners, and generally lasted half a day.[13] In addition to the above-mentioned universities at Bologna, Paris, and Salerno, other medieval universities were founded at Padua, Naples, Florence, Pisa, and Rome, Italy; Oxford and Cambridge in England; Heidelberg and Erfurt in Germany; and also at Prague and Vienna.

New Types of Schools

Characteristics. The period from the end of the twelfth through the fourteenth centuries witnessed the rise of schools controlled and administered by secular interests. In Europe during this period the urge to read and write was becoming a cultural phenomenon. Various kinds of schools were founded, and chief among these were: (1) burgher schools, (2) writing and reading schools, (3) guild schools, and (4) chantry schools.

Burgher Schools. Burgher Schools were established by municipal authorities throughout Germany principally to train the sons of the burgher commercial class in the conduct of business, government, and guild matters. These schools were conducted in the vernacular and taught this everyday language in both reading and writing. Arithmetic was also stressed. Some business law also was taught, and sometimes even elements of commercial Latin. Among the first municipalities in Germany to establish burgher schools were Muhlhausen (1232), Cologne (1234), and Munich (1239).

Writing and Reading Schools. Ghent and Brugh in the Netherlands may have been the first municipalities to establish vernacular writing and reading schools. The school at Brussels was founded in 1320. There were separate elementary schools for boys and girls. The city selected the teachers and supported the schools. The specialty of these schools was the teaching of a sleek and readable hand. Simple numbers and reading were also taught. The language of instruction, of course, was the vernacular.

Guild Schools. Guilds were medieval associations for craftsmen and for merchants founded for the purposes of mutual aid, regulation of commerce, and for social and charitable motives. They were in a sense precursers of modern trade unions and chambers of commerce. It should be noted that federated guilds of scholars or teachers, or both, of which the universities were composed, performed the same functions in regard to higher education as the later medieval guilds performed for the merchant and the craftsman. The growth of the system of apprenticeship during the twelfth and thirteenth centuries was basic to the development of medieval guilds. Many guilds employed one or more priests to minister to the members of the fraternity, and in time the practice arose for these priests to keep school for children of members or of the whole town. In time, also, money was left to guilds for the express purpose of providing schooling. Many guilds founded and/or took charge of free grammar schools. The great English Public School, Merchant Taylors', for example, is a prestigious secondary school that owes its origins to the medieval guild system.

Chantry Schools. Chantires were philanthropic foundations in England founded by wealthy patrons or by associations to provide funds for religious and charitable purposes. Probably the earliest schools founded by chantries date back to the early 1300's. Chantry schools were nearly all from the beginning tuition-free. Chantry Latin grammar schools were intended to do the same work as the great cathedral and collegiate schools, and prepare boys for the universities.[14]

Conclusion

The growth of manufacture and trade in medieval cities, and the rise of the guild system were conditions of changing times that helped to challenge the near monopoly which the Church enjoyed in educational affairs throughout most of the thousand-year medieval period. Although the Church continued to dominate education in the universities and in most Latin grammar schools, feudal nobles, local governments, the guilds, philanthropic individuals and associations, all developed schemes of education.

Court and burgher schools developed particularly in Italy and Germany, respectively. In England private education under the auspices of associations and individuals was to become a traditional practice. On both the continent and in England during the late medieval period a steady trend can be noted toward lay control of education. Other educational trends of the period were the following: the development of a richer course of study in the Latin grammar schools; the use of the vernacular in certain schools; and a wider diffusion of learning in all classes of society.

Chapter II
Footnotes

[1] St. Mark 8:36.

[2] St. Luke 20:25.

[3] George Chatterton Richards, "Martianus Capella," *The Oxford Classical Dictionary* (1964), p. 543.

[4] Robert Mitchell Henry, "Boethius," *The Oxford Classical Dictionary* (1964), pp. 139-140.

[5] Theodore Johannes Harnhoff, "Education," *The Oxford Classical Dictionary* (1964), p. 305.

[6] Adolphe E. Meyer, *An Educational History of the Western World* (New York: McGraw-Hill Book Company, 1965), pp. 74-75.

[7] Meyer, *op. cit.*, p. 153.

[8] *Ibid.*, p. 91.

[9] *Ibid.*, p. 130.

[10] *Ibid.*, p. 131.

[11] *Ibid.*, p. 132.

[12] *Ibid.*, p. 134.

[13] *Ibid.*, pp. 132-134.

[14] A. F. Leach, "Chantry Schools," *A Cyclopedia of Education*, I, (1919), pp. 567-569.

Selected References

Beck, Robert Holmes. *A Social History of Education.* Englewood Cliffs, New Jersey: Prentice-Hall, Inc., 1965.

Bolgar, R. R. *The Classical Heritage.* New York: Harper and Row, Publishers, 1964.

Butts, R. Freeman. *A Cultural History of Western Education.* New York: McGraw-Hill Book Company, 1955.

Cary, M. and others, eds. *The Oxford Classical Dictionary.* London: Oxford University Press, 1964.

Cole, Percival Richard. *A History of Educational Thought.* London: Oxford University Press, 1931.

Cubberley, Ellwood P., *Readings in the History of Education.* Boston: Houghton Mifflin Company, 1948.

Eby, Frederick and Charles Flinn Arrowood. *The History and Philosophy of Education Ancient and Medieval.* Englewood Cliffs, New Jersey: Prentice-Hall, Inc., 1964.

Good, H. G. *A History of Western Education.* New York: The Macmillan Company, 1960.

Marrou, H. I. *A History of Education in Antiquity.* New York: The New American Library of World Literature, Inc., 1964.

Meyer, Adolphe E. *An Educational History of the Western World.* New York: McGraw-Hill Book Company, 1965.

Monroe, Paul (ed.). *A Cyclopedia of Education.* 5 Vols. New York: The Macmillan Company, 1911.

Mulhern, James. *A History of Education.* New York: The Ronald Press Company, 1959.

Nakosteen, Medhi. *The History and Philosophy of Education.* New York: The Ronald Press Company, 1965.

Chapter III
EDUCATION DURING THE RENAISSANCE AND REFORMATION

Education During the Renaissance

Introduction

The thirteenth century marked the summit of the Middle Ages as the Age of Faith. The Italian scholastic philosopher, Saint Thomas Aquinas (1225?-1274), was the systematizer of Catholic theology and the philosophical system known as Thomism. His great work, *Summa Theologica,* best illustrates the scholastic method of logic wherein he takes up each point in church doctrine and examines and proves it to the satisfaction of most of his contemporaries. The Florence-born Italian poet Dante Alighieri (1265-1321) in his *Divina Commedia*—a philosophical poem recounting an imaginary journey of the author through Hell, Purgatory, and Paradise, also helped to characterize the thought of the greatest century of Chiristian faith. Dante is also the bridge between the medieval and the modern world.

In the fourteenth century the scholasticism of the Middle Ages gave way to a new spirit of scientific inquiry in which old ideas were undermined and new ideas were accepted, new institutions developed, and learning was carried out in a broader spirit, unrestricted by the narrow limits previously set up by the Church. The change was not revolutionary but gradual. Humanism was the name given to the new learning. The term may be defined as that school of thought in which human interests, activities, values, and dignity predominate. This world-view is in contrast to medieval scholasticism that stressed doctrine and theory. Humanist scholars of the Renaissance sought out the classical authors and writings of antiquity to find answers to their questions about the hopes and desires of man. The teachings of such ancients as Socrates, Cicero, Quintilian, and Plutarch profoundly affected the thought of humanist philosophers and educators.

The man who best characterized the new age was the Italian poet and scholar Francisco Petrarca (Petrarch) who lived between the dates 1304-1374. He has been aptly named the "Father of Humanism," because it is he who led Europe back to a full realization of the value of Greek and Roman literature. Born at Arezzo and educated at Avignon, he studied law at Montpellier and Bologna before devoting himself to the study of the ancient classics. He urged the study of Greek and Roman authors and greatly influenced the movement to recover lost and forgotten works of ancient authors. He was largely responsible for making Latin classics the basis of a liberal education. Through Petrarch's enthusiasm, libraries were founded, intellectual ambitions aroused, and the ancient classics were again given an important place in education.

Humanistic Education

In humanistic education the ancient languages and literatures of Greek and Latin were studied. Italian scholars rediscovered the Greek language. Few Latin translations of the Greek classics had been in existence. In the Renaissance these scholars went to Constantinople to study Greek, and after the capture of this thousand-year-old capital of Greek culture by the Turks in 1453, many Greek scholars went to Italy. In Italian Renaissance schools more emphasis was placed on the study of mathematics, grammar, and rhetoric, and less on logic. Physical education combined Athenian and knightly ideals. Education was aristocratic and secular in nature. The courts of the nobles, the homes of wealthy merchants, and the palaces of princes of the Church became centers of humanistic study and teaching. Lay teachers replaced churchmen in the schools. The purpose of the humanistic curriculum was to prepare the student for the life he would lead as a cultured gentleman or nobleman. Jacob Burckhardt, historian of the Italian Renaissance, has written:

> There were Latin schools in every town of the least importance, not by any means merely as preparatory to higher education, but because, next to reading, writing, and arithmetic, the knowledge of Latin was a necessity;... It is to be noted particularly that these schools did not depend on the Church, but on the municipality; some of them, too, were merely private enterprise.[1]

Humanist educators were greatly impressed with Quintilian's theory of education. The great Roman rhetorician had insisted upon the development of an all-round education of man, but had recognized the necessity of adapting both subject matter and methods of instruction to the basic needs, age, and bent of the learner.[2] In time, however, preoccupation of the humanists with the mechanics of grammar and literature, led to the academicians' worship of Latin grammar and style. The works of Cicero became sacrosanct. The cult of Cicero reached the peak of its development in the fifteenth century when style became the chief end of scholarship.[3] The following Renaissance scholars were largely responsible for the development of the humanistic curriculum.

Italian Renaissance Educators

PIETRO PAOLO VERGERIUS (c. 1370-1445). Born at Capo d'Istria, he studied at Padua and Florence and may have obtained degrees in the arts and medicine. Vergerius was the author of the first and one of the most widely read educational tracts of the Renaissance: *De Ingenuis Moribus et Liberalibus Studiis* (On the Manners of a Gentleman and on Liberal Studies). This manuscript, addressed to Abertinus, son of Francesco Carrara, lord of Padua, is essentially a Christian adaptation of Quintilian's theory of education. In this work Vergerius shows much insight into the nature and the handling of boys. He defines liberal education as, "Those studies . . . which are worthy of a free man; those studies by which we attain and practice virtue and wisdom; that education which calls forth, trains and develops those highest gifts of body and mind which ennoble men, and which are rightly judged to rank in dignity to virtue only."[4] This treatise passed through some forty editions before 1600.[5] Vergerius served as professor of logic at Padua and was also head of the court school at Ferrara. Classical literature, he maintained, "is a most delightful and at the same time most profitable study for youth."[6]

VITTORINO DA FELTRE (1378-1446). The views of Vergerius were implemented and expanded by his contemporary the humanist scholar and teacher da Feltre. Born at Feltra, Vittorino pursued the arts course at the University of Padua. He remained at Padua for twenty years where he taught grammar and mathematics. He was, perhaps, the most famous pedagogue of the Renaissance, and it is he who formulated the Renaissance ideal of the complete man—l'uomo universale—health of body, strength of character, and wealth of mind. He was invited to become the tutor to the children of Giovan Francisco Gonzaga, princely ruler of Mantua. Later he also established a school at Mantua for children of the aristocracy and gifted youth of the poor. He expected all his pupils to show serious purpose and industry. The pupils varied in age from six to over twenty.[7]

Vittorino was influenced in his attitude about education by the theories of Plutarch, Quintilian, and Vergerius. He was wholly dedicated to the task of reconciling the Christian ideal with the literature of the classics. The curriculum of the Mantua school was broad and liberal. The pupils read widely in Latin and Greek, were trained in grammar, composition, literature, and history of classical antiquity; they studied arithmetic, geometry, astronomy, natural science, and music. Physical education played an important part in the school, but the ultimate purpose was not athletic skill so much as hardiness and good health.[8]

Vittorino and his school gained fame, and word of it spread throughout Italy and into Germany as well. Through Vittorino, who in a sense may be referred to as the first modern schoolmaster, the ideal of the scholar and gentleman found its way into educational thought.[9]

GUARINO OF VERONA (1374-1460). Guarino Dei Guarini Da Verona was a scholar of Greek and a Renaissance schoolmaster. He studied in turn at Padua, Venice, and Florence. For five years he studied Greek at Constantinople, and upon his return to Italy he opened a school at Florence. Some time later he moved to Venice where he taught Vittorino Greek, and the two pedagogues became life-time friends. He was summoned to Ferrara to act as tutor to the son of Niccolo d'Este, and he was also permitted to take additional pupils, who included sons of the aristocracy and a select class of indigent scholars. His presence at Ferrara attracted many distinguished scholars from all over Europe. In 1442 the municipality obtained rights to establish a university, and Guarino was appointed professor of rhetoric. He was an eager collector of Greek manuscripts, and he also transcribed numerous Latin works. As a schoolmaster he emphasized the value of eloquence and pure scholarship in his teaching. He divided school studies into three stages: (1) elementary, including reading Italian, Latin, and grammar of both languages; (2) grammatical, including formal Latin and Greek grammar, and reading of the classics for content and style; and (3) rhetorical, consisting mainly of Cicero and Quintilian for style and composition. Guarino's educational theories are set forth in a letter to his pupil Leoncllo d'Este and in the *De Ordine Docendi et Studendi,* edited by his son Battista Guarino.[10]

AENEAS SILVIUS (1405-1464). Aeneas Silvius was largely responsible for the spread of the Italian humanist system of education north of the Alps into Germany. Born at Corsignano, near Siena, this typical humanist and future Pope first studied law at Siena, but changed to literary studies at Florence. He lived a versatile life, was consumed by ambition, but his interests were basically literary. As a diplomat he was secretary of the antipope Felix V and represented the Vatican for a time at the Imperial court in Germany. He was made Bishop of Trieste in return for his diplomatic services. Later he became a Cardinal, and in 1456 he was elevated to the Papacy as Pius II.

A patron of learning and a prolific writer, his works include a novel written in the manner of Bocaccio, which was translated into nearly every European language, poems in Latin, and treatises on history, geography, and education. He wrote nearly always in Latin. His book *De Liberorum Educatione (A Liberal Education)* was dedicated to his royal pupil Ladislas, King of Bohemia and Hungary, whom he met at the imperial court. This long letter intended for publication sums up the educational ideals of the Renaissance, and the following quotation from this work is typical of humanists' style and thought:

> *Therefore greatest attention and zeal must be given to letters. It was once asked at what age boys ought to be assigned to learning? Hesiod thought not before the age of seven since "that seemed the earliest age" capable of instruction and susceptible of labor; Eratosthenes likewise enjoined the same. But Aristophanes and Chrysippus, with whom Quintilian agrees, held that "no time should be free from care."*[11]

Aeneas emphasized the importance of physical training of the would-be 'cultured gentleman.' Nature, training, and practice he thought were the three factors of education. The curriculum he advocated which is typical of the Renaissance includes training in philosophy, but centers around the study of grammar.

Northern Humanist Educators

GERHART GROOTE (1340-1384). Born at Deventer in Holland, Gerhart Groote was the man who inspired the establishment of the Brethren of the Common Life, an organization which had the greatest influence in religious and educational reform. Born of wealthy parents, he studied at Paris, entered Church service, and undertook a mission for the Pope at Avignon for which he was awarded two rich stipends out of the estate of the cathedral at Cologne. Beginning in 1374 he renounced his worldly goods, and although remaining scrupulously orthodox in doctrine, he attacked the abuses of the clergy, and began to preach throughout Holland in the vernacular. During his retirement at Deventer he began to collect manuscripts and hire poor scholars to copy them. At the suggestion of a friend, Florentius Radewynius, Groote agreed that the copyists should place their earnings in a common fund and live together. Florentius gave his house for this purpose. Pope Gregory XI approved the order that was called Brethren of the Common Life, and soon houses were established throughout the Netherlands and Germany.[12]

From the beginning the Brethren took a deep interest in education. They were invited to take charge of schools or to open new ones. One of their more important schools was opened at Brussels in 1460. By 1470 they were operating a total of fifty schools, and by the end of the fifteenth century the whole educational system of northwestern Europe was under the influence of the Brethren. In their work the Brethren blended the desire of northern Europe for moral and religious reform with the literary renaissance of the south. The Brethren introduced discipline, orderliness, and humanistic studies into the schools of northern Europe. Each school operated by the Brethren was under the direction of a Rector, and the schools were divided into two sections: (1) elementary, for reading, writing, arithmetic, and Latin grammar; and (2) classical, for Greek, rhetoric, dialectic, and other humanities. The Brethren also introduced the modern subjects of history and geography into their schools. Many scholars of the age were educated in Brethren schools, including Erasmus, Sturm, Melanchthon, and Martin Luther. During the Reformation their houses were closed, and many of their schools were taken over by Protestant municipalities.[13]

DESIDERIUS ERASMUS (1466-1536). Erasmus was perhaps the most renowned man of letters of the Northern Renaissance. This Dutch scholar was born at Rotterdam and was educated at Brethren schools at Deventer and Bois-le-Duc. He joined the Augustinian monastic order and was sent to Paris to study theology, but the ancient classics became his chief interest. He edited the Greek text and made a Latin translation of the New Testament. His most popular work was the *Morioe Encomium (Praise of Folly)*, which delivers up to ironical praise scholastic divines and grammarians; and by deriding the old order of learning, it opened the way for the new ideas of the Renaissance.[14]

The works that best reveal Erasmus' educational philosophy are the: *De Pueris Statim ac Liberalites Instituendis* or Liberal Education of Boys; *De Ratione Studii* or the Method of Right Instruction; and the *Institutio Christiani Principis* or the Education of a Christian Prince. *The Method of Right Instruction* is a plea for the study of the Greek and Latin languages in which emphasis would be placed more on style and content rather than grammar. Erasmus also suggests that the good teacher must understand the nature of the child and know the psychology of learning. In the *Liberal Education of Boys* he points out that education must begin early, that care must be taken in the proper selection of a teacher, and that the liberal arts are the handmaidens of conduct. Concerning the education of the Christian Prince in the arts of peace, he wrote:

> *A prince who is about to assume control of the state must be advised at once that the main hope of a state lies in the proper education of its youth. This Xenophon wisely taught.... Pliable youth is amenable to any system of training. Therefore the greatest care should be exercised over public and private schools and over the education of the girls, so that the children may be placed under the best and most trustworthy instructors and may learn the teachings of Christ and that good literature which is beneficial to the state. As a result of this scheme of things, there will be no need for many laws or punishments, for the people will of their own free will follow the course of right.*[15]

Erasmus recommended a diversified school curriculum that would include the study of the humanities, languages, grammar, composition, religion, and morals. Education, he thought, is a process of individual development, and that individual differences were important considerations in determining the direction which education should take. Erasmus helped to introduce into the schools of northern Europe the traditional humanist methods that Vergerius, da Feltre, and Guarino of Verona had brought to Italy. The great northern humanist and scholar resembled Quintilian in that he believed in the deep influence of the years of infancy in the shaping of the future man. On the subject of secondary education, and in particular in the realm of classical studies, his knowledge was profound and inclusive.

Education During the Reformation

Characteristics of the Reformation

During the sixteenth century much of northern and western Europe was wrested from the control of the Roman Catholic Church in religious affairs. But the Protestant Reformation was not only a revolt against the existing church, it was also a series of reforms that affected political, social, economic, philosophical, and education concepts. Among the factors that contributed to the Reformation were inventions, civil law, growth of towns and cities, and economic and political conditions.

The invention of printing from movable type by Johann Gutenberg at Maintz in Germany in 1438, and the development of the paper making process were two salient contributions made to the Reformation. The strengthening of civil law and civil government restricted church-made law to jurisdiction in matters only of religious concern.

In the Netherlands and Germany free cities grew up with expanding populations. Manufacture and trade increased, and considerable wealth was created. Contacts with Italian cities resulted in the growth of arts, culture, education, and spread of humanism. Cities were also largely responsible for the decline of feudalism. Serfs who fled from the estates of the nobility became workers in the cities, and with the invention of gun powder, the common people were given a measure of equality with the feudal knight.

During the Middle Ages the Church exercised temporal authority over vast areas. At one time it is estimated that the religious establishment owned approximately one-third of the land of Germany. Church wealth attracted the greedy eyes of secular rulers, and as greater power was concentrated in the hands of temporal princes, church lands were appropriated by these authorities.

On the eve of the Reformation there was growing protest in northern Europe against the wealth, power, and corruption of the Roman Church. There was wide-spread fear and even hatred of priests. Dogmas of the Church were being questioned, and the Holy Bible was printed and circulated in Latin and in several of the vernaculars.

While the Reformation was basically a religious movement, Protestant educators were interested in the general education of the masses so that everyone might read and interpret the Bible. The teaching of Latin and Greek and Hebrew was also considered important by Protestant leaders because, then, students could read the Bible and the writings of the early Church Fathers in the original languages. The following Reformation figures were largely responsible for the development of education in Protestant lands.

Protestant Educators

MARTIN LUTHER (1483-1546). Martin Luther, the leading figure of the Protestant Revolt, also advocated the development of schools and the reformation of school subjects. He was born at Eisleben in the state of Saxony in Germany. He was educated at Brethren schools at Mageburg and Eisenbach before studying logic at the University of Erfurt. Instead of entering law school he joined the Augustinian order of monks. When the University of Wittenberg was founded, he was appointed professor there where he lectured on dialectics, physics (Aristotelian), and the Scriptures. After long soul-searching and meditation he re-examined church dogma and practices and began to preach a doctrine of salvation by faith rather than by works. He attacked such Church practices as the sale of indulgences which are church pardons of sin that remove or reduce punishments which were expected to be undergone in purgatory. On October 31, 1517, Luther nailed to the Castle Church door at Wittenberg his ninety-five theses that questioned the value of indulgences and condemned the means used by agents selling them, such as Tetzel who hawked them in Wittenberg. On June 15, 1520, Pope Leo X issued a papal bull excommunicating Luther.

Luther wrote profusely setting forth his ideas. Among his important works must be included his translation of the Old and New Testaments into German; the *Letter to the Mayors and Alderman of all the Cities in Behalf of Christian Schools;* and *Sermon on the Duty of Sending Children to School.* Educational reforms advocated by Luther included: (1) compulsory elementary education for boys and girls; (2) religious instruction and bible-reading in the vernacular; (3) advanced education for those capable of further training for careers in the church, teaching, law, medicine, and public service; and (4) instruction in the classical languages above the elementary level of schooling. On the question of compulsory education, Luther wrote:

> *If the government can compel such citizens as are fit for military service to bear spear and rifle, to mount ramparts, and perform other martial duties in time of war; how much more it has a right to compel the people to send their children to school, because in this case we are warring with the devil.* [16]

The respect Luther felt for those who teach is shown in the following quotation from one of his sermons:

> *A diligent devoted schoolteacher, who faithfully trains and teaches boys, can never receive an adequate reward, and no money is sufficient to pay the debt you owe him.* [17]

The Protestant leader favored the learning of classical languages because, he said:

> *The languages are the scabbord in which the Word of God is sheathed ... If through neglect we lose the languages ... we will not only lose the Gospel, but it will finally come to pass that we will lose also the ability to speak and write either Latin or German.* [18]

Luther was a strong advocate of study of the liberal arts. He said the study of dialectic shows order, reason and grounds of forming judgment, and rhetoric should be studied to show how to be effective in putting points to others. Mathematics, he thought, should be taught in the universities, and music, he said, is a noble gift of God.[19]

Luther was concerned with many aspects of educational theory and practice. He condemned existing grammar schools as teaching the student "only enough bad Latin to become a priest and read Mass . . . and yet remain a poor ignoramus."[20] The prime purpose of education he thought was to prepare the pupil for life in the home, vocation, civic life, and the church. Educational reform and church reform he thought of as aspects of the same problem arising out of the conditions of his times.

PHILIPP MELANCHTHON (1497-1560). Melanchthon was one of the earliest and most renowned of the Protestant scholars. Born at Bretten in the province of Baden in Germany, he received a careful education at Latin schools at his home and at Pforzheim before attending the universities of Heidelberg and Tubingen where he studied such diverse subjects as the classics, mathematics, astronomy, physics, medicine, and Roman law. He was appointed professor of Greek and Theology at the University of Wittenberg where he became a close personal friend of both Luther and Erasmus. His popularity as a teacher was high, and he trained a large number of scholars who became teachers throughout Germany. The revival of education was one of his main tasks, and he wrote textbooks of Latin and Greek grammar, rhetoric, logic, psychology, ethics, and theology. So great was his fame that he was named *Praeceptor Germaniae,* the Educator of Germany. Melanchthon also published the first great treatise on Protestant theology, *Loci Communes Rerum Theologicarum,* based on the Epistles of St. Paul.

Melanchthon prepared the most important and far-reaching educational report of the Reformation, called the *Saxony School Plan.* Done at the request of the Elector of Saxony for the purpose of reorganizing the schools of that state, the Plan placed education in the hands of civil authorities and held that the purpose of schools was to prepare men for church and for civil offices. Under his blueprint there was to be a Latin school consisting of three grades in each Saxony town. The first grade was to provide for reading, writing, singing, and religion; the second grade was designed for the study of Latin grammar and literature and for advanced instruction in both singing and religion; and the third grade was for advanced instruction in Latin, logic, and rhetoric. The Plan received widespread attention, and more than fifty cities in Germany sought Melanchthon's counsel in founding grammar schools.[21]

Melanchthon's reputation as a theologian and educator is shown by the fact that he received invitations to join the faculties not only of other German universities but to those in France and England as well. But he preferred to remain at Wittenberg where he dovoted himself to the task of building the foundations of Protestantism on the solid basis of humanistic studies.[22]

JOHANN STURM (1507-1589). Johann Sturm was perhaps the most important Protestant pedagogue of the Reformation period. Born at Schleiden in Germany, he was educated by the Brethren of the Common life at Liege from whence he moved to the University of Louvain as a student, remaining there to teach Latin for a number of years. He also lectured on the classics and dialectic for six years at the University of Paris. In 1537 he was appointed Rector of the new gymnasium at Strassburg, where he also embraced the Protestant faith. After inspecting the schools of Strassburg, he recommended in the *Ratschlag an die Schulhern* one strong school with ten grades to replace the three existing Latin schools—a plan that was adopted.[23]

Wise piety was the chief educational aim of Sturm, and the curriculum of his new school was completely classical in which the work of each grade was carefully planned. Seven years was devoted to the study of Latin style, and five years to Latin grammar and rhetoric. Imitation of classical orators such as Cicero and Demosthenes was the chief objective of the school. The fame of the school was spread by its graduates throughout Europe, and Sturm was asked to draw school ordinances for other Germany communities. He was the author of numerous textbooks and several other educational works. The school at Strassburg became the prototype of the modern Germanic classical school—<u>the Gymnasium.</u>

Protestant School Reorganization

School Reorganization in Germany. Luther had advocated educational reforms; and many of the free cities in Germany heeded his appeal for public education, and under Melanchthon's guidance established Latin grammar schools. It was not an uncommon practice for Protestant states to use the wealth they seized from Catholic Church foundations and monasteries for the support of education. Sturm's Gymnasium at Strassburg became the model for the new type of Latin grammar school.

School Reorganization in Switzerland. ULRICH ZWINGLI (1484-1531). This Swiss cathedral preacher of Zurich became the leader of the Protestant Revolt in Switzerland. Educated at schools at Basle and Berne in Switzerland, he became an enthusiast for classical studies before attending the universities of Vienna and Basle. After his university studies in philosophy he started teaching classics in the school of St. Martin's church at Basle. Later he became parish priest at Glarus where he began the study of Greek in order that he might learn the teachings of Christ from the original sources. Then in 1518 the call came from Zurich where he was invited to be the people's priest at the Great Minster. As the cathedral preacher of Zurich, he attacked practices of the church which he considered evil, and he led the citizens of Zurich out of the Catholic Church.

Zwingli also reorganized the schools of Basel and Zurich. In his school plan he fused humanistic studies with religion, which included the sciences, Hebrew, Greek, Latin, gymnastics, arithmetic, surveying, and vocational training. His early death left his work to be finished by others.

JOHN CALVIN (1509-1564). Zwingli's unfinished educational program was carried on and implemented by the great Protestant theologian and educator John Calvin. Calvin was born at Nylon in the Picardy province of France. Born the second son of Gerard Calvin and the daughter of an innkeeper at Cambrai, he was brought up in the household of the noble family of Hangest de Montmoor and destined for an ecclesiastical career. In Paris he studied theology, and he studied the classics and law at Orleans. A convert to reformation doctrine, he fled France and took refuge in Basel, Switzerland, where he published his famous exposition on Protestant doctrine, the *Institutes of the Christian Religion* (1536). Invited to Geneva to take charge of the city's civil administration, he made that community into a powerful Protestant center. Acquainting himself with Zwingli's educational reforms in Switzerland, and those of Melanchthon and Sturm in Germany, Calvin established a modified system of gymnasiums which he called "colleges." These institutions were Latin grammar schools which were supported by tuition fees but were under supervision of the civil authorities. The seven year curriculum included the study of religion, singing, Latin and Greek literature, and the traditional trivium. Calvin thought everyone should learn catechism and religion, but that schools were for only boys of superior abilities.

School Reorganization in the Netherlands. The people of Holland overthrew their Spanish rulers, became Protestant, and set up the Dutch Republic. The Dutch Reformed Church adhered to the teachings of Luther and Calvin, and cooperated with civil authorities in the establishment of schools. Many Dutch towns established Latin grammar schools, which taught, in addition to Latin, the subjects of French, Greek, mathematics, and philosophy. The schools of the Netherlands influenced the development of education in England and the American colonies. The Pilgrims who had lived for a time in Leyden brought many Dutch ideas to America and incorporated them into their educational structure.

School Reorganization in England. The Act of Supremacy in 1534, which put the church under the control of the king, was the culmination of a long struggle between the English crown and the Papacy. Implementing the act, monasteries and preaching orders were abolished, their wealth was confiscated, and church schools were put under royal patronage. Thomas Elyot (c. 1490-1546), scholar and diplomat during the reign of Henry VIII, in his work called *Boke Called the Governour,* designed a program of studies to train a young man in manners, morals, Latin, Greek, history, and physical training. The Elyot plan became the English pattern for training the aristocracy.

The School at Saint Paul's Cathedral became the humanistic center for secondary education in England. St. Paul's was established as early as the twelfth century. In 1505 the English classical scholar and theologian John Colet (c. 1467-1519) reorganized the school along humanistic lines. The objective of the school was to offer a humanistic and religious education for boys. No tuition was charged. Religion was taught in English, and manners and morals were stressed.

Many individuals and philanthropic groups in England endowed Latin grammar schools to provide free education for poor but worthy boys. Nine of these institutions became England's prestigious "public schools": Winchester, Eton, Westminster, St. Paul's, Merchant Taylors', Shrewsbury, Charterhouse, Rugby, and Harrow. These most famous secondary schools are boarding schools which accept and prepare boys from wide areas of England. Graduates of these schools even today form the British ruling establishment.

Education During the Counter-Reformation

Characteristics of the Counter-Reformation

The attacks on the Roman Church by Protestant theologians, such as Luther and Calvin, and the educational achievements by such humanists as Erasmus, Melanchthon, Sturm and others were instrumental in awakening the Catholic Church to the need to bring about reforms in theology and education. The Catholic Counter-Reformation began with the convening of the Council of Trent

(1545-1563), which attempted to find means to: (1) spread the Catholic faith to non-Christian lands; (2) destroy heresy within Catholic countries; (3) win back Protestant territories; and (4) discipline the priesthood and settle differences in theology. The Council also recommended school reforms and encouraged the establishment of teaching orders within the Church.

The Society of Jesus (Jesuits)

IGNATIUS LOYOLA (c. 1491-1556). The reforms sanctioned by Church authorities were initiated at the beginning by dedicated persons whose only aim was service to God and man. Among them Saint Ignatius Loyola was the earliest and most influential. Loyola was born at the castle of Loyola in Guipuscoa, one of the Basque provinces of Spain. Brought up as a page in the residence of a high official of the state, he later entered the army as an officer in the military service of the Duke of Najera. Wounded at the siege of Pampeluna in the war against the French in 1521, during his slow recovery he read the lives of Christ and the saints and resolved to live a religious life. He visited the Holy Land, and later he studied philosophy and theology at Paris. In 1539 he organized a band of able and dedicated students into a religious order he called the Society of Jesus and offered their services to the Pope. The order was officially recognized by Pope Paul III on September 27, 1540, and Ignatius was elected General of the order and governed it 'til his death in 1556. He was cannonized by the Church in 1622.

Early History. The Jesuits were organized along military lines and were devoted to the tasks of teaching, study, and pastoral care. Chiefly because of their efforts, southern and western Germany and Austria were returned to the fold of the Roman Church, and the Catholic faith was sustained in such countries as France and Spain. In time the Jesuits became so powerful and influential and wealthy that they made many enemies within the Church. Finally, as a result of built-up opposition, the Pope in 1773 suppressed the order, and it was not until 1814 that it was allowed to regroup.

Jesuit Education. From the beginning, education occupied a most prominent part in the work of the Society of Jesus, and, in fact, education was such an important activity that the order can be called a teaching order. The Jesuits were, however, interested only in secondary and higher education. They established what were called 'lower colleges', which were similar to Latin grammar schools. What they called 'higher colleges' were similar to the universities. In St.

Ignatius' lifetime, colleges were founded throughout Italy, Spain, Portugal, France, and many parts of Germany. In 1599 the *Ratio Studiorium* was issued. It was drawn up by a committee of Jesuit scholars under the direction of Francisco Borgia, grandson of Pope Alexander VI, and general of the Society. This document laid down the educational program and method of the order. All teachers in Jesuit schools were required to follow the same curriculum and methods. The method of teaching philosophy, the sciences, and theology was nearly identical to the system prevailing at the University of Paris where Loyola had studied.

Jesuit schools accepted boys between the ages of eleven and fourteen years for a six year course. Instruction was free, and all students were treated equally regardless of the social status of their parents. The course of study included three years of Greek and Latin languages and literatures, but provision was made for time devoted to the mother tongue and its literature as well. The remaining time was given over to the studies of philosophy, natural science, logic, metaphysics, ethics, and mathematics, geography, and history. Philosophy was regarded as the most desirable of subjects, and it certainly should be noted that careful attention was also given to religious indoctrination.

Jesuit schools were founded and endowed by secular authorities, ecclesiastical leaders, or philanthropists, but Jesuits kept full control. Jesuit teachers were generally better trained than their Protestant counterparts. Jesuit schooling was rigorous. The school day was five hours in length divided equally between morning and afternoon sessions. Morning periods consisted mostly of reviews of previous lessons and presentations of new material. Afternoon sessions concentrated on correction of exercises in grammar and reviews of morning lessons. A formal final examination was given at the end of each school year.

Jesuit education was a carefully thought-out and worked-out system at a time when few schools had any system at all. Although Jesuits borrowed ideas from other educators and schools, they did so intelligently. The most important aim of Jesuitical education and the one emphasized for all grades was moral and religious training. The 1599 *Ratio Studiorum* admonished Jesuit instructors as follows:

> He [the instructor] shall take every precaution and consider it a matter of the greatest importance that there be in our schools no books, of poets or others, which may harm uprightness and good morals, unless they have been expurgated of all improper words and statements; or if they cannot be completely expurgated ... they shall not be read, lest the nature of their statements offend purity of mind.[24]

At the beginning of the seventeenth century the Jesuits operated 372 colleges, and at the time of the suppression the Society had over 700 higher schools throughout the world with an enrollment of approximately 200,000 students. Some of the foremost men of learning and public affairs were educated in Jesuit schools. In Catholic countries such as Portugal, Spain, and France secondary education was almost entirely in their hands.

Conclusion

The aim of education in Renaissance Italy seemed to be the advancement of human interests, activities, and values. Ancient languages were studied, and considerable emphasis also was placed on rhetoric, literature, and physical education. Scientific inquiry was also one of the basic characteristics of the Renaissance.

In northern Europe the aim of Renaissance education was moral reform through the study of the Bible, languages, and history. The teaching order, Brethren of the Common Life, adopted the new humanistic studies, and in England, Public Schools were founded.

During the Protestant Reformation general education of the masses was advocated so everyone might read and interpret the Bible. Philipp Melanchthon, "Preceptor of Germany," reformed the German educational system, and Johann Sturm organized the first Gymnasium at Strassburg in 1537. In Switzerland, John Calvin at Geneva founded the college, a Latin grammar school.

In the Catholic Counter-Reformation that began with the convening of the Council of Trent in 1545, new religious teaching orders were set up within the Catholic Church, the most prominent of which was the Society of Jesus. The Jesuits set up a world-wide system of secondary and higher education. Jesuit schools trained some of the most renowned scholars and public men of their times.

Chapter III
Footnotes

[1]Jacob Burckhardt, *The Civilization of the Renaissance in Italy,* Vol. I (New York: Harper and Row, 1965), p. 220.

[2] Mehdi Nakosteen, *The History and Philosophy of Education* (New York: The Ronald Press Company, 1965), p. 227.

[3] *Ibid.*, p. 228.

[4] "Pietro Paolo Vergerius," *A Cyclopedia of Education* (1917), V, p. 713.

[5] *Ibid.*

[6] Nakosteen, *op. cit.*, p. 228.

[7] "Vittorino da Feltre," *Cyclopedia of Education* (1917), V, p. 737.

[8] *Ibid.*, p. 738.

[9] *Ibid.*

[10] "Guarino Dei Guarini Da Verona," *Cyclopedia of Education* (1918), III, pp. 191-192.

[11] Bro. Joel Stanislaus Nelson (translator), *Aeneae Silvii De Liberarum Educattione* (Washington, D.C.: The Catholic University of America Press, 1940), p. 127.

[12] Isaac L. Kandel, "Brethren of the Common Life," *Cyclopedia of Education* (1919), I, p. 446.

[13] *Ibid.*, pp. 446-447.

[14] Foster Watson, "Erasmus," *Cyclopedia of Education* (1915), II, p. 474.

[15] Lester K. Born, ed., and trans., Desiderius Erasmus, *The Education of a Christian Prince* (New York: Columbia University Press, 1936), pp. 212-213.

[16] Martin Luther, *Sermon on the Duty of Sending Children to School* and *Three Thousand Years of Educational Wisdom* (Cambridge, Massachusetts: Harvard University Press), as quoted by Robert Ulich, p. 249.

[17] Frederick J. E. Woodbridge, "Martin Luther," *Cyclopedia of Education* (1918), IV, p. 95.

[18] Martin Luther, *Letter to the Mayors and Aldermen of All the Cities of Germany in Behalf of Christian Schools,* as quoted by Robert Ulich, *op. cit.*, p. 227.

[19] Woodbridge, *op. cit.*, p. 95.

[20] *Ibid.*

[21] "Philip Melanchthon," *Cyclopedia of Education* (1918), IV, p. 190.

[22] *Ibid.*, p. 191.

[23] "Johann Sturm," *Cyclopedia of Education* (1917), V, p. 443.

[24] From *St. Ignatius and the Ratio Studiorum,* edited by E. A. Fitzpatrick. Copyright, 1933, McGraw-Hill, Inc. Used by permission of McGraw-Hill Book Company.

Selected References

Beck, Robert Holmes. *A Social History of Education.* Englewood Cliffs, New Jersey: Prentice-Hall, Inc., 1965.

Bolgar, R. R. *The Classical Heritage.* New YOrk: Harper and Row, Publishers, 1964.

Butts, R. Freeman. *A Cultural History of Western Education.* New York: McGraw-Hill Book Company, 1955.

Cole, Percival Richard. *A History of Educational Thought.* London: Oxford University Press, 1931.

Cubberley, Ellwood P. *Readings in the History of Education.* Boston: Houghton Mifflin Company, 1948.

Good, H. G. *A History of Western Education.* New York: The Macmillan Company, 1960.

Meyer, Adolphe E. *An Educational History of the Western World.* New York: McGraw-Hill Book Company, 1965.

Monroe, Paul (ed.). *A Cyclopedia of Education.* 5 vols. New York: The Macmillan Company, 1911.

Mulhern, James. *A History of Education.* New York: The Ronald Press Company, 1959.

Nakosteen, Mehdi. *The History and Philosophy of Education.* New York: The Ronald Press Company, 1965.

Ulich, Robert. *Three Thousand Years of Educational Wisdom.* Cambridge, Massachusetts: Harvard University Press, 1959.

Chapter IV

EDUCATION FROM THE REFORMATION THROUGH THE NINETEENTH CENTURY

Development of Educational Philosophy

Introduction: The Age of Reason

The sixteenth and seventeenth centuries comprised the era of the beginnings of experimental and natural science. More than a thousand years earlier the Greeks had laid a foundation in science and mathematics, and during the Middle Ages the Italians brought from the Arabic lands to Europe algebra, arabic numerals, the compass, and other contributions of useful scientific knowledge. Then in 1543 the Polish astronomer Nicolaus Copernicus (1473-1543) published *Revolutions of the Celestrial Bodies.* The universe envisaged by Copernicus with the sun, not the earth at its center, sparked a revolution in man's image of the cosmos and thus opened the door to the Age of Reason. The German scholar Johann Kepler (1571-1630) developed further the Copernican theory, and the Italian astronomer Galileo (1564-1642) helped to publicize the heliocentric hypothesis and gain for it wide acceptance in learned circles.

Scientific reasoning was further enhanced by the works of Francis Bacon in England and Rene Descartes in France.

FRANCIS BACON (1561-1626) served as a pivotal figure in the Age of Reason living as he did during the close of the English Renaissance. Orthodox in his religious beliefs, he believed people should look to the authority of the Church in matters of purely religious concern, but in all other areas of life and thought he advocated the more scientific and analytic means of self-questioning. He supported and popularized the inductive method of reasoning that consists of a thought process of estimating the validity of observations of a part of a class of facts as evidence for a proposition about the whole class, and a conclusion reached by this process. Bacon's principal writings are *Advancement of Learning, New Atlantis,* and *Novum Organum.* In the *Novum Organum* he states his case for careful observation. He wrote: "Man, as the minister and interpreter of nature, does and understands as much as his observations on the order of nature, either with regard to things or the mind, permit him, and neither knows nor is capable of more."[1] Bacon defended a general education, including literature and philosophy, as promoting wise judgment of ends to accompany the scientific improvement of means. Man, he thought, could be remade by an enlightened education if society were willing to draw first-rate people into pedagogy by providing them adequate pay and honor.

RENE DESCARTES (1596-1650), who had a Jesuit education in France, built on the ideas of Bacon and attempted to establish an intellectual system on which philosophy, science, and religion would not necessarily be antagnostic to one another. He conceived the idea of applying mathematical logic to philosophy, and he wrote on such diverse subjects as mathematics, physics, astronomy, physiology, metaphysics, epistemology, ethics, and theology. He stressed the observation of fact, as did Bacon, and felt that the opinions we form of the external world through our senses can be considered valid. He stated his basic premise as, "Cogito ergo sum"—I think therefore I am. The intellect, he believed, if correctly used, is sufficient to find truth. In his *Discourse on the Method of Rightly Conducting the Reason and Seeking for Truth in the Sciences,* he rejected all dogmas and doctrines and explained his procedure of reasoning as follows:

> The first of these [Laws of logic] was to accept nothing as true which I did not clearly recognize to be so . . .
>
> The second was to divide up each of the difficulties which I examined into as many parts as possible . . .
>
> The third was to carry on my reflections . . . commencing with objects that were the most simple and easy to understand, in order to rise little by little . . .
>
> The last was . . . to make enumerations so complete and reviews so general that I should be certain of having omitted nothing.[2]

JOHANN AMOS COMENIUS (1592-1670)

The broad and systematic educational philosophy of this Moravian theologian and educator is a landmark in the history of education. He is perhaps the leading Protestant philosopher of education and most certainly is one of the great reformers of educational practice. Comenius was born in Moravia, then a vassal state of the Hapsburg dynasty in what is now Czechoslovakia. Educated at the universities of Herborn, Nassau, and Heidelberg, he was ordained pastor of the dominant but persecuted Protestant sect of his native region, The Bohemian Brethren. He spent much time working out a theory of education to be applied in schools of a Protestant country.

For several years he taught Latin and the classics in villages of his native land before being summoned to Poland where he gained fame for his innovations in methods of teaching languages. He devised theories and wrote textbooks for the teaching of languages. He had also worked on a dictionary for the Czech language. His writings made him the most sought after educator in Protestant Europe. Invited to Sweden, he worked out improvements in that country's educational system. In his later life he was elected bishop in the Moravian Church, and he spent his last years at Amsterdam in the Protestant Netherlands where he conducted church business and continued his educational writings.

The principal works of Comenius include: *Pansophiae Prodromus; Janua Linguarum Reserta; Didactica Magna;* and *Orbis Sensualium Pictus.* Comenius believed education ought to be universal—open to all regardless of sex or means; that it also ought to be uniform, and through the lower schools, compulsory. Education, he maintained, must be kept realistic—that ideas should at every step be kept in touch with things, he said:

> To the rational soul that dwells within us, organs of sense have been supplied, which may be compared to emissaries and scouts, and by the aid of these it compasses all that lies without. These are sight, hearing, smell, sound, and touch, and there is nothing whatever that can escape their notice. For since there is nothing in the visible universe which cannot be seen, heard, smelt, tasted, or touched, and the kind and quality of which cannot in this way be discerned, it follows that there is nothing in the universe which cannot be compassed by a man endowed with senses and reason.[3]

Human nature, he said, is identical in all persons and consequently educational methods and materials ought to be uniform. "The art of teaching," he wrote in *The Great Didactic,*". . . demands nothing more than the skillful arrangement of time, of the subjects taught, and of the method. As soon as we have succeeded in finding the proper method it will be no harder to teach school-boys in any number desired, than with the help of the printing-press to cover a thousand sheets daily with the neatest writing . . ."[4]

Comenius recommended the establishment of separate schools based upon what he considers as the psychological development of the child. The first school he referred to as the "mother school." During the first six years of his life, the child's sense organs develop making possible sensory knowledge of the environment. During this period the family should habituate the child in the correct use of his native language, in social conduct, religious belief, and in the arts of music and poetry.

From six to twelve the child ought to attend a vernacular school. In this period of his life, the child's abilities to imagine and remember what has been sensed come into existence. In the vernacular school six classes, one for each year, and in each he should use only one book encompassing the amount of knowledge, virtue, and piety which is compatible with the child's emerging powers of imagination and memory.

In the third period of the child's life, from twelve to eighteen, the ability to reason emerges in its full power. For those who are fitted for it, Comenius recommended further training at the Latin school. In the Latin school there again should be six classes. The curriculum of the school would comprise, in addition to Latin grammar and literature, the seven liberal arts, and the languages of Greek and Hebrew, and he provided the first textbook with pictures—his famous *Janua linguarum.*

In the fourth stage of life, from eighteen to twenty-four, the will becomes strong, enabling the harmonization of desires and the self-direction of one's life. During this period of time those students who can profit from it should attend a university. The purpose of the university is to carry on research to increase specialized knowledge, and to train for the professions.

Comenius combined in his thinking both the mysticism of the Church and a strong belief in the empirical method. He believed man had many good qualities as well as bad ones, but that he (man) is steadily improving and will eventually reach a divine state. Man is, he said, a rational creature created in God's image. As a Utopian theorist, he visualized the creation of an ideal Protestant Christian republic where an elementary school would be found in every village; a Latin school in every township; and a university in every province. Comenius with his systematic presentation of his educational views influenced European concern for the development of good textbooks, good teachers, and good methods of teaching. The impact of his ideas was felt in schools of both Protestant and Catholic countries.

JOHN LOCKE (1632-1704)

The political and social philosopher, John Locke, lived during the English revolutionary era extending from the reign of Charles I to the accession of William and Mary. Locke's ideas have influenced social and political philosophy and educational thought throughout the world but particularly in Great Britain and the United States.

Locke was born in Wrington, Somersetshire. He received his early education at Westminster school before moving on to Christ Church at Oxford where he did experiments in chemistry and read Descartes. He also tutored at Christ Church in Greek, rhetoric, and philosophy. In 1667 he was employed as confidential adviser and tutor of Lord Ashley, first earl of Shaftesbury, a prominent politician of the day. Suspected of complicity in plots against the crown, he fled England; but he returned during the 'Glorious Revolution' of 1689 and became an important adviser in the government during the reign of William and Mary.

As a follower of the ideas of Bacon and Descartes toward experimental science and rational philosophy, Locke is known as the father of English empiricism. His principal writings include: *Essay Concerning Toleration; Essay Concerning Human Understanding; Two Treatises on Government;* and *Some Thoughts Concerning Education.* As a rationalist, Locke's ideas represent practical aims. He believed government should be by the consent of the governed, that all but atheists should have religious toleration; and that education should be more wide-spread. Locke's educational theory is dispersed throughout his writings. Most of his recommendations for education occur in *Some Thoughts Concerning Education,* but others appear as well in the *Essay Concerning Human Understanding,* and the *Second Treatise of Civil Government.*

Locke's prominent *Essay Concerning Human Understanding* embodies his philosophy. Without ideas, Locke thought knowledge is impossible. The human mind before any ideas are presented to it is a tabula rasa. He classified ideas in several ways. Some ideas, he believed, come from sensation, others from reflection. Through the sense organs, some object acts upon the nervous system, setting up in it a train of neurological events which terminates in the brain, and whose terminal event causes an idea of the object that initiated the event. Ideas of reflection are found not through sensation but through introspection.[5] But he maintained that all human ideas, however complex, abstract, or sublime, ultimately depend upon 'experience.' Knowledge Locke defined as perception of relations among ideas. These relations include: (1) relations of identity and difference; (2) mathematical relations; (3) assertions that one quality does or doesn't coexist with another in the same substance; and (4) with reality independent of our perceptions, such as that God exists.

In his *Thoughts* Locke described certain general principles of child growth and development as they relate to habitual forms of preference and of action. These principles are six in number: (1) the child desires to secure the approbation of others and to avoid their disapprobation; (2) that rewarding the child with bodily pleasure and punishing him with bodily pain neither establishes the actions rewarded nor disestablishes those punished; (3) the child prefers to perform those actions with respect to which he is free over those with respect to which he is compelled; (4) if all of the desires expressed by the child are given approval, he will become overly aggressive and incapable of socialized behavior; (5) if the child is to continue to prefer doing something, he must have occasional relief from it in the form of an activity of some other kind; and (6) if the child is to know something, he must have been curious about it.[6]

Education meant to Locke the development of moral discipline and self-control. He wrote: "the great principle and foundation of all virtue and worth is placed in this, that man is able to deny himself his own desires, cross his own inclinations and purely follow what reason directs as best, though the appetite lean the other way."[7] He agreed with ancient Greek and Renaissance educators that physical training is an important aspect of education. "A sound mind in a sound body," he wrote, "is a short but full description of a happy state in this world."[8]

Educating is a function, Locke said, that parents may and frequently do transfer to others. He advocated that children of the unemployed poor between the ages of three and fourteen be compelled to go to vocational day schools in order that they may learn best to assume their position in society.[9] But Locke thought the most important means for achieving national welfare and prosperity is the preparation of children of 'gentlemen' for their role in the state. He proposed private tutoring as the best preparation for a gentleman's son: ". . . I cannot but prefer breeding of a young gentleman at home in his father's sight under a good governor as much the best and safest way to this great and main end of education—[Virtue]."[10]

Locke advocated three main points concerning the method of moral training for the attainment of 'Virtue': (1) one must first discover the relative strengths of natural desires; (2) one must frustrate those desires which are incompatible with good character; and (3) although one must frustrate the natural desire for bodily pleasure, one cannot dispense with pleasure of all kinds; therefore, the habits of virtue, wisdom, and good breeding and the actions which manifest them must be made pleasant for the agent.[11]

The subjects Locke recommended for the secondary school included: English, French, Latin, arithmetic, geography, anatomy, astronomy, chronology, history, political theory and law, rhetoric, logic, and philosophy. The languages he thought that had the most importance in addition to English were French and Latin. He put French ahead of Latin because, he said: ". . . French is a living language and to be used more in speaking . . .," but he maintained Latin, ". . . as absolutely necessary to a gentleman."[12]

John Locke was the philosophical apologist for the English revolutions of 1640 and 1689, and he exercised an influence that was far-reaching. In England the ideas of the social philosophers Hume and Berkeley reflected his theories, and in America Jefferson and Franklin implemented in practice many of his ideas. In France, also, his theories affected the pre-Revolutionary period known as the 'Enlightenment.' Yet despite his liberal political and social ideas, Locke adhered to the principle that education was primarily for the aristocracy or propertied middle class. Although Comenius had pleaded for universal education in his lifetime, it would not be until the eighteenth century—the Age of Englightenment—and the formulation of the educational philosophy of Jean Jacques Rousseau that the egalitarian doctrine in education would begin to gain acceptance.

JEAN JACQUES ROUSSEAU (1712-1778)

The eighteenth century known as the Age of Enlightenment was a time when many great men worked in the fields of science and philosophy. It was also an age of criticism of political, social, religious, and educational practices. Jean Jacques Rousseau was one of the leading figures and critics of the times.

Rousseau was born to a French Protestant family of Geneva. At the age of sixteen he left Geneva and spent time in Italy and elsewhere wandering about in the capacity of servant to various wealthy persons. His adventures introduced him to several wealthy women who installed him in their households as lover. Converted to Catholicism, he moved to Paris where he quickly ingratiated himself into literary circles. Through his friendship with Diderot, publisher of the *Encyclopedie,* he met and quarreled with most of the enlightened minds of his day. He also began to write profusely. He formed a union with an illiterate inn-servant, Therese Le Vasseur, whom he married near the end of his life. Some scholars have suggested that Rousseau never had any children, despite his boast to have had five by Therese, and to have sent them all to a foundling hospital. It is hypothesized that he invented this story to hide his impotence. But his many apologies for this shirking of responsibility make this theory implausible.

Rousseau ideas were the inspiration for the early years of the French Revolution. His principal works include: *Discourse on the Arts and Sciences; Discourse on Inequality; La Nouvelle Heloise; The*

Social Contract; Emile; his famous *Confessions;* and *Considerations on the Government of Poland.* Rousseau's educational theory is dispersed throughout several works. The *Emile,* a simple romantic tale of a child reared apart from other children by methods of experimentation, pertains to the private education of men; the public education of men is discussed in part in his *Considerations on the Government of Poland;* and the education of women is dealt with in Book V of the *Emile.*

In Rousseau's educational theory there are statements about human nature and human history. The theme most commonly associated with Rousseau is the idea of the need to return to the state of nature. "All things are good as they come out of the hands of their Creator," he wrote, "but everything degenerates in the hands of man."[13] What he was saying, in effect, was that society is evil and needs to be reformed by beginning anew, that it must reeducate itself by returning educationally to childhood. In the *Emile* he wrote:

> *All our wisdom consists in servile prejudice; all our customs are nothing but subjection, confinement and restraint. Civilized man is born, lives and dies in slavery; at his birth he is bound up in swaddling clothes, and at his death nailed in his coffin. As long as he wears the appearance of the human form, he is confined by our institutions. But should mothers again condescend to nurse their children, manners would form themselves, the sentiments of nature would revive in our hearts, the state would be repeopled; this principle point, this point alone would reunite everything.*[14]

Rousseau believed that each child as he grows up to maturity goes through various stages, and that it is the task of the educator to understand each of these stages and realize that each stage has a complete life of its own. The first stage is infancy and begins at birth. This stage is dominated by feeling, by the feeling of pleasure and pain. Education at this time of life should allow for the free play of nature:

> *The only habit in which a child should be indulged is that of contracting none; he should not be permitted to exercise one arm more than another... he should not be used to eat, sleep, or do anything at stated hours... Prepare early for his enjoyment of liberty, and the exercise of his natural abilities...* [15]

The second stage is boyhood and extends from two to twelve. It is dominated by the exercise of the faculty of sense:

> *Everything they see, or hear, appears striking, and they commit it to memory. A child keeps in his mind a register of the actions and*

conversations of those who are about him; every scene he is engaged in, is a book, from which he insensibly enriches his memory, treasuring up his store till time shall ripen his judgment and turn it to profit.[16]

Intellectual reason emerges as dominant in the third stage of youth, covering the years between twelve and fifteen. During this time the youth learns to form concepts and begins to think about learning a trade:

At twelve or thirteen years of age, the faculties of a child display themselves more rapidly than his wants... This, however, is the only time, during life, in which he will be in such a situation... but when the correction of his ideas obliges you to speak of the mutual dependence of mankind,... divert his attention... to industry and the mechanic arts, which render men useful to one another.[17]

In the fourth stage between fifteen and twenty, the quality of life is altered greatly by the emergence of the sexual desire. It brings with it an interest in other persons and a genuine affection for them. Now ends the period when the pupil is educated apart from society. Because of his prolonged innocence, "it enables us by means of his growing sensibility, to sow the first seeds of humanity in his heart: an advantage of infinite importance, because it is the only time of his life when this care will be attended with equal success."[18]

Rousseau's consideration of private education in the *Emile* culminated with the recommendation that the young adult, seeing the corruption of contemporary society, should retire from it so far as possible.[19] Toward the end of his lifetime Rousseau was asked to make suggestions for reform of the Polish government. In his reply he recommended among other things a system of public education. The purpose of public education, he said, is to reproduce the national culture from one generation to another, and to develop in the student the national character. Freedom is achieved, he maintained, through submission to the general will. Rousseau ordered the curriculum and administration of public education to promote adherence to the general will. The curriculum should be administered through schools whose teachers and administrators are public officials. The schools, he insisted, should be administered by a central commission whose function it should be to inspect teachers in order to make certain that national objectives are being realized.[20]

Rousseau held that private education in societies whose institutions are corrupt should aim at providing an inner happiness in withdrawal from public affairs, but that in societies where there is hope for reform, public education should aim at the same inner peace by fostering an inclination to serve the public good through institutions responsive to the general will.[21] Everything, he insisted, depended upon the extension of education. To promote freedom faster than intelligence and moral character, he warned, would be to open the door to chaos.

Rousseau, a convinced republican in politics, had no formal training in political theory, but what he saw under the French monarchy was the greatest misery of the greatest number. But it was as a literary man that Rousseau was most noteworthy. The beauty and sincerity of his writing is not lost in translation. His ideas were enormously influential on educators such as Pestalozzi and Froebel, who advocated the "child-centered" school, and on the American pragmatic progressive educators of the twentieth century.

JOHANN FRIEDRICH HERBART (1776-1841)

The ideas of Rousseau, Pestalozzi, and Froebel were most influential in reforming elementary education in the nineteenth century, but the theories of the great German philosopher-psychologist-educator Herbart were most strongly felt in the field of secondary education. Herbart rejected the concept of the "child-centered" school, but reemphasized the importance of the teacher as the key to the instructional process.

Johann Friedrich Herbart was born at Oldenburg, Germany, and was educated at the gymnasium of his native city. At the University of Jena he briefly fell under the influence of the great German idealist philosopher, Fichte. He left Jena to become tutor to the sons of the governor of Interlacken in Switzerland, where he met Pestalozzi and became acquainted with Pestalozzian teaching methods. After three years in Switzerland he returned to Germany to study for his doctorate at the University of Göttingen. After receiving his degree, he remained at Göttingen where he taught education and philosophy. Later he was invited to succeed to the chair of the great Immanual Kant at the University of Königsburg, where he remained until he fell out of favor with the Prussian government. Leaving Königsburg he returned to Göttingen, where he continued to teach and to write up to a few days before his death.

The principal works of Herbart in psychology and education include: *ABC of Sense-Perception; Outline of Pedagogical Doctrine; The Science of Education; Application of Psychology to the Science of Education;* and *Textbook of Psychology.*

Herbart is considered to be the father of the modern science of education and modern psychology. He was the first to recognize that education was worthy of being a science, not just a depeartment of philosophy. He organized a psychology of the educational process that fused psychology and ethics. Psychology is to provide a knowledge of the human mind to be educated, and ethics is to provide a knowledge of the social ends to which education is to be dedicated. The aim of education he considered to be the building of personal character and social morality. Character he thought is dependent upon knowledge and hence, the first duty of the teacher is filling the mind, "because it is the content of the mind that regulates behavior." The foundation of the moral life, he said, is in "a sober, clear, firm, and determinate judgment."[22] To achieve this result he said, "the teacher must foresee the future man in the boy," and:

> *Consequently the teacher must try to envisage the purposes which the pupil will pursue after he has grown up. It is the teacher's task to prepare beforehand in his pupil the desirable facility for achieving his goals.*[23]

What Herbart in effect was saying is that the teacher, by a pre-conceived method, would impart these supreme ethical ideals to his pupils, and his pupils as a result of this instruction would develop the desire to do good. Full knowledge, he wrote, is the ground of virtue.

The disciples of Herbart, known as Herbartians, synthesized his ideas into the "five formal steps" of classroom instruction and learning. These steps are: (1) Preparation, the recalling of past ideas in connection with the lesson; (2) Presentation, presenting the new material with clarity so that it is understood by each pupil; (3) Association, associating the new idea with older known ideas; (4) Generalization, formulating abstract principles based on sensory observations; and (5) Application, applying new ideas in pursuit of further learning.

The teacher is the key in the Herbartian system of education, and the secondary school subjects of history and literature are the most important ones for achieving the social purpose of education, *i.e.,* citizenship training through the inculcation of moral and ethical values.

Summary

The educational theories of Herbart, Rousseau, Locke, Comenius as well as the ideas of Descartes and Bacon assisted the development of a science of education. During the course of the three centuries following the Reformation, the Church lost its monopoly in the field of education, and the purpose of education changed from that of indoctrinating a morality based on theology to the inculcation of an ethic of civic efficiency. Science gave man a new source for truth and a method for discovering it. The coming of the Industrial Revolution and the growth of the spirit of nationalism turned men's eyes away from religiousity and other-worldiness to a concern for life, and a better life on this earth here and now. The nation-state displaced the Church as the supreme allegiance of men.

Development of National Systems of Education

Early Secondary Schools

The cathedral and monastic schools in England, France, and Germany provided secondary instruction for some 600 years prior to the nineteenth century. Other grammar schools were founded through private means including philanthropy, guilds, and churches. Secondary "court schools" were set up in Italian towns during the Renaissance with the Latin and Greek languages and literatures as the core of the curriculum. In France secondary schools like the court schools of Italy were known as colleges, and many were founded after 1500. In Germany the Brethren of the Common Life adapted the Italian humanistic ideas and reformed many existing institutions. The classical-humanistic curriculum was instituted in the schools of England as well.

The Effects of the Industrial Revolution and Nationalism on Education

The mechanization of the economies of the nations of Western Europe was a prime requisite for the building of national systems of education. The Industrial Revolution began in the latter years of the eighteenth century and changed fundamentally the economic, political, social, and educational life of the Western world. The term narrowly defined means the application of machinery to manufacturing, mining, transportation, communication, and agriculture, and the changes in economic organization that accompanied these innovations. With the Industrial Revolution, all countries with advanced economies developed programs of elementary education available to all children as well as plans for a comprehensive system of secondary schooling that would serve most adolescents.

Schooling on such a large scale did not exist prior to the Industrial Revolution. Secondary education up to the middle of the eighteenth century was not conceived of as schooling for all youth. The classical-humanistic Latin grammar school was for the sons of the upper class or from the deserving poor. The gradual entry into secondary schools of a large number of youth from the middle and lower classes is a prime historical fact of modern education. A corollary fact is the addition of subjects of study to the curriculum that would not have been thought of as education in earlier times. Vocational subjects certainly would have been repugnant to the educators of ancient Greece and to their intellectual descendents during the Middle Ages and the Renaissance.

Attendant with the Industrial Revolution was the outbreak of the spirit of nationalism and revolution that Napoleon unleashed on the European continent at the beginning of the nineteenth century. Education became a prime concern of modern government because loyalty to the state became the supreme purpose of man. The citizen of the modern nation-state needed to be educated to perform great national tasks. Every citizen had to be trained in the role each was to play in the social order. In the democratic societies that developed in America, France, and Britain, such education included the ethic of respect for the dignity of the individual and for the rights of others; whereas, in the developing totalitarian societies found in Germany and Russia, education remained fundamentally and broadly vocational in the widest sense of that word in that it emphasized and meant the development of skills and talent for service to the state.

Great Britain

Education Prior to 1870. In the nineteenth century years that preceded passage of the first public school law in England in 1870, various charity-school organizations carried the major responsibility for English educational support. Mainly interested in the religious instruction of the poor, these societies provided their own texts, trained and paid their own teachers, and administered these schools. Education of upper class children remained the business of the great English public schools, mostly founded before 1600, and the Latin grammar schools which numbered some five thousand at the time of the American Revolution. English secondary education, training as it did the leaders of the British social order, emphasized the classical -humanistic studies of the Renaissance. But education was not considered to be the business of the state.

The English conscience was slowly awakened during the course of the nineteenth century, and various steps were taken that culminated with the passage of the Education Act of 1870. The Factor Act passed by Parliament in 1802 regulated children's employment. In 1816 a parliamentary committee investigated the educational status of lower classes in London and other metropolitan centers. The government began to subsidize educational societies in 1833 with annual appropriations of 20,000 pounds. In 1839 the Committee of Privy Council on Education was established to advise on nondenominational education. Annual grants for establishment of schools of design in manufacturing districts were started in 1841, and in 1846 annual appropriations to educational socieities were increased to 30,000 pounds per year. In 1847 a government proposal for nationalizing education was carried in Parliament despite bitter religious opposition, and in 1856 the Education Department was created that would remain in existence until replaced by the Ministry of Education in 1944. The Newcastle Commission was appointed in 1858 to inquire into the state of British education. The Commission's report in 1861 revealed that only one person in seven in the population was attending school, while in Prussia the ratio was one in six, and in France one out of nine. While the Commission did not recommend compulsory tuition-free education, it did nevertheless pave the way for increasing government grants to educational groups. The National Education League was formed in 1869, and that society was instrumental in forcing the Parliament to establish a secular tuition-free compulsory national education system in England the following year.

Education Act of 1870. The Education Act of 1870 was the first major step in developing a national system of education in Great Britain. The Act provided for division of the country into districts and established local school boards. These school boards were to inventory the educational needs of the districts and establish needed public elementary schools where voluntary societies failed to rectify the deficiency in elementary education within a year. The Act also empowered the school boards to compel school attendance of children between the ages of five and twelve, and to make provision for religious instruction of a nondenominational character in the public schools.

The Act of 1870 was in keeping with the British character because it was a typical British compromise. It let the churches retain any schools they had before the law was passed; yet it established school boards to supplement voluntary educational efforts. Gradually with time after the passage of the Act the burden of elementary education passed from the backs of private groups to public authorities. Subsequent legislation imposed fines upon parents who failed to send their children to school. It was not, however, until the year 1902 that school boards were authorized under law to offer any education beyond the elementary level at public expense, although many of them did.

Education Act of 1902. The Education Act of 1902 was the second major step in the development of a national system of education in Great Britain. It was the most important piece of educational legislation between 1870 and 1944. In 1902 the powers of the school boards were transferred to local educational authorities. Every council of a county or borough was given authority over the elementary schools of their districts. The newly constituted local education authorities were also required to see that, in addition to elementary education, secondary and further education was offered in their areas. Thus for the first time, in 1902, public secondary education was provided for in Great Britain.

France

Jesuit Control. In the development of a national system of education France was almost a century in advance of Great Britain. Until the outbreak of the French Revolution in 1789 French education was dominated by various religious groups, of which perhaps the most significant was the Society of Jesus. The period of Jesuit influence over education in France extended from 1550 to 1764 when their labors were suppressed. Jesuit schools, still the best in Christendom, were organized into "lower colleges" and "upper colleges." The former admitted pupils at the age of ten, and the curriculum was five to six years in length; the latter offered university training. Jesuit education emphasized rigid discipline, keen competition, and teaching through precepts and example.

Elementary education until the time of the Revolution was largely in the hands of the religious group known as the Brothers of the Christian School founded in 1684 by Jean Baptiste de LaSalle (1561-1719), educational reformer and priest at Reims. This order was instrumental in founding many charity schools throughout France for poor children. During the Revolution the Order was suppressed and their schools closed.

Napoleonic Laws of 1802 and 1808. During the pre-Napoleonic phase of the Revolution initiatory steps were taken to establish a national system of public schools. In 1792 the Marquis Marie Jean Antoine Nicholas de Caritat de Condorcet (1743-1794), the philosopher-mathematician, and president of the Legislative Assembly of 1792, advocated tuition-free public education for the first four grades in his school plan of 1792. The French Constitution of 1792 also provided for the creation of a system of common public instruction. Events of the Revolution, however, precluded the implementation of these provisions.

In 1802 when Napoleon served as First Consul of France, he published a school law making secondary education the responsibility of the state. This act led to the establishment of a number of lycees and colleges. These schools, patterned after the Jesuit "lower colleges," maintained a classical-humanistic curriculum and were state supported. Inasmuch as Napoleon was not interested in elementary education, primary schools remained local and limited in scope, and received no state subsidy.

In 1808 Napoleon, now Emperor, united all secondary schools and higher educational institutions into one corporate body known as the *Universitie de France*. The nation was divided into twenty-seven educational administrative units called "academies," each headed by an official known as the "rector." At the top of the pedogogic hierarchy was the Grand Master. He was directly responsible to the Emperor. This administrative pattern remained relatively unchanged until 1875.

Law of 1833. The next important step in establishing a national system of education in France occurred under the reign of the "Citizen King" Louis Philippe (1773-1850). The law of 1833 represents the beginnings of a national system of elementary schools in France. This act was based on the observations of Victor Cousin (1792-1867), the French philosopher and pedagogue who, while studying in Germany, prepared a report on the Prussian *Volkschule*. The Act provided that a primary school be established in each French commune or local community. The state fixed the salary of the teacher, and the schools were to be supervised by state officials. In 1881 elementary education was made free, and in 1882 it was made compulsory between the ages of six and thirteen. By the turn of the century the French had established an extensive and efficient and centralized system of state-controlled primary and secondary schools. In 1904 the schools of the various religious orders were closed.

Germany

Background. The organization and character of German education was developed during the period of the Reformation. The old Latin grammar cathedral and burgh schools of the Middle Ages were reorganized by such Protestant educators as Melanchthon and Johann Sturm. It was Sturm who first used the term "Gymnasium," and who formulated the nine-year humanistic-classical curriculum that became the model for Germany and the rest of Europe. As the German principalities and states evolved through the course of the seventeenth and eighteenth centuries, the kingdom of Prussia slowly emerged as the political, cultural, and educational leader of the German "Vaterland."

Prussian School Legislation. The foundations of the Prussian school organization were laid during the reign of the second Prussian Hohenzollern king, Frederick William I (1713-1740). In 1713 a regulatory code was published urging school attendance. This exhortation was followed in 1717 by a decree from the king directing the authorities of the realm to assist each other in their efforts "to relieve ignorance at last." The *Principia Regulative* of the king, issued in 1737, contained detailed instructions for those who had to contribute to the building of schoolhouses, other instructions concerning the schoolmaster's income, and advice for the nobility and clergy to the effect that they were expected to contribute to the sustenance of the pedagogues in their respective areas. Through the decrees of the government under Frederick William I, the king expressed his earnest concern for schools, and the people adjusted themselves to possess a certain respect for schooling.

Considerable educational progress was made under the reign of the old king's son, Frederick the Great (1740-1786). On September 23, 1763, King Frederick II issued the General Regulations for Elementary Schools and Teachers. This famous document was prepared under the Great Frederick's direction and marks the first general school code for the kingdom. School attendance was made compulsory from five to thirteen for those who could pass the state examinations, and from five to fourteen for those who failed them. Special examinations and licensing of teachers were set, and adult education was provided on Sundays by school teachers for those beyond school age. Improvements also were made in secondary education, academic freedom guaranteed for universities; and church schools were placed under state supervision. In 1765 a state code was adopted for the Catholic schools in Silesia. In 1748 as a result of the War of the Austrian Succession, Frederick the Great wrested the province of Silesia from Maria Theresa of Austria. Silesia was a Catholic province, and in 1765 the king issued a code much like the previous code for Prussia (1763).

Frederick the Great's successor, Frederick William II (1786-1797), put all Prussian schools except the universities under a central administrative board of education. Frederick William III

(1797-1840) completed the codification of Prussian laws begun by Frederick the Great. The twelfth chapter of the new code dealt with education. It reaffirmed state regulation and centralization of the school system, including the universities. Also, it provided for compulsory attendance, appointment of teachers by the state, state supervision of church schools, and guaranteed the practice of religious instruction in church schools.

Nineteenth Century Developments in Prussian Education. The defeat of Prussia by Napoleon in 1806 created a new impulse for German nationalism. Philosophers such as Johann Gottlieb Fichte (1762-1814) stressed the importance of education as a national regenerative force. "I hope," Fichte proclaimed to the Germans during the winter of 1807-08, "that I convince some Germans, and that I shall bring them to see that it is education alone which can save us from all the evils by which we are oppressed."[24] Fichte and others revolutionized the elementary schools and introduced Pestalozzian methods. In 1808 the Department of Public Instruction was created in the Prussian state, and the German philologist and diplomat Baron Wilhelm von Humboldt (1767-1835), brother of Alexander von Humboldt the great cosmologist, traveler, and statesman, was selected as its first head. The Department became a Ministry in 1817, and by 1825 provincial school boards were organized and made responsible to the ministry.

In the seventy years of the nineteenth century that preceded the unification of Germany, secondary education in the state of Prussia was reorganized and unified. Baron Wilhelm von Humboldt, the first Education Minister, reconstructed the Gymnasium and made it into a school that placed emphasis on university-preparatory courses in Greek and mathematics and on training persons for high positions in the civil service.[25] The curriculum of the Gymnasium was further intensified in the years 1858 and 1859 when scientific and technical courses were added to the studies of Greek and Latin literatures and languages. The years 1858-1859 also witnessed the acceptance of the Realschule as a necessary public secondary school. The first Realschule had been opened by Julius Hecker (1707-1768) in Berlin in 1747. This school contained many practical courses for training in trades and business. Revised and upgraded, the Realschule was outfitted with a cultural-practical curriculum.

Prussian military victories over Austria in 1866 and France in 1871 intensified the spirit of nationalism throughout Germany. Under the leadership of Prussia the German peoples were unified into the empire of the first German Reich. The Prussian king Wilhelm I

(1861-1888) became the first German Kaiser in 1871. The purpose of all German schools now became the training of all citizens of the Reich for the performance of great national tasks. German education was to play its role in the idealization and glorification of the German state.

German Education 1871-1919. The school structure in Germany between the years 1871-1919 appeared as follows: ELEMENTARY EDUCATION. The Volkschule was an eight-year compulsory common school that had been reorganized in 1807 by the Prussian Minister of Education, Baron Wilhelm von Humboldt. SECONDARY SCHOOLS. The Vorschule was also a preparatory department attached to the secondary school that trained children of compulsory school age who expected to attend the secondary school. The Gymnasium was the secondary school that had the nine-year curriculum emphasizing Latin and Greek languages and literatures. The Realgymnasium was a secondary school that offered a nine-year curriculum which included both humanities and modern subjects, but required only Greek and not Latin. The Oberrealschule was a nine-year secondary school that offered courses in modern subjects including sciences, mathematics, and modern languages, but without requirements in either Greek or Latin.

Several secondary schools evolved from the Realschule above described. These schools offered curricula that ranged in length from six to nine years. The Realprogymnasium included modern subjects and prescribed Latin but not Greek. The Progymnasium was a modern school that prescribed both Greek and Latin. The Realschule itself emphasized scientific and technical courses, and the Burgerschule stressed the study of modern languages.

During the life of the first German Reich (1871-1919) within the German school structure above described, four basic educational trends were apparent. These were: (1) the increase of central state support and control; (2) the elimination of church jurisdiction; (3) general improvement in teacher education and in instruction; and (4) the domination of the entire school system by nationalistic aims and ambitions.[26]

Russia

Background. Russia is the largest country in the world, and geographically it is a vast lowland stretching from the Baltic and Black Seas eastward to the Pacific Ocean. It covers about one-sixth of the earth's inhabited surface. The history of Russia has been a dramatization of struggle between a drive for individual independence and a trend toward a God-king ideology, which manifested itself first in the worship of the Czar and later in the adulation of Lenin and Marx.[27] Until the seventeenth century the only schools in Russia were elementary schools. These schools prepared persons to become clerks and priests.

Peter the Great (1689-1725) introduced European culture and education into Russia. Peter's "window on the west" was the great northern capital city he ordered built and that was named St. Petersburg. It is now known as Leningrad. Under Peter's successor, Catherine I (1725-1727), a Gymnasium was added to the school structure that educated mostly sons of government officials. In 1755 the first Russian university was founded in Moscow. Attached to the University were two Gymnasiums, one for training the children of the nobility, and one for children of other classes. Catherine the Great (1762-1796) set up a Commission for the Creation of Public Schools, and in the year 1802 under Alexander I (1801-1825) the Ministry of Education was established. In 1802, Nakosteen reports, there were 315 schools in Russia with an enrollment of 20,000 pupils.[28]

Russian Education During the Nineteenth Century. Under Czar Alexander I Russia was divided into six educational districts. Each district was headed by an official called the "curator." A university, under the Czar's plan, was to be founded in each district, a Gymnasium in each provincial capital, and an elementary school in each county. When Alexander I died in 1825, Nakosteen reports, there were 3,375 schools, including 48 Gymnasiums with a student enrollment of 5,500.[29]

The nineteenth century was the golden age in Russian literature and art. Such literary and artistic figures as Pushkin, Dostoevski, Tolstoi, Gogol, and Tchaikowski received world acclaim. The high state of Russian culture was also reflected in the founding of such schools as the Demidov Law School in Iaroslave in 1805; the Philological Institute of Prince Bezborodko in Niezhim in 1820; and the Imperial Lyceum in Tsarskoe, founded in 1811, and the school from which Russia's most famous poet, Alexander Sergeevich Pushkin (1799-1837) was graduated.

The Russians in the nineteenth century helped to pioneer industrial arts and technical education. The Institute of Technology of St. Petersburg was founded in 1828, and the Institute of Technology in Moscow was opened in 1844. The building of the Trans-Siberian Railroad (1891-1905) was one of the great technological achievements of the nineteenth century. The number of Russian scientists and inventors during the latter decades of the nineteenth century compared favorably with Europe and America.

Russian educational progress during the course of the nineteenth century was mainly evidenced in higher education. Most of the universities, higher institutes, and schools were comparable to their European counterparts. The empire of the Czars had also made some advances in elementary and secondary education, but the educational structure was set up to favor the children of the nobility and of the other elite in Russian society. Until the Russian Revolution of 1917 the land of the Czars was characterized by an infinitesimal educated and enlightened elite on the one hand, and on the other by an almost wholly illiterate rural peasantry and urban laboring class.

Conclusion

The renaissance had been a landmark in the history of Western education. One of its principal characteristics was a revival of the learning of ancient times, but no less strong was the yearning for a new world with a fuller and more interesting way of life. In the seventeenth century, the classical languages and literature still remained the only essential elements of secondary education. Francis Bacon in England and Rene Descartes in France foresaw the need to include science and knowledge of the scientific process in the curriculum. Johann Amos Comenius, the great Czech educator, sought to bring a new note of realism into educational thought. John Locke's writings on education became important educational doctrine on both sides of the Atlantic.

The eighteenth century was a period of great activity in reformulating educational principles. There was a ferment of new ideas, some of which wrought a transformation in secondary school practices. Of those who thought and wrote about education no one has had as much influence as Jean Rousseau. His version of education inspired others to continue the revolution which he initiated. The German philosopher-psychologist-educator Johann Friedrich Herbart was perhaps the first to recognize that education was worthy to be a science and not just a department of philosophy.

There were in the nineteenth century several general trends that are still influencing education in all Western countries during the second half of the twentieth century. Of these, the most significant is the gradual acceptance of the view that education ought to be a responsibility of the nation-state. England hesitated a long time before allowing the state to intervene in educational affairs. It was in France that the idea that the state would control education first took hold. The Prussian educational system became the mainspring of German recovery after its crushing defeat by Napoleon at Jena. Feeble beginnings of public education in the Russian state can be traced back to actions taken by the Czars in the latter part of the nineteenth century.

Chapter IV
Footnotes

[1] Francis Bacon, *Novum Organum,* as quoted by Robert Ulich, *Three Thousand Years of Educational Wisdom* (Cambridge, Massachusetts: Harvard University Press, 1959), p. 306.

[2] Rene Descartes, *Discourses,* as quoted by Robert Ulich, *op. cit.,* p. 319.

[3] Kingsley Price, *Education and Philosophical Thought* (Boston: Allyn and Bacon, Inc., 1962), p. 210.

[4] *Ibid.,* p. 215.

[5] *Ibid.,* p. 231.

[6] *Ibid.,* pp. 238-239.

[7] John Locke, *Some Thoughts on Education,* as quoted by Robert Ulich, *op. cit.,* p. 356.

[8] *Ibid.*

[9] Price, *op. cit.,* p. 241.

[10] Locke, *op. cit.,* p. 361.

[11] Price, *op. cit.,* pp. 248-249.

[12] Locke, *op. cit.,* p. 376.

[13] Jean Jacques Rousseau, *Emile,* as quoted by Robert Ulich, *op. cit.,* p. 383.

[14] *Ibid.,* p. 388.

[15] *Ibid.,* p. 392.

[16] *Ibid.,* p. 403.

[17] *Ibid.,* pp. 407-415.

[18] *Ibid.,* p. 419.

[19] Price, *op. cit.,* p. 322.

[20]*Ibid.*, pp. 323-324.

[21]*Ibid.*, p. 324.

[22]Percival R. Cole, "Herbart," *A Cyclopedia of Education* (1912), III p. 252.

[23]Johann Friedrich Herbart, *Science of Education,* as quoted by Robert Ulich, *op. cit.*, p. 520.

[24]Johann Gottlieb Fichte, *Addresses to the German Nation* (Boston: Houghton Mifflin Co., 1920), p. 480.

[25]Medhi Nakosteen, *The History and Philosophy of Education* (New York: The Ronald Press, 1965), p. 378.

[26]*Ibid.*, p. 381.

[27]Arthur H. Moehlman, *Comparative Educational Systems* (Washington, D.C.: The Center for Applied Research in Education, Inc., 1963), p. 33.

[28]Nakosteen, *op. cit.*, p. 409.

[29]*Ibid.*

Selected References

Beck, Robert Holmes. *A Social History of Education.* Englewood Cliffs, New Jersey: Prentice-Hall, Inc., 1965.

Butts, R. Freeman. *A Cultural History of Western Education.* New York: McGraw-Hill Book Company, 1955.

Cole, Percival Richard. *A History of Educational Thought.* London: Oxford University Press, 1931.

Cubberley, Ellwood P. *Readings in the History of Education.* Boston: Houghton-Mifflin Company, 1920.

Good, H. G. *A History of Western Education.* New York: The Macmillan Company, 1960.

Meyer, Adolphe E. *An Educational History of the Western World.* New York: McGraw-Hill Book Company, 1965.

Moehlman, Arthur H. *Comparative Educational Systems.* Washington, D.C.: The Center for Applied Research in Education, Inc., 1963.

Monroe, Paul (ed.). *A Cyclopedia of Education.* 5 vols. New York: The Macmillan Company, 1911.

Mulhern, James. *A History of Education.* New York: The Ronald Press Company, 1959.

Nakosteen, Mehdi. *The History and Philosophy of Education.* New York: The Ronald Press Company, 1965.

Ulich, Robert. *Three Thousand Years of Educational Wisdom.* Cambridge, Massachusetts: Harvard University Press, 1959.

Chapter V

COMPARATIVE EUROPEAN SECONDARY SCHOOL SYSTEMS: GREAT BRITAIN AND FRANCE

England and Wales

Background

In the early nineteenth century there arose a strong desire for general reform of the British grammar and public schools. The public school, a characteristic British institution, dating from the sixteenth century or earlier, is a grammar school controlled completely by its own board of governors. The reforms that came about were largely the result of efforts of such famous headmasters as Thomas Arnold of Rugby, Edward Thring of Uppingham, and Haig Brown of Charterhouse.[1]

THOMAS ARNOLD (1795-1842) was the greatest of the nineteenth century headmasters. A graduate of Oxford (1814), and ordained in the Church of England (1818), he was appointed Headmaster of Rugby in 1828. Arnold reorganized Rugby School and broadened its curriculum. He introduced mathematics, modern history and modern language. His practices of entrusting responsibility to subordinates and of using organized games and sports as instruments in character building were strongly influential in giving public school education in England its unique character. He also made attendance at chapel services an integral part of school life.[2]

The work of pioneering headmasters improved the standards of the old public schools. There was, however, no publicly provided system of secondary education and the need for it grew increasingly throughout the course of the nineteenth century. Three important commissions were established as the century proceeded. The first was the Public Schools Commission (1861-1864), which investigated the administration of the public schools. The Schools Inquiry Commission (1864-1868) dealt with other secondary schools. The third was the Bryce Commission (1894-1895), which was instructed to consider what were the best methods of establishing a well-organized system of secondary education in England. The Bryce Commission recommendations form the basis for some of the main British educational developments of the twentieth century.[3]

The Education Act of 1902 became the foundation of the State educational system in England and Wales. It abolished the School Boards and made the county councils, county borough councils, and certain borough and urban district councils into local education authorities. It also lessened the financial difficulties of the voluntary schools by requiring the local education authorities to maintain them in return for assuming control of the instruction (other than religious) given in them. Finally, it gave county councils and county borough councils power to supply or assist secondary and technical education. The ultimate results of the 1902 Act and its elaboration in later legislation included the establishment and rapid development of secondary schools wholly provided and maintained by local education authorities; the granting of financial assistance by local education authorities to a number of secondary schools (grammar schools and others) already in existence; the development of technical education; and the establishment of a number of teacher-training colleges wholly provided and maintained by local education authorities.[4]

Characteristics of British Secondary Education

Statistics. Secondary education in Britain is being progressively reorganized on comprehensive lines. Following passage of the Education Act of 1944, the main types of secondary schools have been "grammar," "modern," and "technical" schools. Until the early 1960's the great majority of secondary schools maintained by local education authorities (LEAs) were organized on a selective basis in which entry into the different types generally depended on the results of tests taken at the age of eleven, and known as the "Eleven Plus." In 1965, out of the 5,873 LEA-maintained secondary schools, there were 1,295 grammar schools for children selected as suitable for an academic education oriented toward university entrance; 3,727 secondary modern schools, originally designed to give a general education with a practical basis, but many of them later widening their approach to include academic courses; and 172 secondary technical schools. Also in 1965 there were 262 secondary comprehensive schools. These are non-selective schools which provide all types of education for all or most of the pupils in a district. In July, 1965, it was announced that eighty-one of the 162 LEA's had, or were, considering schemes for comprehensive schools.[5]

Compulsory Education. All children in Britain between the ages of five and fifteen must by law attend school or be otherwise educated in a way approved by the local education authority. The statutory school-leaving age is to be raised to sixteen in the 1970-1971 year. About a quarter of all pupils in England and Wales stay for an extra school year after reaching the age of fifteen. Pupils may stay till nineteen. The usual age of entry to universities is eighteen or nineteen, and the first degree course of study lasts three or four years. All children must by law receive some form of secondary education.[6]

Free Public Education. In England and Wales most of the publicly supported schools are county schools. The largest groups are provided and maintained by local education authorities or by voluntary schools provided by voluntary bodies (usually religious denominations) assisted, however, by the local education authorities. In addition, there are a few direct-grant schools, mostly grammar schools, which are independent of local education authorities, but which receive direct grants-in-aid from the Ministry of Education. These direct-grant schools charge fees, but up to fifty per cent of their enrollees must be accepted free.[7] All education in state-maintained schools is now free.

In Great Britain no tuition fees are charged to parents of children attending schools maintained wholly or partly by local education authorities, and books and equipment are supplied free. A small number of maintained schools have boarding facilities, and boarding fees charged are nominal. Also, local education authorities may help parents with these fees to the extent needed to prevent hardship. Each authority decides the extent of its help. Direct-grant schools still charge fees but as noted above, they must offer each year a fixed number of free enrollments.[8]

Religious Instruction. Religious instruction distinctive of any one denomination may not be given in any school fully supported out of public funds. Yet religious instruction is a vital aspect of British secondary education. All British school-children attending schools that are wholly maintained by local education authorities receive religious instruction of an undenominational Christian character in accordance with an agreed syllabus and take part in a daily corporate act of worship unless their parents object. The syllabus is agreed to by a conference representing the religious denominations, the teachers, and the local education authorities. In schools partially supported out of public funds, denominational religious instruction may be given subject to parents' approval. In certain circumstances clergy have a right of access to county schools in order to give denominational instruction to children of their persuasion for a limited period each week.[9]

Religious instruction in direct-grant schools is given in accordance with the school's trust deed; or, if no mention is made of this in the deed, in accordance with the established practice of the school. There is also a daily collective act of worship at direct-grant schools.[10]

Types of Secondary Education

Characteristics. Public provision of secondary education is being greatly extended to provide all children with a secondary education appropriate to their particular needs. Since the organization of publicly supported secondary schools in England and Wales (1902) is the responsibility of local education authorities, subject to the approval of the Ministry of Education, the type of provision made for secondary education varies to some extent between areas. In some areas different types of schools specialize, particularly in the later years, in different types of courses, with arrangements for the transfer of pupils between schools where desirable. In others, flexibility is achieved by an overlap of the courses provided in different types of schools. There are today, however, four broadly discernable types of publicly maintained secondary schools in Great Britain: grammar schools, secondary modern schools, secondary technical schools, and comprehensive secondary schools.

Grammar Schools. Grammar schools are designed for pupils likely to profit from an academic type of education. These schools offer a university preparatory program of six to seven years in length. The age range of pupils is eleven to eighteen years. These schools recruit the upper twenty-five per cent in ability of the secondary school pupil population. Grammar schools are either maintained by local education authorities or operated as direct-grant schools.

Secondary Modern Schools. Secondary modern schools still form the largest group of secondary schools in Great Britain. They emphasize general education and give some vocational training consciously related to the interests and environments of their pupils. Modern schools enroll approximately three-fifths of the secondary school children. The age range of the pupils is from eleven to sixteen years, with most leaving at fifteen. Pupil range of abilities in secondary modern schools is wide.

Secondary Technical Schools. Secondary technical schools are a smaller group that offer an education largely related to industry, commerce, and agriculture. The curricula of these schools is general in intent and not vocational in purpose. It might be stated that they offer general education through technical studies. Pupil age range in technical schools vary, depending upon local arrangements, but it may extend from eleven to seventeen. These schools generally contain well-equipped laboratories and workshops.

Comprehensive Schools. Comprehensive secondary schools were introduced into England about fifteen years ago. They are not selective and provide a wide range of secondary education for all or most children of a district. All pupils follow the same general education curriculum for the first two years. In 1965 the British government announced that as a matter of national policy all secondary education should be reorganized on a comprehensive basis, and in July of that year it was announced that eighty-one of the 162 LEA's had, or were considering, plans for comprehensive schools. The comprehensive school will in time replace the separatist system of schooling in Britain.

Independent Secondary Schools

Although independent schools are completely self-supporting and independent of public funds, all such schools must be registered with the Ministry of Education. These schools are attended by about six per cent of the school children in England and Wales.

The largest and most important of the independent schools are known as public schools. There are just under 300 public schools, about half of which are for girls. The boys' schools, in particular, include a high proportion of boarding schools, and it is among these that the nine great public schools are numbered.

The nine great English public schools, dating from the sixteenth century or earlier, are: Eton, Shrewsbury, Harrow, Rugby, Merchant Taylors, St. Paul's, Charterhouse, Westminster, and Winchester. The largest (1,200 students), and perhaps most socially selective of them all, is Eton. Over 500 years old and a bastion of aristocracy, Eton admits as much as seventy-five per cent of its students from among the sons of old Etonians, many registered at birth. Etonians still wear striped trousers, black tailcoats, and white ties that their predecessors first donned in the nineteenth century. The cost of attending Eton is $1,600 a year, including board.[11]

The public schools admit between three to six out of each one thousand secondary school pupils. The usual age of entry is thirteen, and the leaving age about eighteen. Public schools have emphasized the importance of character-building and have developed the perfect system, whereby day-to-day discipline is largely maintained by the pupils themselves, and the house system, in which a school is divided into groups of about fifty, each under the care of a housemaster. The public school is also characterized by a high staffing ratio and a high proportion of pupils doing advanced work often leading to the university. Services in the school chapel and religious teaching are essential parts of the life and education of the public schools.[12] Traditionally, the public schools have educated the leaders of the British church, government, and business. Chief complaint against the public school is that admissions are based on wealth and family ties, rather than ability. Education Minister Anthony Crosland says that these schools are "a major cause of social inequality. It is no accident that Britain, the only country in the world with this stratum of private and privileged education, is the most class-conscious, snobbish and stratified country in the world."[13]

Late in 1965 the British government announced the appointment of a Public Schools Commission to advise on the best way to integrate the public schools within the state system of education. The objectives of the Commission are: (1) to ensure that the public schools make their maximum contribution to the national educational needs, particularly for boarding education; (2) to create a socially mixed entry into the schools; (3) to move toward a wider range of academic attainment in order to conform with the national policy for comprehensive education; and (4) to see that the public schools become progressively open to boys and girls irrespective of their parents' income.[14]

Secondary School Curricula and Practices

Grammar Schools. The grammar school is older than any other English institution except the Church. St. Peter's School in York is the oldest and was founded in 627 A.D. Many grammar schools were organized by the Church during the Middle Ages to train young boys in the Latin language so they could take part in Church services. At the time of the English Renaissance during the reign of the first Elizabeth the schools adopted the classical-humanistic curriculum.

The grammar schools include the public schools, above described, independent day schools and independent boarding schools, direct-grant schools, and schools built by local education authorities. Each grammar school has its own board of governors that selects the headmaster, who in turn draws up the curriculum and prescribes methods of teaching.

Grammar schools offer nonvocational general education suited for pupils with an interest in academic learning. In grammar schools the study of English language and literature, Latin and one foreign language, geography, mathematics, chemistry, and physics have become firmly entrenched. The proportions of time spent on each of these subjects vary, as does also the somewhat more generous proportion allotted to games, gymnastics, singing, and fine arts. Only religion, taught according to the approved syllabus, is a compulsory subject for all schools. The last two years of the curriculum, after the foundation of a good general education has been laid, is called the "Sixth Form" and involves some degree of specialization and separation between arts and science subjects.

Secondary Modern Schools. No two secondary modern schools have identical curricula or set courses of study. The heads of these schools, like those of grammar schools, arrange their own curricula. Since, in contrast to the grammar school, only a small proportion of their pupils take any external examination (see pp. 86-87), they have greater freedom in arranging curricula. In the secondary modern school it is common for more time to be given to industrial arts, domestic science, and other practical activities than is possible in grammar schools because the curriculum is designed to meet the needs of all and is influenced by local circumstances. In a rural district, for example, agricultural science may be taught. In other places a pre-nursing or commercial course may be instituted. In all locations, however, the general subjects required for passing the examination for the General Certificate of Education are offered (see pp. 86-87). General education courses include the following: mathematics, geography, history, French, German, Spanish, physical education, and nondenominational religious instruction.[15]

Modern secondary schools attempt to relate life within the school to life without and to help pupils make better social adjustments. Curricular programs are designed in such a way that faster pupils are grouped together and proceed at their own pace, and slower school children are grouped together and follow a less academic and more practical curriculum. The trend in the modern secondary school towards a comprehensive system received a tremendous boost when the Government circular of 1964 was issued.[16]

Secondary Technical Schools. In secondary technical schools the curricula are generally similar to those of the grammar schools except that the emphasis in general education is to relate pupils' schooling to the scientific and industrial background of society, and through general studies to create an interest in culture and philosophy which are fundamental to good design, taste, and craftsmanship. More attention is given to science, mathematics, practical, and technical subjects. Latin and Greek are not usually given. The curriculum varies from school to school according to the particular field of interest.[17]

In the first two years of the secondary technical school the primary emphasis is on the basic skills of learning. The course of study is the arts and sciences and a modern foreign language. During this period of time the final determination is made on the type of secondary course which the pupil will pursue, either technical, grammar, or modern. If the pupil remains in the technical school, his third and fourth years of study will consist mostly of the liberal arts with approximately ten per cent of the time devoted to technical studies. During the final two years cognizance is taken of the pupil's future requirements, and necessary options are provided. Most pupils enter for the General Certificate of Education examination at the Ordinary level, and an increasing number at the Advanced level (see p. 87).[18]

Secondary School Examinations

Common Entrance Examination. The Common Entrance Examination, commonly known as the "Eleven Plus," generally has been required of public school entrants. It has been the normal method of passing from a preparatory school to a public school. A preparatory school, which is usually a boarding school, is for boys from about eight to thirteen years of age who are preparing to enter a public school. There are preparatory schools for girls also. The curriculum of the preparatory school is very different from that of a state-maintained primary school because its purpose is to prepare pupils for the General Certificate of Education.[19]

The Common Entrance, or "Eleven Plus" Examination, is a comprehensive test that includes—besides English—history, geography, and scripture, subjects such as Greek or Latin, French and mathematics (divided into arithmetic, algebra, and geometry). The public schools are beginning to drop the requirement that their entering students must know some Latin.

General Certificate of Education Examinations. There is no national secondary school-leaving examination in Great Britain, but secondary pupils and candidates not attending school may take the General Certificate of Education Examination (GCE). Examinations for the GCE were introduced in 1951. The examinations replaced the former School Certificate and Higher School Certificate examinations. Nine independent examining bodies, eight of which are connected with universities, are responsible for conducting the examinations.[20]

These examinations are set at two levels: Ordinary ("O"), and Advanced ("A"). The O-level examination is usually taken at the end of a five-year course in a secondary school. Nearly half the candidates for the O-level come from other than grammar schools. The A-level examination is usually taken after a further two year's study in the sixth form of the grammar school. The A-level results are used to determine eligibility of candidates for most universities other than Oxford and Cambridge, whose colleges have their own entrance examinations.

There are no compulsory subjects at either level, and candidates may take as many or as few subjects and as many times as they wish. They do not need to take the same subject at both O- and A-levels. Universities and professional bodies determine for themselves what constitute the level of achievement required of their entrants. The normal minimum age of entry for the GCE examinations is sixteen. There is no upper age limit. There are about eighty subjects to choose from at the O-level, and about sixty at the A-level. Normally, the candidate chooses a minimum of six subjects.

Certificate of Secondary Education Examinations. A new examination, the Certificate of Secondary Education (CSE), was introduced in 1965 as the result of the need for an examination below the level of the GCE. The CSE, like the GCE, is on a single subject basis. Unlike the GCE, the CSE is controlled by the participating schools and reflects the work of the schools without imposing a pattern on the curriculum. There are fourteen regional examining boards composed of practicing teachers. The CSE is open to pupils of any school who have completed, or about to complete, five years of secondary education.[21]

Administration of Secondary Education

Administration of the public system of primary, secondary, and further education is divided between the central government, local education authorities, and various voluntary organizations. Relations between these three groups are based on consultation and cooperation, both by direct contact between the parties and through school inspectors who act as liaison officers between local education authorities and the Ministry of Education.

Ministry of Education. The Ministry of Education is presided over by the Minister who is appointed by the Prime Minister, and he serves as a cabinet member. The staff of the Ministry consists of headquarters administrative officers and school inspectors whose work mostly lies in the districts of the local education authorities.

It is the duty of the Minister of Education to promote the education of the people of England and Wales; to promote the progressive development of institutions devoted to that purpose; and to secure the effective execution by local education authorities, under his control and direction, of the national policy for providing a varied and comprehensive educational service in every area. He issues his main requirements in the form of statutory regulations and in circulars addressed to local education authorities and other bodies.

The Minister is concerned not only with formal full-time education other than university education but also with the encouragement of adult education, the maintenance of certain museums, and the promotion of youth services. He has powers that enable him to foster educational research and to make grants for this purpose.[22]

Local Education Authorities. In England and Wales there are 162 local education authorities. These are fifty-nine county councils and 102 county borough councils, besides one joint board representing the areas of a county and a borough. In order to use local knowledge and initiative, certain of the educational functions of county councils may be delegated to specially constituted divisional executives (some of which are called 'excepted districts'). These executives are individual county districts (borough or urban or rural districts) or combinations of districts or parts of districts. Each local education authority must establish an education committee to which it entrusts its educational work, with the exception of certain financial transactions. Education committees must contain a number of persons of experience in education who may or may not be members of the council.[23]

The local education authority has the responsibility of providing, apart from the independent and private schools, the educational facilities of its area, and it is primarily responsible to the Ministry of Education for the conduct of the schools in its area. The local education authority submits to the Ministry of Education development plans for approval, observes the rules on teacher certification, and are guided by the ministry-negotiated official schedule of teacher salaries. In return, the local authority receives national funds that help to defray more than one-half of their current expenditures; it can also obtain professional advice and educational publications from the ministry's inspectorate.

Education Act of 1944. The Education Act of 1944 superseded all existing educational legislation. It reframed the public system of education and brought the first triparte legislation of secondary education for all. The plan called for extending compulsory school attendance to the age of sixteen, and part-time attendance to eighteen, and for building up the nonacademic wing of modern schools. The remainder of the school population not selected for the grammar or technical stream had been placed in these modern schools in which the curriculum was meant to be geared to the practical needs of the pupils. The right of a full-time secondary education for all adolescents was guaranteed by the Act. All tuition fees in secondary schools maintained by local education authorities were abolished, and provision was made for scholarships and maintenance grants, and for the payment of fees at fee-paying schools under some circumstances. Further Acts were passed in 1946, 1948, 1953, and 1962 to preserve and to supplement the intentions of the Act of 1944.[24]

Some Educational Practices

Teachers. Teachers are appointed by local education authorities or school governing bodies. Teachers in government-aided schools must be approved as 'qualified' by the Ministry of Education.

Secondary teachers obtain their qualified status by virtue of their training by university faculties of arts and science and in departments and institutes of education. The undergraduate candidate for his degree will take a pass or honors in one to three academic subjects. The undergraduate degree usually takes three years to earn. Graduates may, however, undertake a one-year training course either at a university department of education or at one of the general training institutes to which graduates are admitted. The postgraduate course includes studies in philosophy, history, psychology, and principles of education and measurement, and methods of teaching special subjects. An increasing number of schools prefer to recruit staffs who have such graduate training. The Ministry of Education has announced its intention of making graduate training in education a prerequisite of qualified status, at some future date.

Salaries. Salary schedules are uniform throughout England and Wales. In Britain agreed salary schedules are submitted to the Minister of Education by joint committees of representatives of local education authorities and teachers' associations. The best known of these committees are the Burnham Committees, named after Lord Burnham, chairman when they were first set up in 1919. It deals with salaries of teachers in primary and secondary schools and in establishments of further education. The Minister can accept or reject, but not modify, the committees' recommendations and make the approved schedules mandatory on local education authorities. Teachers in England and Wales also are under a national pension system to which they and local education authorities are required by law to make contributions.[25]

Health and Welfare Practices. Before the 1944 Education Act, local education authorities in England and Wales had permissive powers to provide school lunches, but the 1944 Act imposed on local education authorities a duty to provide milk and meals for pupils at state-maintained schools. About fifty-four per cent of pupils in such schools take a noon-time school meal. A nominal charge is made for a meal, but this may be partially or totally remitted according to need.

The British Government has recognized for over fifty years that special medical care, both preventive and curative, is essential to the welfare of growing children, and that a school health service is the best means of providing it. The School Health Service is closely co-ordinated with the National Health Service but continues as a separate entity under the responsibility of the Ministry of Education. All the medical and dental services are free of charge to parents. Child guidance centers or clinics for the treatment of pupils with psychological problems are provided by many local education authorities.[26]

Special Education for Handicapped Children. Educational services are provided in special schools for children between the ages of five and sixteen on account of any physical or mental handicap. The 1944 Education Act prescribed that every local education authority provide for the needs of pupils suffering from a disability of mind or body. A handicapped child can sometimes be given special educational treatment in an ordinary school, and no child is sent to a special school who can be educated satisfactorily in an ordinary school.[27]

Youth Employment Service. Pupils leaving schools between the ages of fifteen and eighteen have the benefit of individual advice on the choice of a career from the local youth employment officers of the Ministry of Labor or of the local education authority. The value of the Youth Employment Service is widely recognized and both young people and employers use it extensively. The service was reconstituted under the Employment and Training Act of 1948 and is well established for fifteen-year-old school-leavers.[28]

France

Background

A major problem of French education in the twentieth century has been the question of pupil access to secondary schools. The dissatisfaction with the functioning of the educational system between the two world wars led to the establishment of the <u>Commission</u> <u>de</u> <u>l'Ecole</u> <u>Unique</u> in 1924 to examine the problem of access to the secondary schools. The preparatory classes attached to the secondary schools known as <u>lycées</u> and <u>collèges</u> were not abolished, but in 1925 the curricula of the preparatory classes and the primary schools were made the same so that all pupils would have equal opportunity for five years (ages six to eleven) to prepare for the selection of examinations for entrance to the secondary schools.

In 1937 direction-finding classes (<u>classes</u> <u>d'orientation</u>) were set up in some <u>lycées</u> in order to help pupils make a better choice of their subsequent course of secondary schooling. Major reform in secondary education received impetus as a result of two post-World War study commissions. The first, the Algiers Commission, reported in 1944, and the second, the Langevin Commission, in 1946. The Langevin report recommended two phases of secondary education, which would begin at the age of eleven years after the completion of primary education. The first phase, termed the <u>cycle d'orientation</u>, was to last for four years and was to be required of all children. It was to be general education together with some optional specialized studies, and its main purpose was to be the exploration of the aptitudes and abilities of the pupils so that the subsequent course of differentiated education could be wisely chosen by the pupils, their parents, and their teachers. The second phase of secondary education was to be a three-year <u>cycle de determination</u>, either full-time or part-time, devoted to specialized vocational training or preparation for the institutions of higher education. The recommendations of the Langevin Commission were drastic and far-reaching and profoundly affected the subsequent thinking of educators both in France and elsewhere.

In 1945 <u>classes nouvelles</u> were formed in a number of <u>lycées</u> that provided an opportunity for experimentation with orientation procedures, activity methods, and optional subjects. Although these classes were abandoned in 1951 when they numbered 800, the experimental findings were spread widely throughout the junior forms of the secondary school, and a few pilot programs continued the work of innovation. In 1956 a new reform proposal was made that reduced the orientation period to two years but emphasized the importance of a common period of education in the first phase of secondary schooling. The plan envisaged the establishment of separate <u>ecoles</u> <u>moyennes</u> to enable all pupils to make a wider choice of subsequent education and extend upward the period of general education for all. The proposal to establish <u>ecoles</u> <u>moyennes</u> was, however, regarded as too costly to be acceptable.

In 1955 Minister of Education J. Berthoin prepared a new school bill, and it was enacted in 1958 for a 1960 (postponed to 1967) implementation. Under the terms of the new education law the school-leaving age was raised to sixteen years, and it was provided that every child would have at least four years of junior secondary education. At the age of eleven years pupils of the primary school were again to be allocated to different types of secondary school, but the curriculum of the first two years in these different schools would be similar. This two-year period was to be devoted to the exploration of the pupils' aptitudes, and at the end of this period the school would advise parents on the best form of continued education for their children.

Under the reorganization of French education the types of secondary school were to be: (1) <u>lycées</u>, both classical and modern, to give a general education leading up to the universities; (2) <u>lycées</u> <u>techniques</u>, to give a general and technical education also leading to the universities and institutions of higher technology; (3) <u>collèges</u> <u>d'enseignement</u> <u>technique</u>, to provide a shorter technical education and trade training to those who would then go out to work; and (4) <u>collèges</u> <u>d'enseignement</u> <u>general</u>, which would conclude the general education of those pupils who intended to leave school at sixteen years of age. In order to facilitate transfer from one type of school to another after the two years of orientation training, special adjustment classes were to be set up.

Characteristics of French Secondary Education

Compulsory Education. Education in France today is compulsory for all children until the age of sixteen. Compulsory schooling has as its object education and basic knowledge, the elements of general culture, and optionally, the rudiments of professional and technical training. Penalties for breaking regulations on compulsory education may be imposed upon members of the teaching corps and persons responsible for the children. In 1965 a decree signed by the Prime Minister and the Ministers of National Education, Economy and Finance, and Social Affairs directs policemen to take pupils of public and private schools out of movie houses and parks during school hours and deliver them to the nearest school. Parents of pupils absent from school for a total of six days in a twelve-month period may be fined up to 400 dollars and put in jail for as long as two months. Parents with less truant children may be fined four to eight dollars and jailed for eight days.

Public Education and Private Schools. The French nation guarantees equal access to the child and adult to instruction, professional training, and culture. The organization of free secular public education on all levels is a duty of the State. Public educational institutions created and maintained by the nation, however, do not have an educational monopoly. Alongside the state establishments are private educational institutions founded and maintained by individuals, associations, professional agencies and religious groups. Since the passage of the 1959 Education Act, private educational institutions may receive public aid. The private schools may request to be integrated into the state education system; or they may keep their separate status and contract with public authorities the extent of state participation in their expenses.[29]

Free Public Education. Free tuition was instituted progressively by the Third Republic (1871-1940). Curricular programs are free in all public educational institutions with the exception of the universities and certain other institutions of higher education. The State, the Departments, and the Communes grant scholarships to students whose scholastic aptitude has been recognized and who belong to families of modest means. For secondary education, these scholarships cover pupils' living expenses (food, clothing, books, etc.).[30]

Religious Instruction. The neutrality of public education in religious, philosophical, and political matters was incorporated in the same law that required compulsory schooling (1882). Separation of Church and State in education was confirmed by the 1905 Education Act. The French firmly believe that secularity in education assures respect for freedom of thought. French pupils at all schools are authorized to practice their religion freely and to receive religious instruction outside of class hours and school buildings. In the lycées and collèges which have boarders, religious instruction, upon the request of families, can be given at the school itself by ministers of the various faiths.[31]

Types of Secondary Education

First Cycle. The first phase of secondary education, four years in length, in France is known as the "Premier Cycle," and every pupil of at least eleven years of age participates in one or another of the educational programs comprising the first cycle. A qualifying examination is prepared in each French department (state) for pupils from private primary schools or for those whose general average is inadequate. These programs are parallel and as similar to one another as possible in order to facilitate transfer from one to another. They all have a basis in general education, but none of them offer vocational training. Each of them, however, has its particularities based on the aptitudes and the objectives of the students it forms.

The first cycle enrolling students between the ages of eleven to fifteen years of age is composed of the following sections: (1) the <u>classical</u> section, characterized by the study of Latin and sometimes Greek; (2) the section known as <u>modern 1</u>, characterized by the intensive study of French and two foreign languages; (3) the section known as <u>modern 2</u>, characterized by the study of French with only one foreign language; (4) the <u>transition</u> section for students whose progress is, for one reason or another, below average. The teachers employed for this section are specially qualified to teach and orient students at this level.

During the entire period of the first cycle, the teachers meet periodically to make evaluations of students and of the type of studies which seem best suited for each pupil. Meeting under the direction of the homeroom teacher, the teachers council coordinates and reviews the observations made by the different teachers on the aptitudes of each pupil. The council establishes the individual record that represents the psychological and academic profile of each pupil. Also, the council establishes useful contacts with parents and transmits its opinions and recommendations to them. At the end of the first two years of the first cycle, pupils may opt for agricultural education offered in the agricultural <u>collèges</u> or <u>lycées</u>.

The schools which offer the first cycle of secondary education are the following: (1) the classical and modern <u>lycées</u>, which offer the classical and modern 1 sections of secondary education; (2) the <u>collèges of general education</u>, which offer the modern 2 and the transition sections; and (3) the <u>colleges of secondary education</u> (C.E.S.) which have just recently been established to meet current needs. The C.E.S.'s are comprehensive schools offering all the different sections of the first cycle.[32]

Second Cycle. Following the first cycle of secondary education, French pupils are guided according to their talents and their previous work into either one of the long educational programs, lasting three years, or toward one of the short programs, lasting not more than two years. The long programs prepare for the diverse baccalaureats or for a technician's baccalaureat or a technician's brevêt. The short programs provide vocational training combined with general education, and are sanctioned by a diploma or certificate of studies.

SHORT PROGRAMS. One type of vocational training which lasts for two years consists of three sections: (1) an industrial section training skilled workers; (2) a commercial section, training qualified employees; and (3) an administrative section, training employees for public administration and private enterprises.

A second type of vocational training lasts for a period of one year. This program can benefit both adolescents who until now have entered life without any vocational training and those who are not capable of higher studies. The certificate awarded in this program will sanction a direct form of training given through apprenticeships and industrial courses.

Schools which offer short programs of the second cycle of secondary education are the technical lycées and collèges of technical education. Sections in these schools offering the short program will qualify their enrollees as either technical agents or skilled workers.

A short program of agricultural training covering a period of one or two years is offered in agricultural collèges and lycées. At the end of the first year when the pupil is generally sixteen (which is the maximum age of compulsory schooling) he can obtain a certificate of agricultural apprenticeship. At the end of the second year he can qualify either as a technical agent or skilled worker.

LONG PROGRAMS. Long programs of the second cycle of secondary education are offered in the classical, modern, and technical lycees, and lead to the baccalaureat diploma. There are three four-year programs: literary, science, and industrial techniques. The literary studies, which always include a modern foreign language, offer seven possibilities, three of which include Latin, and four which include a second modern foreign language. The science program also offers a choice of Latin or a second modern foreign language. In addition, the optional study of Greek permits the best students to combine the classical tradition and science.

The first year of each long program in the second cycle is a common program of liberal arts studies. The relative specialization of each program becomes apparent gradually. These diversified programs with their numerous options provide a balance between literary and scientific studies at the same time that they enrich the pupils' training by taking into account their interests and their aptitudes. It is to be noted that technical training is an integral part of the second cycle of secondary education, along with the other types of training. A technical agricultural program is offered in the agricultural lycees which leads to an agricultural technician's diploma.[33]

Some Educational Practices.

General Aims of Education. France, since the time of the French Revolution, has set supreme value on the exercise of intellect. Clear, cold, deep, logical and analytical thinking have characterized French education. The emphasis on culture, brilliance of mind, elegance, and matters spiritual permeates the French school system. M. Edouard Morot-Sir, Cultural Counselor in the United States for French universities, has written of the French desire for culture as follows:

> ... *modern man is hungry for universality, and culture is the sole vehicle that can lead men to this universality ... French thought was strived since the Middle Ages to give its ideas and theories a universal quality ...*
>
> *For France the desire for culture and the quest for universality have been lived within the framework of that dialogue which still continues today between the Ancients—the Greeks and the Latins—and us ... What French thought has not ceased to repeat for four centuries is this: the differences among men are infinite; and it is good to cultivate these differences; but in going to the source of these differences, one discovers a need for universality which makes the unity of men, not an ethnic, or a historic, or a political, or a religious unity, but a cultural one, not imposed from the outside, but felt and lived inside each conscience and in the heart of each national experience.*[34]

Civic Education. The teaching of civics in the French secondary schools is so unusual that it warrants some special note. Civic education is separate from the traditional subjects and is taught by itself. The program lasts a period of seven years. In the first cycle of secondary education covering pupil ages eleven to fifteen years civic education is simple. It accustoms the adolescent to look at and to understand the world around him. It consists of a study of the environment; the town, county, and the state; the important services (postal and tele-communications, railroads, gas and electricity, food, etc.), and the administrative organization of the nation.

In the second cycle of secondary education (fifteen to eighteen years of age) the pupils study some of the important problems of the present world such as the political, economic, and social organization of France; international cooperation and international world organization. The fundamental aim of this training is not so much to inculcate knowledge of all problems as it is to develop awareness that they exist, to know how they became problems, and to have reasoned and informed opinion on them.[35]

Dimond found a weakness in the civics program to be the time allotment of one hour each two weeks, and the fact that teachers had no training in the political or other social sciences. He also reported that the subject seemed remote from students' lives. He quotes an official of the French Ministry of Education as saying: "Our program in civics does not work; we have failed to teach politics or political institutions. This is a weak spot in French education." Dimond said similar comments were offered by teachers and directors of schools.[36]

Physical Education and Instruction in the Arts. Physical education and sports training is compulsory at all levels of public education. It is designed for all students but is adapted to the age and individual capacities of each one under medical supervision. Instruction in the arts is offered in the secondary as well as elementary schools. New programs during the first year of the long second cycle have introduced an arts option with three hours a week of art theory and application.[37]

Adult Education. To make it possible for everyone to add to the general knowledge acquired during compulsory schooling, and to make possible the means of personal development more readily available to all, educational authorities are making an effort to promote a broad movement of cultural education and vocational advancement throughout the French nation. Cultural education open to all is offered: (1) in special centers, directed or recognized by the State; (2) in the various educational institutions; and (3) by private associations, which, because of their purpose, receive state aid.

Vocational advancement has the goals of contributing to job promotion and keeping workers abreast of modern technical developments. Courses in vocational advancement are given either in schools or in special public or private centers.[38]

Teaching Methods. Teaching strategies in France are aimed toward the maximum development of each pupil through what the French call active methods. Active methods may be defined as all methods which put truly creative activities into practice and make the pupil participate "actively" in the discovery of the knowledge which he must acquire. Active methods, which are a part of the observation, orientation, and educational coordination instituted by recent French educational reforms, require an atmosphere of reciprocal freedom and trust in the classroom.[39]

Teacher Education

Teachers of general education (the classical, modern, or technical sections) must have a university degree in the subject they teach. The teachers of the lycees are recruited through competitive examinations. Those candidates who pass the competitive examinations are titled certified teachers and are qualified to teach in all the classes of the long form of secondary education.

About twenty-five per cent of the secondary school teachers are known as "agréges." These persons are teachers who have passed the examination called the "Agregation." Candidates for the "agregation" will have had an academic year of advanced preparation. There are nineteen different sections of the "agregation" to correspond to the respective teaching fields of the secondary school. Passing the "agregation" entitles the teacher to certain financial privileges and a reduction of teaching load. He must teach fifteen class hours a week as opposed to eighteen for the other teachers.

The French secondary school teacher enjoys almost complete freedom of thought and expression in the classroom. He must, however, observe religious and political neutrality in his classes. His freedom is assured by French law. No disciplinary action can be taken against any teacher unless the accusations made against him are examined by a jury which include a number of his colleagues.[40]

Administration of Secondary Education

Ministry of National Education. In France, the administration of education is rigidly centralized and in the hands of career civil servants. These civil servants, the directors of departments in the ministry of education, the school inspectors, the rectors of the academies, were once teachers or educational administrators at lower levels. In their hands is a centralized machinery of control begun by Napoleon. The French educational administrative machinery exercises powers to provide a uniform curriculum, control the selection, salaries, and promotion of teachers; and furnishes strict legal supervision over the financial outlay, even though school buildings are largely financed from funds raised by the local communities.

The Minister of Education is a member of the Council of Ministers of the Fifth French Republic and participates in the deliberations and political decisions of the government. He is primarily responsible for the policy and activities of the ministry and is its spokesman during the debates at the Chamber of Deputies and the Senate of the French Parliament. He is appointed by the Prime Minister.

Academies. Under the 1964 education reforms approved by the Council of Ministers, the Fifth French Republic is divided into twenty-two geographical units known as academies. Each academic district (academy) is composed of a number of French departments (the basic administrative political unit of France of which there are a total of eighty-nine.) The head of an academy is called the Rector. He is appointed by the Council of Ministers upon the recommendation of the Minister of Education. The Rector is assisted by inspectors—one for each of the departments in the academy.

1964 Educational Reforms. M. Christian Fouchet, Minister of National Education, in a press conference held on September 9, 1964, described the educational reforms approved by the Council of Ministers. He told the press, in part:

> *The educational reform enacted in 1959 has accelerated the democratization of secondary education. It has had the result that increased numbers of students are enrolling for the second cycle of secondary education . . . But orientation has functioned badly. Due to pressures from their families and social milieus, too many students who have been merely wasting time enter the second cycle only to continue wasting time. Some of them eventually get the baccalaureate at the age of twenty or twenty-one, but by being practically forced to it. More rigorous orientation . . . is necessary. The main advisers should be the teachers. It is up to them and the school principals to take the responsibility.*
>
> *The current programs . . . of secondary education are out of touch with present realities and are too categorical. Under the new system, there will be . . . sections more clearly differentiated . . . The only subjects common to all sections will be French, modern languages, and history.*[41]

Practical results of the new educational reform include closer orientation of pupils toward studies which correspond best to their aptitudes. Enrollment in classical and modern programs is to be narrowed down. The baccalaureate will be maintained and enforced. Examination questions will be drawn up and distributed by each academy, and all subjects will be recognized by the baccalaureate. Only candidates who obtain better than passing grades on the baccalaureate examination will be admitted to the faculties or preparatory classes of institutions for higher studies. Special institutes will be opened for training of the middle ranks of civil servants, and they will admit students holding the baccalaureate who received only passing grades.

Conclusion

The purpose of this chapter has been to trace the twentieth century educational developments of the national secondary school systems of Great Britain and France. Because of the great empires once controlled by these two European nations, education in many parts of the world such as Africa, the Near East, and Asia has been greatly influenced by the educational policies of these two powers. In the following chapter the national systems of two other important European countries will be viewed—*i.e.*, Germany and the Soviet Union. The secondary school systems of Germany and the Soviet Union have also, during the course of the twentieth century, strongly affected trends in secondary education throughout the world.

Chapter V

Footnotes

[1] *Education in Britain*, British Information Services (Harrow: H. M. Stationery Office, 1964), p. 7.

[2] *Ibid.*

[3] *Ibid.*

[4] *Ibid.*, pp. 8-9.

[5] *Education in Britain*, British Information Services (Harrow: H. M. Stationery Office, 1966), p. 18.

[6] *"Education," Fact Sheets on Britain*: British Information Services (New York: July, 1966).

[7] *Education in Britain*, British Information Services (Harrow: H. M. Stationery Office, 1964), p. 7.

[8] *Ibid.*, p. 20.

[9] *Ibid.*, p. 21.

[10] *Ibid.*

[11] News item in *Time Magazine,* April 28, 1967.

[12] *Education in Britain,* British Information Services (Harrow: H. M. Stationery Office, 1964), pp. 31-32.

[13] *Time Magazine,* April 28, 1967.

[14] *Education in Britain,* British Information Services (Harrow: H. M. Stationery Office, 1966), p. 21.

European School Systems: Great Britain - France 101

[15] *Education in Britain*, British Information Services (Harrow: H. M. Stationery Office, 1964), p. 26.

[16] That Circular stated that, as a matter of national policy, all secondary education should be reorganized on a comprehensive basis.

[17] *Education in Britain*, British Information Services (Harrow: H. M. Stationery Office, 1964), p. 26.

[18] *Ibid.*, p. 31.

[19] *Ibid.*, pp. 31-32.

[20] *Ibid.*, p. 27.

[21] *Education in Britain*, British Information Services (Harrow: H. M. Stationery Office, 1966), p. 24.

[22] *Education in Britain*, British Information Serivces (Harrow: H. M. Stationery Office, 1964), pp. 15-16.

[23] *Ibid.*, pp. 16-17.

[24] *Ibid.*, p. 10.

[25] *Ibid.*, pp. 36-37.

[26] *Ibid.*, pp. 44-45.

[27] *Ibid.*, pp. 45-46.

[28] *Ibid.*, pp. 47-48.

[29] "French System of Education," *Education in France*. Cultural Services of the French Embassy, Revised Edition (New York: 1965), p. 4.

[30] *Ibid.*, p. 5.

[31] *Ibid.*

[32] *Education in France*, No. 37, Cultural Services of the French Embassy (New York: September, 1968), pp. 10-13.

[33] *Ibid.*, pp. 13-15.

[34] "French System of Education," *op. cit.*, pp. 10-11.

[35] Stanley E. Dimond, "Social Studies in French Secondary Schools," *Social Education* (March, 1966), pp. 175-178.

[36] *Ibid.*, p. 178.

[37] *Education in France*, no. 37, *op. cit.*, p. 21.

[38] *Ibid.*, p. 22.

[39] *Ibid.*, pp. 22-23.

[40] *Ibid.*, pp. 24-26.

[41] "French System of Education," *op. cit.*, p. 28.

Selected References

Bereday, George Z. F. *Comparative Method in Education.* New York: Holt, Rinehart and Winston, 1964.

Capelle, J. "The Observation and Guidance Phase in French Secondary Education," *Comparative Education* 1:171-179, June, 1965.

Council for Cultural Cooperation of the Council of Europe. *Education in Europe: School Systems: A Guide.* Section II, General and Technical Education, No. 5. Strasbourg: the Council, 1965.

Cramer, John F., and Browne, George S. *Contemporary Education: A Comparative Study of National Systems.* Second edition, revised. New York: Harcourt, Brace and World, 1965.

Dimond, Stanley E. "Social Studies in French Secondary Schools," *Social Education* 30: 175-178, March, 1966.

Fahmy, M. S. "Technical Education in Western Europe," *Comparative Education Review* 9:155-162, June, 1965.

Fraser, Steward, editor. *Governmental Policy and International Education.* New York: John Wiley and Sons, 1965.

Fraser, William R. "Progress in French School Reform," *Comparative Education Review* 7:273-278, February, 1964.

Great Britain. British Information Services. *Education in Britain.* Harrow: H. M. Stationery Office, 1964.

France. Cultural Services of the French Embassy. *French System of Education.* Revised edition. Washington, D.C.: the Embassy, 1965.

Gross, Richard E., editor. *British Secondary Education.* London: Oxford University Press, 1965.

Halls, W. D. "Educational Planning in an Industrial Society: The French Experience," *Comparative Education* 1:19-28, October, 1964.

_____. *Society, Schools and Progress in France.* New York: Pergamon Press, 1965.

Hanky, L. H. A. "The Independent School in British Education," *Teachers College Record* 65:423-429, February, 1964.

Hansen, Gary B. " 'Separate But Equal': Some Myths and Realities of English Secondary Education," *Comparative Education Review* 9:356-365, October, 1965.

Reed, John R. *Old School Ties: The Public Schools in British Literature.* Syracuse, N.Y.: Syracuse University Press, 1964.

Thut, I. N., and Don Adams. *Educational Patterns in Contemporary Socieities.* New York: McGraw-Hill, 1964.

UNESCO. *World Trends in Secondary Education.* Paris: the Organization, 1962.

Wilkinson, Rupert. *The Prefects: British Leadership and the Public School Tradition.* London: Oxford University Press, 1964.

Chapter VI

COMPARATIVE EUROPEAN SECONDARY SCHOOL SYSTEMS: GERMANY AND THE SOVIET UNION

West Germany

Background

In 1871 the German states were unified under the able leadership of the iron-fisted Prussian chancellor, Otto von Bismarck, and the king of Prussia became the emperor or "Kaiser" of Germany. The German Empire held together until the end of the First World War. During the period of empire, education in the various German states was chiefly the concern of the Ministries of Education and Religious Affairs, and of other ministries depending on the traditions of the state concerned. Education had reached a high level in each of the member states before the empire was formed. The common origins, language, and other cultural forces such as religion had influenced educational developments, and so similar institutional forms were found throughout the empire.[1]

Several educational conferences were held late in the nineteenth century from which were derived the German school reforms of 1892 and 1901. They defined three parallel types of secondary education, each with a nine-year curriculum designed to prepare candidates for the school-leaving or maturity examinations. The curricula differed chiefly with respect to the study of languages and time spent on the study of mathematics. The <u>Gymnasien</u> required both Latin and Greek; the <u>Realgymnasien</u>, Latin and two modern languages; and the extended Realschulen, known as the <u>Oberrealschulen</u>, required only modern languages but emphasized mathematics and sciences.

An abbreviated form of each of the three nine-year curricula that offered the first six years of the official course of study was used in schools known as <u>Progymnasien</u>, <u>Prorealgymnasien</u>, and <u>Realschulen</u>. Students who finished studies in these six-year schools could complete preparation for one of the maturity examinations by transferring with advanced standing to the appropriate nine-year school.[2]

The years immediately preceding the outbreak of World War I witnessed a substantial expansion of educational opportunity. Gymnasien for girls were opened; a common elementary education was established for all children in their first years of schooling in what was called a <u>Grundschule</u>; also steps were taken in secondary education to establish programs which combined the common elements in the first years of the <u>Gymnasien</u>, <u>Realgymnasien</u>, and <u>Oberrealschulen</u>. From such efforts there emerged a type of secondary school called the <u>Reformagymnasien</u>.[3]

The defeat of Germany in the First World War resulted in the abolition of the monarchy and the establishment of the Weimar Republic. Under the Republic the organization of schools was much the same as under the Empire. However, liberal forces were at work in Germany, and certain educational reforms were instituted, among which the more important were the following: (1) abolition of the selective primary school known as the <u>Vorschulen</u>; (2) establishment of a common primary education for all children in the <u>Grundschulen</u>; (3) education made compulsory in full-time schools for all children from the age of six to fourteen; (4) creation of a Department of General Culture in the Federal Ministry of Interior to consider educational problems of interest to the nation as a whole; (5) establishment of two new types of secondary schools, the <u>Deutsche Oberschulen</u> and the <u>Aufbauschulen</u>, which reached into the middle and lower social classes for their students and gave more attention to 'modern' subjects.[4]

In January 1933 when Adolph Hitler became Chancellor, Germany had no national ministry of education. One year later control of education had been transferred from the individual states to the national government. A law of May 1, 1934, confirmed this fact by establishing the National Ministry of Science, Education, and Public Instruction. The ministries of education in the individual states continued to exist mainly to carry out orders and decrees of the national ministry.[5]

The Nazi educational program emphasized the doctrines of race, German superiority, and revenge for defeat in World War I. Under fascist leadership German history and geography with strong nationalistic overtones became major school subjects. The study of Latin and Greek was deemphasized, and English became the major foreign language. The school day was reduced to make time for physical fitness programs and Nazi party propagandistic activities. Under the Nazis education became a major instrument in preparing the nation for aggressive warfare.[6]

With the end of World War II in 1945 the national educational administrative machinery was abolished and the functions of the Ministry of Education returned to the state governments. In 1947 the Allied Control Council issued general guidelines for the several states to follow in rebuilding their educational systems. School reorganization by 1953 represented to a great degree the old pattern of twenty years earlier, which in turn had retained many features of former stages of its development. In 1955 the Minister-Presidents of the West German states approved the proposals presented by the Conference of the Ministers of Education for a unified plan that envisaged a four-year primary school, followed by two alternatives: (1) a six-year shorter middle school (Mittleschulen), and (2) the traditional nine-year secondary school.

Characteristics of West German Education

Compulsory Education. Education has been compulsory in the Federal Republic of West Germany since April 1, 1955, for all children between the ages of six and fourteen. While the minimum duration of full-time schooling is eight years, some West German states have nine years of full-time compulsory schooling, while others offer a ninth year on a voluntary basis. West Germany, comprising an area of nearly 96,000 square miles, is approximately the size of the American states of New York and Pennsylvania combined. It had a population of over fifty-eight million in 1964. In 1963, 5,506,373 pupils were enrolled in primary schools, 869,992 in secondary schools, and 1,895,834 in vocational schools.[7] It is expected that in the period from 1961 to 1970 the probable increase in enrollment will be as follows: primary schools – 1,314,000; intermediate schools – 251,000; grammar schools – 207,000; and vocational schools – 325,000. Altogether there is expected to be about 2,300,000 more pupils in school in 1970 than in 1961, and that the ratio of schoolchildren to the population as a whole is likely to increase from 15.4% in 1961 to 18.6% in 1970.[8]

Private Education. The right to establish private schools is guaranteed by the federal constitution of the West German Republic. Article VII of the Basic Law states:

> Private schools as substitute for state schools shall require the sanction of the state and shall be subject to legislation. The sanction must be given if the private schools, in their educational aims and facilities, as well as in the scholarly training of their teaching personnel, are not inferior to the state schools and if a separation of the pupils according to the means of the parents is not encouraged.[9]

Religious Instruction. In West German schools provision is made for religious instruction. In Article VII of the Federal Constitution which relates to education it is stated:

> Religious instruction shall, without prejudice to the state's right of supervision, be given according to the principles of the religious societies. No teacher may be obliged against his will to give religious instruction.[10]

Types of Educational Programs

Volkschulen. The Volkschule is an eight-year elementary school, free and public and coeducational. Comprising the first four years of the Volkschule is the Grundschule that all children are compelled to attend before entering a more specialized course of study. From eighty to ninety per cent of the pupil age group continue in the Volkschule to the age of fourteen years. Upon graduation from the Volkschule the pupil may attend a part-time vocational school or a full-time trade school. In most West German states school attendance is compulsory on a part-time basis until the age of eighteen for those who do not attend full-time schools.

Mittleschulen. The Mittleschule is generally a six-year school which accepts, upon examination, pupils from the Grundschule and which combines an academic and a practical curriculum through grade ten. The curriculum requires two modern languages, stresses science and mathematics, and includes practical and vocational courses. Upon completing this curriculum and passing the school-leaving examination known as the Mittlere Reife, the student receives a middle-level maturity certificate which enables him to find employment in the lower business or governmental positions. These schools turn out much sought after young people. These middle schools are expanding rapidly, and it is expected that by 1970 there will be 694,000 intermediate school pupils as compared with 430,000 in 1956. These schools are not easy to get through. In 1954 only eighteen per cent of any one year group successfully completed an intermediate school education. In 1963 the corresponding figure was 23.5 per cent.[11]

Vocational Education. Vocational education was initiated and promoted in Germany as early as the Bismarck era. About eighty per cent of the pupils who remain in school beyond the compulsory age of fourteen enter some form of commercial or vocational apprenticeship or training. Students are committed to part-time further education until approximately the age of eighteen. Berufsfachschulen are full-time trade schools which students attend for one, two, or three years, depending on the length of the course they are pursuing.

Fachschulen are generally part-time trade schools which complement apprenticeship programs in which students remain until reaching the age of eighteen. These vocational training institutions, both part-time and full-time, are run today by a community, by an industry, or by private individuals.[12] The full-time schools are attended more by girls than by boys, because the boys prefer to leave the academic environment to start an apprenticeship as soon as possible.[13]

Gymnasien (Secondary Education)

Traditionally Germany has had three types of secondary schools through which students passed to enter institutions of higher education. In order of historical development they were the Gymnasium which stressed Latin and Greek; the Realgymnasium which omitted Greek but emphasized Latin and modern languages; and the Oberrealschule, with neither Greek nor Latin, which gave its main attention to mathematics, science, and modern languages. Each was a nine-year school. Some schools, however, offered only the first six years of the secondary curricula, and these were the Progymnasium, Prorealgymnasium, and the Realschule. During the Weimar Republic two new secondary schools were added: the Deutsch Oberschule, which stressed German life and culture, and the Aufbauschule, which enabled able pupils who had completed the seventh year of the Volkschule to prepare for university admission by attending this six-year school.[14]

In addition to the prescribed language requirements of the respective secondary schools, other required subjects include the following: history, geography, botany, chemistry, physics, music, art, and gymnastics. Each subject is given at least two periods a week. Entrance to the secondary school is based on an examination when the candidate has completed the Grundschule and is at least ten years of age. The examination consists of an intelligence test and tests in arithmetic and German. An appraisal is also made of the candidate by his teachers. Only about ten per cent of the graduates of the primary school are admitted to the secondary schools. The lecture method of instruction is used almost exclusively in the secondary school. The student remains with his class, and the instructors move from classroom to classroom. A final examination is given in each required subject each year. The written examinations are prepared by state officials, and oral examinations are conducted individually by the teachers following the written examinations. The pupil is required to repeat the entire year's work if he fails two or more subjects. There is no organized program of student activities in German secondary schools.

After completing the nine-year course, the student takes the school-leaving examination for the certificate of maturity called the Abitur. Only about twenty-five to thirty per cent pass it on first trial. This certificate is the regular requirement for admission to a university or other institution of higher education.

Educational Practices

Rahmenplan (masterplan). In 1959 an all-state committee was named by the West German federal government to study reform of educational practice. The committee set up three guide-lines for its use: (1) the structure of the school system must help to preserve the intellectual unity of the nation and establish the general awareness of this unity on a broad basis; (2) the obligation to establish social equality and the increased demands of modern society render it necessary to offer every child the opportunity corresponding to his intelligence and ability; and (3) our specialized society requires different levels of education among members of the future generation.[15]

On July 1, 1965, the committee published its recommendations on the reorganization of secondary education. It recommended two different, clearly defined types of grammar school: (1) a grammar school with seven-year courses, which after three years would have a 'science stream' (with English and French as languages) and a 'language arts stream' (with English, Latin, and French); and (2) an academic type of grammar school lasting for nine years in which in the last four years there would be a 'French' or 'modern language stream' (Latin, English, and French), and a 'Greek' or 'classical stream' (Latin, English, and Greek). The committee based its recommendations on the following reasoning:

> The grammar school of today serves a double function: on the one hand it must cover the constantly increasing demand by modern civilization for qualified people; on the other hand it must continue to serve its old educational function of handing down our classical heritage of European culture from one generation to the next ... For we must not purchase our entry into the world of technology by cutting down our intellectual and historical horizons.[16]

The Rahmenplan has not introduced any revolutionary changes into the German system of secondary education. It does, however, envisage the bringing together of the several types of secondary schools within a unified educational structure. Also, and most significantly, it has as its aim the increase of the nation's manpower capability and more equitable distribution of educational opportunity.

Teaching of History. The effort of Germany to re-enter the family of nations after World War II has focused attention on how the German schools deal with the subject of history and particularly the history of the Nazi period. Between 1950 and 1962 the Ministers of Education of the respective West German states have repeatedly published guiding principles and directives as aids to those responsible for the teaching of history and 'Gemeinschaftskunde' (a new subject for senior classes in which the study of history, geography, and social studies are combined). There are also regulations concerning the treatment of totalitarianism in history lessons and the content of history books. In addition, various ministries of education have published recommendations and suggested literature for history teachers in their official journals.[17]

The German press has frequently exercised a controlling and purifying function in postwar Germany, and a number of newspapers have carefully scrutinized the history textbooks used in the schools. The individual school, in fact the teacher himself, is free to choose which history book is to be used out of the many offered by educational publishers. The process of selection is facilitated by the above mentioned directives and recommendations of the Ministries of Education and also by the International School Book Institute, which organizes conferences of German and foreign historians. The aim of these conferences is to begin with the task of reconciling the nations at the point where in the past young people frequently acquired their first prejudices—the school textbook.[18]

Teacher-Training. In Germany teacher-training schools are rapidly climbing to the university level, and many insist on the Abitur as a prerequisite of admission. Preparation for qualification as a secondary schoolteacher of academic subjects, however, is still a function of the universities. Admission of the teacher-candidate to study at a university requires presentation of the Abitur from a secondary school. The length of training is at least four years of undergraduate work plus two years of inservice training. The nature of the training consists of undergraduate credits in one or more academic subjects and the study of philosophy, psychology, pedagogy, and political science. The examination for the Studienreferendar marks completion of the four-year period of general education. The examination for Studienassessor is taken after the two years of inservice training. When after several years of successful service in a secondary school the teacher attains permanent appointment (tenure), he becomes a Studienrat.

Administration of Education

Public control of education in the Federal Republic of West Germany is exercised by the respective eleven states that comprise the territory of the nation: Schleswig-Holstein, Hamburg (city-state), Lower Saxony, Bremen (city-state), North Rhine-Westphalia, Hesse, Rhineland-Palatinate, Saarland, Baden-Wurttemberg, Bavaria, and West Berlin (city-state). At the head of the government in each state is the Minister-President (Ministerprasident), called in West Berlin the Governing Mayor (Regierendar Burgermeister), and in the city-states of Hamburg and Bremen, the President of the Senate (Prasident des Senats). While the organization of school administration in the states varies in detail, there are three basic levels of administration: state or central, middle or government district level, and local district or lower level.

The Minister of Education of each State exercises central control over the public and private schools within his area. He represents the schools in the state legislature as well as in the executive branch of his government. His office maintains careful control over educational finances, over inspection of physical plants, and over academic programs of schools throughout the state. Teachers are appointed and salaries are regulated and paid by the state ministry. Curricula of the schools are determined, and some control in adoption of texts is exercised also at the state level. Instruction is supervised, and end-of-school examinations are devised and partially administered by the ministry.[19]

Between the state ministry and the local level in the large German states there are from three to six governmental districts established mainly to facilitate liaison in specific functions between individual communities and the ministry. The local districts (Kreise) form the smallest unit of self-administration in the German Federal Republic. They include rural districts consisting of several small towns. City districts for cities with a population of more than 50,000 generally form a district of their own. The local district office for schools is headed by an appointed representative from the ministry. Local districts are mainly responsible for constructing and maintaining their own schools.

The state generally is responsible for financing personnel. Beyond this the state makes grants-in-aid for school building, compensates the municipalities for the loss of income from school fees resulting from the introduction of free education, and gives loans and scholarships to able but needy students.

To coordinate educational practices and insure uniform standards, the ministers of education in the various states began to meet periodically, and in 1948 formed the Permanent Conference of Ministers with a general secretariat at Bonn, the capital city of the Federal Republic. The Conference of Ministers meets at regular intervals to discuss educational problems of common interest to the states. Decisions and recommendations passed with unanimous agreement are referred to state authorities.[20]

The Soviet Union

Background

During the nineteenth century Russian secondary schools and universities were patterned after Western European practices. The secondary school code of 1864 recognized the already established division into the classical Gymnasium and the Realgymnasium, the latter oriented to modern languages and science. In the late nineteenth century and the opening decade of the twentieth, the literacy rate in the land of the Czars steadily mounted. From 1906 to 1911 the Russian parliament known as the Duma passed legislation raising the salaries of primary school teachers, and establishing the principle of free primary school education. More than ninety per cent of the youths of elementary school-age were in some form of school when the Revolution began in 1917.

Education under Communism in the Soviet Union has undergone four distinct phases. Phase one was the adjustment years between 1917 and 1921. During this period educational changes were part of the total revolutionary reform. Communists speeded up the effort to eliminate illiteracy;[21] they introduced free tuition and materials, and provided school lunches, and for the needy, clothing. Schools were removed from control of churches, the central ministry of education replaced by ministries in the fifteen union republics.

The second phase of Soviet education occurred during the decade from 1921 until Stalin came to power. This was the progressive period of Communist education. The ideas of the American pragmatic educator, John Dewey, were popular. The drive to eliminate illiteracy also was pushed hard. Lenin proclaimed there could be no politics without ABC's, and school primers were filled with propaganda content, including anti-religious material.[22]

The third phase of Soviet education occurred during the Stalinist era from about 1930 until 1953. The ideas of Dewey fell into disfavor. Emphasis was placed on the writings of Marx. The role of the teacher in the classroom was upgraded, but a prescribed syllabus had to be followed without deviation. During World War II, in an effort to inspire patriotism, history books were rewritten to include more of Russia's glorious past. After the war, and with the descent of the iron curtain, cultural life in the Soviet Union was strongly controlled. The fourth phase of Soviet education extends from the death of Stalin in 1953 to the present time and is the subject of the remainder of this chapter.

Characteristics of Soviet Education

Compulsory Education. Education is compulsory in the Soviet Union for all children between the ages of six and fourteen, or through the eighth grade in school. Coeducation is the rule at all levels including the university. It is expected that universal schooling until the age of eighteen will be instituted. Over 48 million pupils attend the Soviet Union's 214,000 schools.

Free Public Education. All education in the Soviet Union from the elementary through graduate school is free and public. There are no private schools. Textbooks are not free, but they are cheap, less than fifty cents in American money. If the student cannot afford to buy his textbooks, the school provides them, but they must be returned when the course is completed.[23]

Religious Instruction. The USSR is an anti-religious state. In the pre-Revolutionary period schools were predominantly run by the Russian Orthodox Church. In 1918 the decree was issued separating the Church from the State, and in 1921 religious education of children was banned. At the same time all monasteries and religious schools were closed. In 1925 the Society of the Militant Godless was formed to combat religion through education. A 1929 law again banned religious teaching in the schools. Since 1946, however, there has been a decline in anti-religious instruction in the official school syllabus. It is now believed that science, properly taught, should make anti-religious instruction unnecessary.[24]

Types of Educational Programs

The Elementary School. The elementary school is four years in length and covers grades one through four. The age range of pupils is from seven to ten. The pupil has but one teacher to a grade who teaches all subjects. In the first to third grade the pupil learns to read and write in his native language and also studies arithmetic. The primers have stories by Chekhov, Tolstoy, Pushkin, Mayakovsky, and other Russian and Soviet classics. Two additional subjects are added to the curriculum in the fourth grade, and these are nature study and the history of the Soviet Union. In all four grades there are also the subjects of drawing, singing, and physical education. The pupils go to school six days a week, lessons are forty-five minutes long, and there are four lessons a day in the elementary school.[25]

The Eight Year School. In addition to the first four years of schooling, the eight-year schools cover grades five, six, seven, and eight. The age-range of pupils in the eight-year school is from seven to fifteen years. Beginning with the fifth grade, each subject is taught by a different teacher. In grade five pupils study their native language, reading, arithmetic, botany, ancient history, physical geography, and a foreign language (English, French, or German). A foreign language is studied in grades five through ten. Drawing, singing, and physical training continue to be studied in grades five through eight.

The native language of the region continues to be studied in grade six, but reading is replaced by a course in literature, which in turn is divided into the literature of the native language and Soviet literature. Arithmetic is replaced by algebra and geometry, and ancient history by medieval history. Geography becomes the study of the physical and political geography of important regions and countries of the world. An introductory course in physics is added to the curriculum, and zoology replaces botany.

In grade seven the study of the grammar of the native language continues. The course in Russian literature emphasizes the nineteenth century writers Pushkin, Lermontov, and Gogol. Students are also introduced to theoretical aspects of literature and the fundamentals of versification, rhythm, comedy, humor, and satire, and the basic principles of plot. Algebra, geometry, physics, geography, a foreign language, and zoology continue to be studied. History now becomes the history of the Soviet Union from ancient times to the beginning of the twentieth century. Chemistry is also introduced at this time.

In the eighth grade the student studies the Russian language and Russian literature of the nineteenth and twentieth centuries. He also takes algebra, geometry, physics, chemistry, human anatomy and physiology, the geography of the USSR, modern history, and a foreign language. Final school examinations are administered at the completion of grade eight. Students are examined in the following subjects: Russian language, oral and written (an essay), algebra and arithmetic (written), and geometry and algebra (oral)—a total of four examinations. In addition, non-Russian schools have oral and written examinations in the native language. Written examinations are three hours maximum. On completion of the eight-year school the student is awarded a certificate that signifies he has completed the period of compulsory formal schooling.

The Secondary School. The ninth and tenth grades in the ten-year school constitute the secondary school. Several years ago an eleventh grade was introduced at a number of secondary schools as an experiment. Soviet school officials did not feel it justified itself, and so beginning with 1966 there has been no more eleventh grade. Subjects studied in the ninth grade are the following: Russian literature of the early nineteenth century, algebra, trigonometry, plane and solid geometry, mechanical drawing, physics (mechanics), biology, chemistry (inorganic), contemporary world history, history of the USSR to mid-nineteenth century, and a foreign language.

Tenth grade students study Russian literature of the late nineteenth and early twentieth centuries, and they also have a complete course in Soviet literature. Other courses they study are mathematics, physics (molecular), chemistry (organic), contemporary world history, history of the USSR from the end of the nineteenth century to the present, economic geography, astronomy, and a foreign language.

School-leaving examinations are held at the close of the tenth year. These examinations include a composition on a literary subject for which six hours is allowed, oral examinations in algebra, geometry, physics, chemistry, the history of the USSR, social science, and the foreign language. The ten-year school completion certificate lists the final marks, determined from the final examinations, and the marks the student received during the course of the tenth year. Students who fail their final examinations in one or two subjects may take a second examination in those subjects the following semester. Students who fail more than two subjects or who fail to pass the second examination in either one or both subjects receive a certificate that they have attended the school. They are permitted to take the examinations once again the year after.[27]

Specialized Secondary Schools. Specialized secondary schools train highly skilled technicians. Students are admitted to these schools after completing the eighth grade and passing the entrance examinations. In addition to learning a trade, students cover the subjects taught in the ninth and tenth grades but in somewhat shorter courses. Graduates receive both school-leaving certificates and certificates attesting to their vocational skill.[28]

Other Specialized Schools. In addition to the schools described, there are several other types of specialized schools which include foreign language schools, specialized mathematics-physics schools, music schools, and experimental schools. At the schools where special emphasis is laid on foreign languages, one foreign language is taught beginning with the first grade. Later, many of the courses are taught in the foreign language. These schools are intended to train future philologists, translators, and interpreters.

The pupils who attend the specialized mathematics-physics schools will later specialize in cybernetics, electronic theory, and theoretical mathematics, and physics. Music schools to which gifted children are admitted from the age of seven are taught to play one or more musical instruments. Graduates of complete secondary music schools may enter a conservatory, and graduates of the eight-year music schools may apply for admission to higher music schools. Projected changes in the curriculum are tested in experimental schools and may later be introduced into all general education schools. Students in all these specialized schools, in addition to their special subjects, cover all the subjects in the general school curriculum, and take the corresponding examinations and receive the same certificates as all other students.[29]

Vocational Training Schools. Established back in 1940, these schools train skilled workers. They accept youths between the ages of fourteen and seventeen who are not in school or employed. Eight years of study at a general school is now a prerequisite for admission. These schools range from factory schools to trade schools, and the training period may range from six months to three years, depending upon the length of the course.[30]

Educational Practices

Stages of Schooling. A. I. Markushevich, Vice President of the Academy of Pedagogical Sciences, and Chairman of the Commission on the Content of School Education has reported the principles which guided the commission in working out the new curricula for USSR schools, and which were put into effect in 1966, as follows:

> *First, we endeavored to bring the content of school education in conformity with the modern level of science, culture, and art. Second, we tried to arrange the ten-year course of studies as a harmonious whole without a repetition of the same topic in the eight-year and ten-year schools. Third, to reduce the overstrain of pupils the commission curtailed the number of hours for the compulsory study of subjects in many grades. Fourth, and this is the most important, we sought new opportunities for*

determining and taking into account the individual inclinations and interests of the pupils as well as the means that would make schoolchildren think instead of memorizing things by heart.[31]

College Entrance Examinations. The student seeking entrance to an institution of higher education must take competitive entrance examinations. The number of examinations and the subjects vary with the type of higher school, except for the examination in the native language and native literature which are required by all schools. Examinations range in number from three to eight. Honor graduates from secondary schools and technical schools are required to take examinations only in the key subjects.[32]

Teacher-Training. Although the universities turn out large numbers of secondary school teachers, the principal burden of teacher training at the elementary and secondary levels fall on the pedagogical institutes. In these institutes there is a four year course for elementary teachers, with an added year for those desiring to teach in secondary schools. All candidates for teacher training are graduates of the complete secondary (ten-year) school and so are also qualified to have entered a university. Each secondary trainee selects a teaching major and minor. In his third year of training the candidate enters a program of student teaching, spending six hours a week conducting classes, increasing to eight hours in the fourth year. The secondary candidate in his fifth year spends twelve hours a week in active teaching practice. A final practical examination is given at the conclusion of the candidate's period of training. No degree is conferred, but a certificate for teaching at his qualified level is issued.[33]

Teacher Salaries. Secondary teachers are hired and assigned to schools by each Republic's Ministry of Education. With few exceptions elementary and secondary teachers are paid less than the average income of other salaried employees and workers in the USSR. The basic wage scale for teachers is based on a twenty-four hour week. Retirement for women teachers is established at age fifty-five, and for men at age sixty.[34]

Academic Standards. The Soviet school system, though universal at the base, does in fact sponsor a stringent form of intellectual elitism. Soviet school practice is largely dominated by solidly conservative academic traditions. The number of pupils who start in the ten-year program and graduate therefrom is comparably as low as in elitist systems of secondary education in Western Europe. In 1954 less than 125 out of one thousand pupils who entered the ten-year program graduated.[35]

Administration of Education

The USSR is divided into fifteen Union Republics of which the Russian Socialist Federated Soviet Republic (RSFSR) is dominant. The RSFSR contains the majority of the nation's population and a greater part of the land area; its capital (Moscow) is also the nation's capital, and what its Minister of Education has to say is indicative of what is going on in the other Republics.

Nominally each Republic is responsible for its own educational system and has its own Ministry of Education. However, the Central Committee of the Communist Party has supreme authority over everything that happens in government, which includes the schools. The Council of Ministers for the Soviet Union commits to law the directives of the Central Committee. Working closely with the Council and the Central Committee in educational affairs is the Academy of Pedagogical Sciences of the RSFS Republic. As a research institution this body formulates details of ordinances and regulations which serve as models for the respective Union Republics.

The education ministers of the fifteen union republics are responsible for education in their areas, and they are also the principal links between the Kremlin and the lower educational echelons. Under the republic ministers are regions, of which there are eighty throughout the USSR, each with its director. Below the regional level is the district of which there are 4,000 in number. Finally there are the local education departments which run municipal schools. Allocation of that portion of national income to be used for financing schools and the administration of these moneys are tasks of the central government at Moscow, although local distribution of funds may be based on decisions made at the community or district or regional or republic level.[36]

Conclusion

In this chapter attention has been focused on the educational systems of West Germany and the Soviet Union. In West Germany the trend is toward an integrated, unified educational system in each of the member states. The social class differences formerly cultivated by the selective secondary schools have been substantially reduced, and an element of mobility has been introduced into the educational system which Thut and Adams claim has resulted in a corresponding degree of social mobility throughout the nation.[37]

In the Soviet Union the half century since the Revolution has changed the old land of the Czars into one of the world's great and powerful nations. Much of this progress might have been achieved under equally vigorous leadership, but nonetheless the Communists have predicted from the outset their ability to change a backward, largely rural nation into a world industrial power. They have regarded education as a major instrument in effecting this change. The words of A. S. Makarenko, one of the Soviet Union's most respected pedagogues, describe well the attitude of Soviet officials toward education:

> *Wherefrom can the aims of education arise? From our social needs, of course, from the aspirations of the Soviet people, from the aims and tasks of our revolution, from the aims and problems of our struggle. And so, obviously, a formula of aims cannot be derived from either biology or psychology, but only from our social history, from our social environment.*[38]

Chapters five and six have been a survey of selected European secondary school systems the purpose of which has been to provide a world setting for the discussion of American secondary schools. For the most part, with the exception of the United States, the school systems of the nations of the so-called Western World, including much of Asia and Africa as well, have been patterned after the school systems of Great Britain, France, and Germany; and the school systems of the countries which lie behind the iron curtain in eastern Europe are to a high degree modelled after the Soviet system. The remainder of this book will now deal with secondary education in the United States, its development, structure and organization, curriculum, problems, etc.

Chapter VI

Footnotes

[1] I. N. Thut, and Don Adams, *Educational Patterns in Contemporary Societies* (New York: McGraw-Hill Book Company, 1964), p. 99.

[2] *Ibid.*, p. 100.

[3] *Ibid.*, p. 101.

[4] *Ibid.*, p. 102.

[5] Alina M. Lindegren, *Germany Revisisted: Education in the Federal Republic*, United States Department of Health, Education, and Welfare, Bulletin 1957, No. 12 (Washington, D.C.: Government Printing Office, 1957), p. 7.

[6] Thut and Adams, *op. cit.*, pp. 103-104.

[7] International Bureau of Education, *Educational Trends in 1963-1964* (Publication No. 276. Geneva: International Bureau of Education, 1965), p. 29.

[8] "Numbers of Schoolchildren Today and Tomorrow,' *Education in Germany*, II (1965), 11.

[9] Lindegren, *op. cit.*, p. 4.

[10] *Ibid.*

[11] "Numbers of Schoolchildren Today and Tomorrow," *op. cit.*, p. 10.

[12] Robert E. Belding, *European Classrooms: Schools of Four Nations* (Iowa City, Iowa: Sernoll, Inc., 1966), p. 69.

[13] *Ibid.*, p. 68.

[14] Lindegren, *op. cit.*, pp. 21-22.

[15] "Legacy of the German Committee for Education: Recommendations on the Reorganization of the Grammar School," *Education in Germany*, II (1965), 17.

[16] *Ibid.*, p. 18.

[17] "The Teaching of History in the Federal Republic: The 1933-1945 Period," *Education in Germany*, I (1956), 6.

[18] *Ibid.*, p. 7.

[19] Belding, *op. cit.*, p. 62.

[20] Lindegren, *op. cit.*, p. 12.

[21] Almost immediately after the Soviets took power, Lenin signed a decree on the elimination of illiteracy in Russia.

[22] Belding, *op. cit.*, p. 86.

[23] "From First Grade Through Graduate School," *Soviet Life*, II (February, 1966), 28.

[24] Belding, *op. cit.*, p. 117.

[25] *Soviet Life, op. cit.*, p. 28.

[26] *Ibid.*

[27] *Ibid.*, pp. 28-29.

[28] *Ibid.*, p. 29.

[29] *Ibid.*

[30] *Ibid.*

[31] Interview in *Tass*, December 8, 1966.

[32] *Soviet Life, op. cit.*, p. 28.

[33] Belding, *op. cit.*, p. 107.

[34] *Ibid.*, p. 108.

[35] George Z. F. Bereday, *Comparative Method in Education* (New York: Holt, Rinehart and Winston, Inc., 1964), p. 76.

[36] Belding, *op. cit.*, pp. 88-89.

[37] Thut and Adams, *op. cit.*, p. 107.

[38] Anton Makarenko, *Problems of Soviet School Education* (Moscow: Progress Publishers, 1965), pp. 32-33.

Selected References

Belding, Robert E. *European Classrooms: Schools of Four Nations.* Iowa City, Iowa: Sernoll, Inc., 1966.

Bereday, George Z. F. *Comparative Method in Education.* New York: Holt, Rinehart and Winston, Inc., 1964.

Bowen, James. *Soviet Education: Anton Makarenko and the Years of Experiment.* Madison, Wisconsin: The University of Wisconsin Press, 1962.

Counts, George S. *The Challenge of Soviet Education.* New York: McGraw-Hill Book Company, 1957.

Deineko. M. *Forty Years of Public Education in the U.S.S.R.* Moscow: Foreign Language Publishing House, 1957.

Heckinger, Fred M. *The Big Red Schoolhouse.* New York: Doubleday and Company, 1959.

Huebener, Theodore. *The Schools of West Germany.* New York: New York University Press, 1962.

Hylla, Erich J., and Frederich O. Kegel. *Education in Germany.* Frankfurt-am-Main: Institute of Studies in International Education, 1958.

Kazamias, Andreas M., and Byron G. Massialas. *Tradition and Change in Education.* Englewood Cliffs, New Jersey: Prentice-Hall, Inc., 1965.

Lindegren, Alina M. *Germany Revisited: Education in the Federal Republic.* United States Department of Health, Education, and Welfare, Bulletin 1957, No. 12. Washington: Government Printing Office, 1957.

Makarenko, Anton. *Problems of Soviet School Education.* Moscow: Progress Publishers, 1965.

Moos, Elizabeth. *Soviet Education Today and Tomorrow.* New York: National Council of American-Soviet Friendship, 1959.

Thut, I. N., and Don Adams. *Educational Patterns in Contemporary Societies.* New York: McGraw-Hill Book Company, 1964.

Chapter VII

AMERICAN SECONDARY SCHOOLS: BEGINNINGS

Introduction: The European Heritage

The idea of universal secondary education was first implemented in the United States. In the school year 1965-1966 there were in the United States 30,500 secondary schools which enrolled more than 16,721,000 students who were taught by more than 796,000 teachers.[1] More than two million students graduate from U.S. high schools each year.[2] The magnitude of the American enterprise in secondary education is staggering and unique, and it is worthy to see how and why such a vast educational undertaking came into being.

Whatever the motives that brought the colonists to America, their settlements in the New World began as European outposts, the frontier of an old and rich civilization. That civilization was the result of a Graeco-Roman legacy, and more immediately it was based on the foundation of Judaeo-Christian thought.

As indicated in Chapter One, education probably predates organized, civilized, literate societies. In primitive societies secondary education consists of inducting adolescents into the mysteries of adult behavior. The initiation rite is the climax of this period of training and is usually followed by a period of fasting or even isolation from the tribe. The experience is so designed as to leave an indelible impression upon the individual.

It was also pointed out in Chapter I that formal education in the tradition of the Western world emerged in the classical culture of ancient Greece. The curriculum favored by the Greeks survived the Romans to pass through countless centuries into the Middle Ages where it became the Seven Liberal Arts, and from which it evolved, altered and enlarged, into modern times.

Chapter II indicated that during the Middle Ages the growth of manufacture and trade in medieval cities and the use of the guild system created conditions to challenge the near monopoly the

Church had enjoyed in educational affairs throughout most of the thousand-year medieval period. Court and burgher schools developed on the continent of Europe, and on the island of England private education under the aegis of associations and individuals became a common practice.

Chapter III has shown that in the Renaissance the pattern was established for the Western European classical Latin school, and that during the Protestant Reformation general education of the masses was advocated so everyone might read and interpret the Bible. The New England Puritan colonists who came to these shores in 1620 were the spiritual scions of the Reformation.

The Grammar School in America

Background. In 1492 the Genoese navigator, Christopher Columbus sailing under the flag of Spain discovered the New World. John Cabot, a Venetian employed by the English, in 1497 reached Canada and established the English claim to North America. In 1517 Martin Luther posted his ninety-five theses on the Wittenberg church door and thus launched the Reformation. In 1533 the English Act of Supremacy was passed which abrogated the pope's authority and made the king (Henry VIII) head of the Church of England. In 1620 Puritan separatists from the Church of England founded Plymouth Colony in Massachusetts, and in 1630 the Massachusetts Bay Colony was established. In 1635 the citizens of Boston founded the Boston Latin Grammar School, the first American secondary school.

Boston Latin Grammar School. In England from whence the puritan settlers had come, there were perhaps more than 300 grammar schools at the time. Many of the leaders of the Bay colony had been educated in these schools, and it would have been strange indeed if they had not made the effort to perpetuate their English educational tradition. A main tenet of the Protestant Reformation had been that every individual is responsible for his own soul, and in order to work out his salvation, he must be able to read the Christian doctrines contained in the Scriptures. The Protestant churches of the period, including those of the Puritans in New England, agreed upon the principle of teaching children to read as a religious obligation.

The Boston Public Latin School was established by the good citizens of Boston on April 23, 1635. The aim of the school was narrow. The school was to prepare a select few to enter college.

Harvard, the first American college, was founded in 1636, the year following the birth of the Boston Latin school. The fathers of the Massachusetts colony wished to insure a source for a trained ministry, and not have to depend upon the importation of ministers from England. The Boston Latin School enrolled only male students between the ages of seven and nine years. The curriculum was classical-humanistic and was seven years in length. Latin was the language of instruction. The most famous schoolmaster of the school was Ezekiel Cheever (c. 1615-1708). Cheever, a graduate of Emmanuel College, Cambridge, emigrated to the American colonies in 1637. He taught for seventy years, and for the last thirty-eight years of his life he was master of the Boston Latin School.

Other Latin Schools. Latin schools were established at many towns in Massachusetts and other New England colonies. These schools were usually small, many enrolling as few as thirty students. Teachers were mostly ministers, or other persons with a Latin education, and those who might be indentured servants or even transported felons.

These Latin schools often received public funds either directly or from income assigned from certain public lands. Families that could afford to do so were expected to pay part of the cost of educating their children, but provision was also made for children of indigent parents.

Very few regularly organized grammar schools were to be found in the southern colonies. Plantation owners often hired tutors who were college graduates, and in larger communities frequently ministers of churches kept school during week days.

Colonial Legislation in New England

Massachusetts Law of 1642. Voluntary efforts to establish schools and provide education were soon buttressed by the passage of a series of colonial laws designed to unify educational efforts and direct them to the ends of religious discipline and civil obedience.[3] The first of these legal efforts was the Massachusetts law of 1642. This act gave town officials power to provide schooling, and it ordered that all children should be taught to read.

Massachusetts Law of 1647. The law of 1647, known as the 'Old Deluder Satan Act,' went one step further and made it obligatory on townships to establish and maintain schools. This act thus initiated the local pattern of public education in the United States. The puritan religious climate of the Massachusetts colony is reflected in the stated purposes of this law which says that one chief object of "that old deluder, Satan," is, "to keepe men from the knowledge of ye Scriptures." The act required those towns of fifty households or more to establish elementary schools and those of 100 families to establish a Latin grammar school. These schools were to be supported by either all the citizens or just by the parents. Other New England colonies, with the exception of Rhode Island, soon adopted similar statutes.

Educational Developments Outside New England

The Southern Colonies. Colonization in the southern English colonies reflected a different spirit from that found in New England. Apart from the Catholics in Maryland and Quakers in Pennsylvania, these colonists were not so much seeking separation from the Anglican church as they were interested in improving their economic condition. In the southern colonies, as in England, education was regarded not as the business of the state but of the person. Education therefore remained in the hands of private agencies with but little public aid. The biggest organization for educational activities was the Society for the Propagation of the Gospel in Foreign Parts, chartered by the Anglican Church in England in 1701. For the Southerner of means there were tutors, and as the years passed a number of good private schools were developed in the southern colonies.

The Middle Atlantic Colonies. Between New England and the Southern Colonies were the colonies of New York, New Jersey, Delaware, and Pennsylvania. Church education was strong in Pennsylvania, the southernmost of these colonies. The Anglican Church through the Society for the Propagation of the Gospel in Foreign Parts opened charity schools, and the Quakers, Presbyterians, Baptists, and other denominational groups also operated schools. In New York, the northernmost of the middle colonies, legislation was enacted to provide for the establishment of free grammar schools; but here, too, education was for the most part carried on by private agencies.

Period of the Academies

Decline of Latin Grammar Schools. The Latin grammar schools satisfactorily achieved the limited objectives of the limited number of pupils they served. As the colonies prospered, new skills were in demand such as accounting, navigation, surveying, and speaking knowledge of foreign languages. At first some persons set up schools as private business ventures to teach these subjects in exchange for tuition. No longer was a classical-humanistic curriculum sufficient to meet the educational needs of the colonies by the middle of the eighteenth century.

Franklin's Academy. Benjamin Franklin was the first prominent American to see that practical subjects as well as classical learning offered a more realistic basis for secondary education in America. In an essay he published in 1749 he proposed the establishment of an academy in Philadelphia. This was to be a secondary school in which would be taught, in addition to the classical languages and literatures, French, Spanish, German, English grammar, rhetoric, literature, history, the sciences, and subjects of a practical vocational nature. Of students attending such a school Franklin wrote:

> ... it would be well if they could be taught <u>everything that is useful,</u> and <u>everything</u> that is ornamental; But Art is long, and their Time is short. It is therefore propos'd that they learn those Things that are likely to be <u>most useful</u> and most ornamental. Regard being had to the several Professions for which they are intended.[4]

Franklin's academy was opened in 1751 with three departments: the classical, the English, and the mathematical-scientific. The school proved popular from the start, and soon other academies were started elsewhere in Pennsylvania and in other soon-to-be states.

Phillips Academy at Andover. Initiated by private effort, most academies were granted charters with broad provisions. Phillips Academy at Andover, Massachusetts, is typical of the schools founded, and it served as a model for others.

The Massachusetts legislature granted a charter to Phillips Academy "for the purpose of promoting piety and virtue, and for the education of youth in the English, Latin, and Greek languages, together with Writing, Arithmetic, Music, and the Art of Speaking; also practical Geometry, Logic and Geography, and such other of the liberal Arts and Sciences, or Languages, as opportunity may thereafter permit ..."[5]

Characteristics of Academies. The academy rose to challenge the narrow and limited curriculum of the Latin school, but it was not, however, adverse nor unprepared to train some of its scholars in the old schooling. The academy generally offered all the academic subjects and came to stress the college-preparatory function. Instruction in the academies was carried on in English. The sciences and mathematics, subjects not often found in the Latin schools, geography, history, and modern languages were academic subjects of considerable importance in the academies.

The two major departments of a typical academy were the classical and the English. Subjects listed under the classical department generally included: Latin, Greek, English, geography, rhetoric, composition, arithmetic, geometry, and ancient history. Subjects commonly found in the English department were: English grammar, ancient and modern history, American history, geography, rhetoric, composition, arithmetic, geometry, algebra, declamation, trigonometry, surveying, navigation, chemistry, philosophy, and logic. The aim of the academy might be defined as schooling to provide training to serve some utilitarian end and/or to provide 'culture' and develop character.

Most academies (as above noted) were granted charters with broad provisions, and were operated by boards of trustees as nonprofit educational enterprises.[6] Academies depended for the major part of their income on tuition receipts. They were often as well the recipient of public support either through fund solicitation or from the sale of confiscated lands, or even outright grants from the public treasury.

Academies varied greatly in size. Many had boarding facilities for pupils. The philosophy of learning centered on the Lockian theory of mental discipline. Drill, textbook memorization, and lecturing were the most common instructional practices. Corporal punishment was not infrequent. The average age of pupils was higher than in Latin schools. Sports, clubs, and societies engaged the attention of pupils in many academies.

Academies which offered courses in pedagogy were few in number, yet many prospective elementary school teachers did attend academies to extend their horizons of knowledge, and many academy students earned their way by teaching the elementary grades. Some academies were opened for women, but the admission of girls to others was infrequent.

Contributions of the Academies. In the century from 1770 to 1870 the secondary education of the few Americans who went beyond the common school was obtained mostly in the academies. The academy was 'the poor man's college.' Only the most ambitious from the middle class aspired to more than an academy education. Much credit must, therefore, be given to the academy movement for the intellectual and cultural level achieved by the United States at the time. The academies served uniquely the educational needs and interests of the aggressive middle class in American life. An appreciable number of academy graduates became leaders in all the major economic pursuits—law, medicine, teaching, the ministry, business, and industry. The basic aim of the academy was preparation for successful living.

Perhaps the greatest contribution of the academy was the fact that it engendered interest in the American people in secondary education. By serving the needs particularly of the middle class, the academy greatly broadened the base of support for secondary education in the new republic. The development of a broad curriculum, the provision of secondary schooling for girls, though meagerly attained at the time, and the establishment of the principle of public financial support of secondary schooling may also be considered as contributions arising out of the academy movement in the youthful nation.

Early American Educational Reformers

BENJAMIN FRANKLIN (1706-1790) Mention must be made of certain Americans who were greatly responsible for founding the American tradition of free universal public education. Benjamin Franklin was without doubt the most progressive and best known public figure of pre-revolutionary America. His life is a nearly perfect biography of the rise of a new middle class of tradesmen and farmers in colonial America. A self-educated man, an inventor, scientist, author, publisher, philanthropist, educator, philosopher, and statesman, he believed that education should aim at utility, but not a narrow utility. Born in Boston, he settled in Philadelphia and obtained employment as a printer. He later acquired a printing business and was publisher of *The Pennsylvania Gazette* for a number of years. He gained a wide circle of readers for his *Poor Richard's Almanac*, which contained a store of witty aphorisms and moral precepts that influenced the thought of the times. He founded in 1727 a debating club called the Junto, a circulating library in 1731, the American Philosophical Society for Promoting Useful Knowledge in 1743, and his famous Academy in 1751—which later developed into The University of Pennsylvania.

As American representative in the court of France in the first decade following the Revolution, he became immensely popular there during his stay. During his latter years of public service he was president of the Pennsylvania executive council (1785-87) and served as a member of the Constitutional Convention of 1787. His partial autobiography which he wrote between 1771 and 1789 covers his life and times between 1706 and 1759.

Franklin's educational views were greatly influenced by the writings of Locke, Rousseau, and other seventeenth and eighteenth-century philosophers. According to Franklin education should prepare one for life in the business and social worlds. In place of the rigid Latin school curriculum with its college-preparatory aim, Franklin favored a curriculum that emphasized the study of the English language, vocational and professional training, and courses contributing to the refinement of living. His basic aim was to create a curriculum directly useful in fitting young men for any trade or profession. Ultimately, Franklin's reforms were directed at the betterment of society through the moral improvement of individuals.

THOMAS JEFFERSON (1743-1826) Jefferson was the most eloquent spokesman among the founding fathers for the cause of education. Of the men closely associated with the founding of the republic, only Benjamin Franklin approached Jefferson in degree of concern for education. Whereas Franklin clearly saw the necessity for education primarily in economic and practical terms, Jefferson, on the other hand, conceived of education as a prerequisite for intelligent popular rule. Jefferson proclaimed that without constant and devoted attention to education, the ideals of the young republic could not be achieved.

Thomas Jefferson was the first American to develop a state plan of universal education. The third president of the United States was born in Albemarle County, Virginia. After graduating from William and Mary College, he was admitted to the bar and was elected a member of the Virginia House of Burgesses. Along with Richard Henry Lee and Patrick Henry, he initiated the intercolonial committee of correspondence. He was a member of the Continental Congress (1775-76); chief author and chairman of the committee that drew up the Declaration of Independence; governor of Virginia (1779-81); member of Congress (1783-84); American minister to France (1785-89); U.S. Secretary of State (1790-93); vice president of the United States (1797-1801); and two-term President of the United States (1801-1809).

While in France, Jefferson became acquainted with French political ideas, particularly those of Rousseau, and on returning to America became an eloquent spokesman for these ideas. Writing to James Madison in 1787, he declared that, "Above all things I hope the education of the common people will be attended to; convinced that on their good senses we may rely with the most security for the preservation of a due degree of liberty."[7]

Jefferson's plan for a system of schooling in Virginia was the first secular plan for universal education in America. The Jefferson proposal was first to provide free elementary schools for all children. Second, free education was to be provided for the best of the scholars through a series of residential Latin grammar schools, which were also to serve the rich on a tuition basis. Third, a university education was to be provided at public expense for a selected few who would benefit from this education.

Jefferson's education proposal was introduced in the Virginia legislature several times and finally passed in the 1796-97 session. Although the bill failed to be implemented, its influence on the movement for free public schools was considerable. In 1818 Jefferson wrote of his devotion to education as follows:

A system of general instruction, which shall reach every description of our citizens from the richest to the poorest, as it was the earliest, so will it be the latest of all the public concerns in which I shall permit myself to take an interest. Nor am I tenacious of the form in which it shall be introduced. Be that what it may, our descendents will be as wise as we are, and will know how to amend and amend it, until it shall suit their circumstances. Give it to us then in any shape and receive for the inestimable boon the thanks of the young and the blessings of the old who are past all other services but prayers for the prosperity of their country, and blessings for those who promote it.[8]

It was the founding of the University of Virginia in 1819, however, that stands as Jefferson's greatest achievement in his efforts to make education a state responsibility. Concerning the University of Virginia, he wrote in the year preceding his death:

I am closing the last scenes of my life by fashioning and fastening an establishment for the instruction of those who are to come after us. I hope its influence on their virtue, freedom, fame, and happiness will be salutary and permanent.[9]

HORACE MANN (1796-1859) While both Franklin and Jefferson recognized the need for equality of educational opportunity in America, both men were mainly involved as public figures with the political and economic problems of the new nation. Horace Mann, however, forsook a promising political career to devote his entire time and abilities to the expansion of public education in the United States. His strong feelings for education are aptly illustrated in this statement:

> *If ever there was a cause, if ever there can be a cause, worthy to be upheld by all of toil and sacrifice that the human heart can endure, it is the cause of Education. It has intrinsic and indestructible merits. It holds the welfare of mankind in its embrace, as the protecting arms of a mother hold her infant to her bosom. The very ignorance and selfishness which obstruct its path are the strongest arguments for its promotion, for it furnishes the only adequate means for their removal.*[10]

Born in Franklin, Massachusetts, he graduated from Brown University, studied law and was admitted to the bar. He was appointed the first secretary of the Massachusetts Board of Education in 1837 from which position he fostered a revolution in public school organization and teaching.

Basic educational reforms in France and Prussia stirred the attention of educational leaders in Massachusetts, and in 1837 the legislature of Massachusetts enacted a bill to create a board to further education in that state. Mann accepted the secretaryship of this board over which he presided for twelve years. Each year he prepared an annual report that contained his basic educational beliefs.

Mann's Third Annual Report (1839) discusses books and libraries, and while his views on the proper contents of libraries are controversial, he reports that, "It seems to be the unanimous opinion of the teachers of all schools, whether public or private, that a School Library would be a most valuable auxiliary in interesting children in their studies."[11] Mann lists what he considers to be the prime requisites of the teacher in his Fourth Annual Report (1840), and they are: (1) knowledge of subject matter, (2) aptness to teach, (3) experience, (4) good behavior, and (5) character.

That education is a natural right of man, he strongly insisted in the Tenth Annual Report (1846):

> *I believe in the existence of a great, immortal, immutable principle of natural law, or natural ethics—a principle antecedent to all human institutions and incapable of being abrogated by any ordinance of man—a principle of divine origin, clearly legible in the ways of Providence as those ways are manifested in the order of Nature and in the history of the race, which proves the <u>absolute right</u> to an education of every human being that comes into the world; and which, of course, proves the correlative duty of every government to see that the means of that education are provided for all.*[12]

Fundamental to his thinking was the idea of the indispensibility of free schools to American liberties. He wrote: "... since the achievement of American independence, the universal and ever-repeated argument in favor of free schools has been that the general intelligence which they are capable of diffusing and which can be imparted by no other human instrumentality, is indispensable to the continuance of a republican government."[13]

The year 1848 was a revolutionary year throughout Europe, and it was appropriate for Mann in his Twelfth Annual Report, and his last one, to emphasize the revolutionary potential in education. "Now, surely," he says, "nothing but universal education can counterwork this tendency to the domination of capital and the servility of labor." He concludes, "Education, then, beyond all other devices of human origin, is the great equalizer of the conditions of men."[14]

In 1848, Mann resigned his post on the Massachusetts Board of Education to take the seat in Congress of former U.S. President John Quincy Adams. Later he was defeated in a race for the Massachusetts governorship. But in 1853 he was appointed president of Antioch College, in Ohio, an institution dedicated to the task of educating Negroes. He remained at Antioch until a year before his death. Mann's greatest contribution was to convince the American people through the medium of his beautifully written reports, that free, public, nonsectarian schools should be financed by the state to the extent of the need for such support, and that such schools should be conducted by teachers well trained in both subject matter and methods of teaching. Mann was a pre-eminent spokesman for the movement to establish free public high schools as a part of the common schools in the United States.

Conclusion

During the colonial period, from the founding of the colonies in the seventeenth century to the Revolutionary War in the latter part of the eighteenth century, American schools generally reflected European educational ideas, but they also began to reveal some distinctive characteristics of their own. Education was one of the powers of government transferred to the New World by delegation from the British crown to stock companies, proprietors, royal governors, and colonial legislatures. The New England colonies exercised more direct control over and support of schools than did the other colonies.

Throughout most of the colonial period the dominant type of secondary instruction was carried on in Latin grammar schools. In general, the Latin grammar school was attended by the children of the more privileged families of the upper classes and was looked upon as providing the preparation necessary for college education. In the eighteenth century, the classical character of secondary education was modified and broadened somewhat by the appearance of new types of secondary schools. Academies were set up to provide instruction in a much wider range of studies including English, modern language, mathematics, navigation, surveying, commercial arithmetic, bookkeeping, geography, history, music and the arts. The curriculums of the academies combined the religious, humanistic, and practical concerns of the latter part of the eighteenth century.

During the years of the early national period, Americans developed educational policies dedicated to the new national ideals of democracy, equality, and freedom. The ideal of public education was fostered by a determined group of educational leaders and statesmen who acquired the support of increasing numbers of middle-class liberals, reformers, and humanitarians. Notable among them were Benjamin Franklin, Thomas Jefferson, and Horace Mann.

Chapter VII

Footnotes

[1] William M. French, *American Secondary Education* (New York: The Odyssey Press, Inc., 1967), p. 1.

[2] *Ibid.*, p. 2.

[3] Mehdi Nakosteen, *The History and Philosophy of Education* (New York: The Ronald Press Company, 1965), p. 430.

[4] Leonard W. Labaree (ed.), *The Papers of Benjamin Franklin,* III (New Haven, Connecticut: Yale University Press, 1961), p. 404.

[5] *Acts and Laws of Massachusetts, 1780.* See also Robert O. Hahn and David B. Bidna, *Secondary Education: Origins and Directions* (New York: The Macmillan Company, 1965), pp. 60-61.

[6] It is true some academies were operated by individuals as profit-making businesses.

[7] John P. Foley (ed.), *The Jefferson Cyclopedia* (New York: Russell and Russell, Inc., 1967), I, 277.

[8] *Ibid.*, p. 274.

[9] *Ibid.*, II, 900.

[10] Louis Filler (ed.), *Horace Mann on the Crisis in Education* (Yellow Springs, Ohio: Antioch Press, 1965), p. 18.

[11] *Ibid.*, p. 64.

[12] Horace Mann, *Tenth Annual Report (1846).* See also Tyrus Hellway, *American Education: an Introduction Through Readings* (Boston: Houghton Mifflin Company, 1964), pp. 34-35.

[13] *Ibid.*

[14] Filler, *op. cit.*, pp. 119-124.

Selected References

Alexander, William M., and Saylor, J. Galen. *Modern Secondary Education.* New York: Holt, Rinehart and Winston, 1965.

Butts, R. Freeman. *A Cultural History of Education.* New York: McGraw-Hill Book Company, 1947.

Cubberley, Ellwood P. *Public Education in the United States.* Revised. Boston: Houghton Mifflin Company, 1934.

French, William M. *American Secondary Education.* New York: The Odyssey Press, Inc., 1967.

America's Educational Tradition. New York: D. C. Heath and Company, 1964.

Hahn, David O., and Bidna, David B. *Secondary Education: Origins and Directions.* New York: The Macmillan Company, 1965.

Hillway, Tyrus. *American Education: An Introduction Through Readings.* Boston: Houghton Mifflin Company, 1964.

Meyer, Adolphe E. *An Educational History of the American People.* New York: McGraw-Hill Book Company, 1967.

Middlekauff, Robert. *Ancients and Axioms: Secondary Education in Eighteenth-Century New England.* New Haven: Yale University Press, 1963.

Nakosteen, Mehdi. *The History and Philosophy of Education.* New York: The Ronald Press Company, 1965.

Sizer, Theodore R. *The Age of the Academies.* New York: Teachers College, Columbia University, 1964.

Chapter VIII

THE MOVEMENT TO ESTABLISH HIGH SCHOOLS

Introduction

The academy reached the height of its importance during the middle years of the nineteenth century at about the time the common or public elementary school was gaining acceptance by the American people. The forces which brought forth the American elementary school also began to impinge upon the secondary school. Many of the elementary schools began to add a higher department, sometimes known as a 'grammar school.' The state of Connecticut in 1798 passed a law that permitted a school district upon approval of voters to establish a higher school to instruct in English and other subjects, including Greek and Latin.[1]

The Boston English Classical High School

The first free American high school was established in Boston in 1821. In a report of the School Committee to the Town Meeting of Boston in January, 1821, it was recommended, in part, as follows:

> Though the present system of public education, and the munificence with which it is supported, are highly beneficial and honorable to the town; yet, in the opinion of the Committee, it is susceptible of a greater degree of perfection and usefulness without materially augmenting the weight of the public burdens . . . .
> The present system, in the opinion of the Committee, requires still further amendment. The Studies that are pursued at the English grammar schools are merely elementary, and more time than is necessary is devoted to their acquisition . . . .
> The Committee for these and many other weighty considerations that might be offered, and in order to render the present system of public education more nearly perfect, are of the opinion that an additional

School is required. They therefore recommend the founding of a seminary which shall be called the English Classical School . . . .[2]

This school was opened in May, 1821, and in 1824 was renamed as the English High School. The high school was an effort to make the advantages of a secondary education available to all youth, since many parents were not able to send their children to an academy.

The purpose of the new school as stipulated by the School Committee in 1821 was "to render the present system of public education more nearly perfect." Originally founded as a school for boys, the school later became the first coeducational public high school in America. The school accepted pupils at not less than twelve years of age. They established a three-year course of studies. The first year of studies included arithmetic, geography, English grammar, the history of bookkeeping, some arts and sciences, composition, and declamation. The second and third years embraced geometry, algebra, trigonometry, philosophy and theology, natural history, chemistry, rhetoric, logic, and political economy.

The same year which witnessed the opening of the Boston school also saw a similar school opened in Portland, Maine, and three years later another in Worcester, Massachusetts. In 1825 New York City also opened what can be considered as a high school.[3]

Massachusetts Law of 1827

What gave the American high school its first real impetus was not these few and scattered efforts, but a law which Massachusetts enacted in 1827. Although this statute made no open reference to a high school, it called upon every town of 500 families to offer tax-supported instruction in the branches of learning of the following subjects: the history of the United States, bookkeeping, geometry, surveying, and algebra. In addition, towns of 4,000 were required to offer the additional courses of general history, rhetoric, logic, Latin, and Greek. In spite of its mandatory provisions, this legislation was not well enforced until the time of Horace Mann, who became Secretary of the State Board of Education in 1837.

Nevertheless, the movement to establish publically supported high schools was launched. By 1840 sixteen Massachusetts towns had established high schools. In Pennsylvania special legislation was enacted in the years between 1838 and 1850 for the establishment of high schools in Philadelphia, Pittsburgh, and Easton. A general law was adopted in 1854. During the period from 1847 to 1853 ten public high schools were authorized by special legislation in New York, and in 1853 the Free School Act gave general authorization for the establishment of high schools. In the new western states such as Ohio, Indiana, Iowa, and California, high schools were established in many larger communities, usually at first under special legislative authorization and later by general law.[4] By the year 1860, over 300 high schools had been opened throughout the length and breadth of the country as far west as San Francisco and as far south as New Orleans.[5]

First Compulsory School Law

Again in 1852 the state of Massachusetts set yet another educational precedent by enacting the first compulsory school law in the United States. By an act of 1850 the legislature had given authority to cities and towns to make any necessary provisions and arrangements concerning children between the ages of six and sixteen not attending school. In 1852 the Massachusetts legislature made school attendance compulsory for children between the ages of eight and fourteen. Section 1 of the Act states:

> Every person who shall have any child under his control between the ages of eight and fourteen years shall send such child to some public school within the town or city in which he resides, during at least twelve weeks, ... in each and every year during which such child shall be under his control, six weeks of which shall be consecutive.[6]

Section 4 of this Act exempted from the provisions of the law the child who had attended school in some other community for the time required by the Act, or, "has been otherwise furnished with the means of education for a like period of time, or has already acquired those branches of learning which are taught in common schools, or if it shall appear that his bodily or mental condition has been such as to prevent his attendance at school, ..."[7] The act also exempted parents who could not afford to send their children to school. This 1852 act was another milestone along the way to establishing free universal education ranging from the elementary through the secondary schools.

Kalamazoo Case and Decision

A landmark in the movement for the establishment of a system of free, public high schools was the decision rendered by the Supreme Court of the State of Michigan in what is called the Kalamazoo decision. In 1872 the citizens of Kalamazoo voted to establish a free high school and to employ a superintendent of schools. Taxes were levied upon property holders to raise the needed funds. A group of taxpayers challenged the right of the school district to collect the additional taxes, alleging that there was no constitutional authority for such action. The complainants charged that although there were no constitutional provisions expressly prohibiting such taxation, the whole course of legislation and the general understanding of the people had been that high school instruction, particularly in classical and modern languages, was not of a practical nature and therefore unnecessary for the general instruction of the people at large. The case was carried to the supreme court of the state.

Mr. Justice Cooley, in rendering the decision of the court, reviewed at some length the history of school legislation in the State of Michigan and the efforts of the citizens to make education available to all the people. The constitution of 1850, he pointed out, had specifically provided for the establishment of free schools in every district of the state and for a state university; he went on to state:

> ... *we have every reason to believe the people expected a complete collegiate education might be obtained. The branches of the university had ceased to exist; the university had no preparatory department, and it must either be understood that young men were to be prepared for the university in the common schools.... The inference seems irresistible that the people expected the tendency towards the establishment of high schools in the primary school districts would continue until every locality capable of supporting one was supplied.*[8]

Justice Cooley concluded that the court could find no reason for restricting the primary school districts in the branches of knowledge to be taught or the grades of instruction to be given, provided that the voters consented, "in regular form to bear the expense and raise taxes for the purpose."[9] The historic Kalamazoo decision contributed to the advancement of free, public secondary education in the United States. In other American states court decisions which established the legality of the public high school were clearly based on this Michigan decision. Earlier court decisions, however, had laid the groundwork for the Kalamazoo ruling. In 1859, the supreme court in both the states of Iowa and Illinois had determined that the high school must be regarded as a common school.

Nature of, Curriculum, and Practices of the Early American High School

After Kalamazoo, the high school was definitely accepted as a part of the common or public school system. Not yet everyone attended it, but there it was, and it was free, and it was available to anyone who could meet the entrance requirements. The main difference between the high school and the earlier academy was mostly in the matter of control and tuition charges. Whereas the high school was controlled by a public body, the academy was under the control of a private board or corporation which set charges for instruction.

High School Population. During the latter part of the nineteenth century more girls than boys attended the high school. The preponderance of girls may be explained by the fact that at the time there were fewer work opportunities for middle class girls than now, and also that girls generally have been more orderly and inclined to accept formal schooling. Boys, in the absence of child labor laws, went to work to augment family incomes. High school students came mostly from middle class homes. The rich and influential families continued to send their children to private schools, and the very poor tended to avoid the high school.

High School Teachers. Teachers in the early high school came either from the liberal arts colleges or the state normal schools and teachers colleges. Most teachers were subject-matter centered in their teaching. Mastery of knowledge was regarded as the aim of learning because knowledge was thought to be power, in the Lockian sense. Both men and women taught in the early high schools, whereas men had held the greater number of positions in the academies. The increase in the number of women teachers is attributed to the breaking of the ancient barrier against higher education for the female sex. And not a small consideration was the fact that it was possible to obtain women teachers of high qualifications for lower salaries than were paid men of equal caliber. Only since World War II have men recaptured a slight majority of the secondary school teaching positions.

High School Curriculum. There was very little uniformity among the early American high schools, either throughout the nation or even within most states. A school report published in 1838 and quoted by Henry Barnard in 1857 states well the functions and purpose of the early high school:

> .... *To be truly a public school, a High School must embrace in its course of instruction studies which can be more profitably pursued there than in public schools of a lower grade, or which gather their pupils from a more circumscribed territory, and as profitably as in any private school of the same pretensions.* [10]

From 1870 to the end of the nineteenth century individual schools developed their distinctive characteristics. The following listing of subjects, however, is typical of high school offerings of this period: Latin, Greek, French, German, algebra, geometry, trigonometry, astronomy, physics, chemistry, geography, geology, physiology, botany, agriculture, domestic economy (home economics), psychology, rhetoric, English literature, history, and civics.

As the high school came to play a progressively larger part in American life in succeeding decades, it was subjected to increasing critical appraisal by college officials as well as by leading educators. Because of the great diversity among high schools, various pressures were exerted to standardize them. With the tendency to tighten up in the secondary schools and with the increased selectivity by the colleges when the number of applicants increased sizeably, the movement to standardize high school offerings gained momentum. Beginning in the 1890's there opened three decades of remarkable professional committee activity which investigated and made recommendations for all aspects of secondary education. Among the more important of these committees were the following: the Committee of Ten on Secondary School Studies, 1892-93; Committee on College Entrance Requirements, 1895-99; Committee on Six Year Courses, 1905-09; Committee on Economy of Time in Education, 1908-13, and 1911-19; Committee on the Articulation of High School and College, 1910-1911; and the Commission on the Reorganization of Secondary Education, 1913-18. The first and perhaps the most prestigious of these committees is called the Committee of Ten.

Committee of Ten

In 1887, at a meeting of the National Council of Education, a leadership committee within the National Education Association, a proposal was adopted to make an investigation of the high school curriculum with reference to uniformity in high school work and consequent uniformity in college entrance requirements. A standing committee of the National Council with James H. Baker, principal of the Denver High School as chairman, investigated the matter and issued a report in 1891. The committee recommended that the National Council join with its parent organization, the NEA, to sponsor a conference of school and college teachers. The NEA then proceeded to appoint a Committee of Ten on Secondary School Studies. The members were leading American educators of the time. They were President Charles W. Eliot of Harvard University, chairman; U.S. Commissioner of Education William T. Harris; John Teglow, principal of the Boston Girls' High and Latin Schools; Oscar D. Robinson, principal, Albany (New York) High School; James C. MacKenzie, headmaster of the Lawrenceville School; Henry C. King, professor at Oberlin College; President James H. Baker of the University of Colorado; President James M. Taylor of Vassar College; President Richard H. Jesse of the University of Missouri; and President James B. Angell of the University of Michigan.

The Committee of Ten undertook the task of creating a unitary system of education for all pupils, with the secondary school serving as the vital link between elementary and higher education. The committee rejected the European practice of having a dual system of secondary education, and formulated a program that would enable the high school to serve both the functions of preparing those who are going on to college, and of preparing those who did not wish to go on to college. The goal of the committee was four years of strong and effective academic training. The committee felt that the best preparation for college or for life was training of the intellect and the development of the powers of reasoning.

The committee recommended four high school courses: the Classical, the Latin-Scientific, the Modern Languages, and the English. The Classical would require Latin, Greek, and one modern language; the Latin-Scientific would require Latin and one modern language; the modern languages would require two modern languages; and the English would require one foreign language.

The prestige of the Committee of Ten gave its recommendations considerable weight and led many high schools to redirect their thinking along the lines laid down by the committee. However, the report of the committee left many problems still unsolved in secondary education, among them the matter of preparing pupils to meet college entrance requirements.

Committee on College Entrance Requirements

In 1895 the NEA appointed a second committee. This committee was composed of five representatives of the secondary schools and five from the colleges and universities. Chairman of the new committee was Dr. A. F. Nightengale, superintendent of the Chicago Public Schools. This committee suggested several educational innovations: (1) it listed a group of subjects that it considered proper for college admission, and it described the work to be covered in these and additional courses; (2) it defined a unit of measure that could be employed to determine the amount of work to be required by the colleges in those subjects; and (3) it recommended development of a six-year secondary school program beginning with grade seven; also, a limited number of free electives, sequential courses in science, and acceleration of gifted students in high school.

In the report of the committee the reference to the term 'unit' signified a subject studied for four or five periods per week for one school year in the secondary school. The committee recommended the following number of units in all secondary schools and in all requirements for admission to college: (1) four units in foreign languages—with no language accepted in less than two units; (2) two units in mathematics; (3) two units in English; and (4) one unit each in history and science. When this concept of unit came to be endorsed by the Carnegie Foundation for the Advancement of Teaching, it was called the "Carnegie Unit." The Carnegie unit is still used in secondary schools to describe one year's study of a discrete subject.

Educational Reformers
of the Nineteenth and Early Twentieth Centuries

The names of certain individuals stand out prominently in the movement to establish and to reform American High Schools during the course of the nineteenth century and into the early decades of the twentieth. These men are Henry Barnard, G. Stanley Hall, and John Dewey.

HENRY BARNARD (1811-1900)   The career of Henry Barnard was in many respects similar to that of Horace Mann's. Born at Hartford, Connecticut, he received his early training in the Hopkins Grammar School and Monson Academy. After graduating from Yale

University he began the study of law, but interrupted it to accept the post of headmaster of an academy at Willsboro in Pennsylvania. He was admitted to the bar in 1835. During the years 1835 and 1836, he was in Europe studying schools and Pestalozzian ideas. Serving as a member of the Connecticut legislature in 1837, he sponsored legislation similar to that of Horace Mann's, and in 1838 he helped secure the passage of the bill which established the State Board of Education. He was appointed secretary of the new board, a position which he held for four years. Although the Board was abolished in 1842, it gave Barnard an opportunity to put through reforms in Connecticut equal in importance to those carried on by Mann in Massachusetts. One of the significant measures of his administration was the organization in 1839 of the first teacher's institute. Extensive use was made of these institutes in the training of teachers. He also founded the *Connecticut School Journal* for the dissemination of knowledge among teachers, school boards, and the general public.

Barnard removed to the State of Rhode Island where he was school commissioner from 1843 to 1849. In 1845 he organized the Rhode Island Institute of Instruction, the oldest state teachers' association in the United States. He was also active in the organization of town libraries and popular lecture courses for teachers and the general public. In 1851 he returned to Connecticut as superintendent of the Connecticut state schools. He was the U.S. delegate at the educational congress held at London in 1854. Active in the organization of the American Association for the Advancement of Education, he was its president in 1855. Also in the year 1855 he began the publication of the *American Journal of Education* which he continued to edit for the next twenty-six years.

In 1858 Barnard was appointed chancellor of the University of Wisconsin. At Wisconsin he also organized the State Normal School and conducted teachers' institutes. At the close of the Civil War in 1866, he was chosen as president of St. John's College at Annapolis, but he resigned this post to become in 1867 the first U.S. Commissioner of Education. During his three-year stay in Washington, D.C., he organized the U.S. Bureau of Education and outlined its policy.

In his long lifetime, which spanned nearly all but one decade of the nineteenth century, Barnard published fifty-two works on the history and theory of education, thirty-two volumes of the *American Journal of Education,* four volumes of the Connecticut *Common School Journal,* and three volumes of the *Rhode Island Institute of Instruction.* He gave the United States its earliest literature of education. Among the more important of his works were several:

Reformatory Education is one of the earliest and best contributions to the literature of the care and treatment of juvenile delinquents. *School Architecture,* published in 1849, the first American book of its kind, set a high standard virtually unrealized by contemporary school buildings. The architect, James Renwick, incorporated Barnard's suggestion in such buildings as the Tryon Park School in New York City. This school provided good light, ventilation, sanitation and safety within the cavernous spaces found in Gothic Revival style architecture. Another work, *Papers for Teachers,* in seven volumes, includes accounts of, and translations from, the great educators and philosophers, together with papers by contemporary educators of his day.

The educational efforts and writings of Barnard assisted in bringing about the great awakening in public education in the United States. His educational philosophy is well summarized in the following sentence from one of his annual reports:

> ...If they [the public] had a proper estimate of the influence of teachers, for good or for evil, for time and eternity, on the character and destiny of their pupils, they would employ, if within the reach of their means, those best qualified to give strength and grace to the body, clearness, vigor and richness to the mind, and the highest and purest feeling to the moral nature of every child entrusted to their care.[11]

G. STANLEY HALL (1846-1924)   G. Stanley Hall was the founder of the psychological movement in education in America. He was concerned with efforts to give a systematic account of how the psychophysiological processes of chilren differ from those of adults, and of the manner in which children develop from birth to the end of adolescence. He was born at Ashfield, Massachusetts. After graduating from Williams College he spent two years studying in Germany. Returning to the United States, he took a degree from Union Theological Seminary. After holding the chair of psychology at Antioch College for four years, he became a student of William James at Harvard for the Ph. D. degree, which he received in 1878. He then returned to Europe for further studies in psychology at Berlin, Bonn, Heidelberg, and Leipzig working with Wundt, Helmholtz, and other noted psychological investigators.

From 1881 to 1888 Hall was professor of psychology at Johns Hopkins University where his laboratory, the first of its kind in America, drew many able students, one of them, John Dewey. In 1889 Hall was appointed first president and was made professor of psychology of the recently organized Clark University at Worcestor, Massachusetts, which under his personal leadership was devoted chiefly to educational research, and for thirty years he was an important contributor to educational literature. Although at times his methods lacked scientific accuracy, his contributions to the process of psychology and education were substantial and important. In 1887 he began editing the *American Journal of Psychology*, which publication he founded and which he continued to edit until 1921. In 1891 he established a periodical, the Pedagogical Seminary, devoted to child psychology and pedagogy.

Hall's numerous works include the following: *The Contents of Children's Minds on Entering School; Youth—Its Education, Regimen and Hygiene; Educational Problems;* and *Life and Confessions of a Psychologist.*

Influenced by Darwin's theory of evolution, Hall sought to reconcile the development of mental life with the evolutionary hypothesis. He held that mental and physical life are parallel. The child, in his growth and development, repeats each stage in the evolution of the race. In this 'recapitulation' theory the stages are: the prenatal, the primitive, the savage, and finally the civilized stage. Hall introduced the child study movement into the United States and became its leader, both here and throughout Europe.

The central interest of education, he asserted, must be those learnings which promote the continuation of the race. In human development, he believed, one sees repeated the history of racial development, and this 'recapitulation,' he held, must control the steps in education. Therefore, education should be based upon the growth and development of the child's nature and lead to a well-balanced whole person. Although the 'recapitulation' theory is rejected today, Hall's life and work mark an important milestone in the development of a science of education in the United States.

JOHN DEWEY (1859-1952) John Dewey is the most renowned American philosopher-psychologist-educator. Born in Burlington, Vermont, he received his bachelor's degree from the University of Vermont and then taught school for two years in Pennsylvania and rural Vermont. He received the Ph.D. degree from Johns Hopkins University, where he studied under G. Stanley Hall. He taught philosophy at the Universities of Minnesota and Michigan before going to the University of Chicago, where he became head of the combined departments of philosophy, psychology, and pedagogy. In 1896 he established the first laboratory school at Chicago University, which he directed until he went to Columbia University as professor of philosophy, where he remained until his retirement in 1930.

Dewey's professional career was long and active. He was president of the American Psychological Association, of the American Philosophical Association, and of the American Association of University Professors which he helped to organize. He was also active in the American Civil Liberties Union. He was guest lecturer in philosophy and education at the University of Peking. He visited Turkey at the request of that government and prepared a report on the reorganization of the schools of that nation. Later he also visited Japan, Mexico, the Soviet Union, and South Africa to study the practices and problems of education in those countries. These visits made him the unofficial American spokesman for American thought to other parts of the world.

The work of John Dewey in psychology and philosophy was largely a result of his interest in educational reform. His distinctive philosophy began to emerge at the turn of the century while he was at the University of Chicago. There his ideas on education were stimulated and tested experimentally in the laboratory school he founded. Dewey's ideas of problem-solving and of using children's interests were developed in his experimental school at Chicago. The slogan "learning by doing" became the key to Dewey's educational theory and the pedagogical counterpart of his attempt to make philosophy relevant to the moral, social, and political problems of the time. After 1900 John Dewey was largely responsible for the flow of progressive educational ideas and practices back to join with the European progressive tradition dating from the times of Comenius and Rousseau. For over sixty years Dewey turned out a series of articles and books on philosophy and education. Among his more important publications are: *School and Society; Democracy and Education; Reconstruction in Philosophy; Human Nature and Conduct; Experience and Nature; The Public and its Problems; The Quest for Certainty; Experience and Education;* and *Education Today.*

The philosophy on which Dewey's educational theories rest has been called pragmatism, though he, himself, seems to have favored the term instrumentalism or experimentalism. Like Rousseau and Plato before him, Dewey conceived of education as an instrument of social reform. Unlike Rousseau, he did not accept nature uncritically as his standard, nor did he, like Plato, seek his standard in some ideal realm beyond nature. Dewey saw reform as basically experimental. He called for the fullest sharing of ideas and resources for the solving of problems. Only in this way, he maintained, could there be continual and effective reconstruction of individual and social experience.

As he saw it, the experimental methods of science provided the most promising approach for the solution of social and ethical problems as well. He found two aspects of modern society of basic importance to education: first, that society is in the process of great change, of which the Industrial Revolution is one of the chief marks; second, that the great advances of modern society are the results of modern science. Ultimately and philosophically, he thought science is the organ of general social progress. In *Democracy and Education,* published in 1916, Dewey wrote the following concerning the importance of education to society:

> *In directing the activities of the young, society determines its own future in determining that of the young. Since the young at a given time will at some later date compose the society of that period, the latter's nature will largely turn upon the direction children's activities were given at an earlier period.* [12]

Conclusion

In this chapter the attempt has been made to describe how that uniquely American institution the comprehensive high school has come into being. The comprehensive high school may be defined as a high school whose programs relate to the educational needs of all youth of the community it serves.

Chapter VIII
Footnotes

[1] William M. Alexander, and J. Galen Saylor, *Modern Secondary Education* (New York: Holt, Rinehart and Winston, Inc., 1965), p. 136.

[2] *Report of the School Committee to the Town Meeting of Boston,* "The Establishment of the First American High School," January, 1821. See also Robert O. Hahn, and David B. Bidna, *Secondary Education: Origins and Directions* (New York: The Macmillan Company, 1965), pp. 62-64.

[3] Adolphe E. Meyer, *An Educational History of the American People* (New York: McGraw-Hill Book Company, Inc., 1967), p. 207.

[4] Alexander and Saylor, *op. cit.,* pp. 138-139.

[5] Meyer, *op. cit.,* p. 208.

[6] *Acts and Resolves Passed by the General Court of Massachusetts in the Year 1852,* "The First Compulsory School Law in the United States, 1852," pp. 170-171. See also Hahn, and Bidna, *op. cit.,* pp. 70-71.

[7] *Ibid.*

[8] *Stuart v. School District No. 1 of Kalamazoo,* 30 Mich. 69-84. See also Hahn, and Bidna, *op. cit.,* pp. 75-78; Tyrus Hillway, *American Education: An Introduction Through Readings* (Boston: Houghton Mifflin Company, 1964), pp. 62-72.

[9] *Ibid.*

[10] Quoted in Henry Barnard's *American Journal of Education,* 3:185 (March, 1857), but original source not given. See also Alexander and Saylor, *op. cit.,* p. 143.

[11] Henry Barnard, *Second Annual Report, 1840.* See also William E. Drake, *The American School in Transition* (Englewood Cliffs, New Jersey: Prentice-Hall, Inc., 1955), pp. 150-245, 373-428; Mehdi Nakosteen, *The History and Philosophy of Education* (New York: The Ronald Press, 1965), pp. 462-463.

[12] John Dewey, *Democracy and Education* (New York: The Macmillan Company, 1916), p. 49.

Selected References

Alexander, William M., and J. Galen Saylor. *Modern Secondary Education.* New York: Holt, Rinehart and Winston, 1965.

Brown, Elmer Ellsworth. *The Making of Our Middle Schools.* New Impression. New York: Longmans, Green and Company, 1921.

Butts, R. Freeman, and Lawrence A. Cremin. *A History of Education in American Culture.* New York: Henry Holt and Company, 1953.

Cubberley, Ellwood P. *Public Education in the United States.* Rev. ed. Boston: Houghton Mifflin Company, 1934.

French, William Marshall. *America's Educational Tradition.* New York: D. C. Heath and Company, 1964.

Hahn, Robert O., and David B. Bidna. *Secondary Education: Origins and Directions.* New York: The Macmillan Company, 1965.

Hillway, Tyrus. *American Education: An Introduction Through Readings.* Boston: Houghton Mifflin Company, 1964.

Krug, Edward A. *The Shaping of the High School.* New York: Harper and Row Publishers, Inc., 1964.

Meyer, Adolphe E. *An Educational History of the American People.* New York: McGraw-Hill Book Company, 1967.

Nakosteen, Mehdi. *The History and Philosophy of Education.* New York: The Ronald Press, 1965.

Price, Kingsley. *Education and Philosophical Thought.* Boston: Allyn and Bacon, Inc., 1965.

Sizer, Theodore R. *Secondary Schools at the Turn of the Century.* New Haven, Connecticut: Yale University Press, 1964.

Chapter IX

TWENTIETH CENTURY DEVELOPMENTS IN AMERICAN SECONDARY EDUCATION

The Junior High School

The idea of reorganizing the eight-year elementary and the four-year secondary schools was in existence even before the end of the nineteenth century. The Committee of Ten (1893) and the Committee on College Entrance Requirements (1899) had proposed to recast the elementary and secondary school studies into two periods of six years each. The rationale for the junior high school was that it would consist of the last two years and the first year of the traditional 8-4 plan of school organization. Although several school systems had introduced some of the features of the junior high school prior to 1909, the first example of a school system organized on a 6-3-3 basis was Berkeley, California, in 1909. The organization of grades 7, 8, and 9 into a separate or intermediate school quickly gained widespread acceptance, particularly during the 1920-1930 decade.

The junior high school has as its first purpose to provide for a more gradual transition from elementary to secondary education. One of the earliest arguments for the junior high school was that pupils in grades 7, 8, and 9 constitute a homogeneous group of early adolescents. The new school would provide the kinds of learnings within an intellectual, social, and emotional environment that would be most conducive to the development of that particular age group. A second justification of the junior high school is the claim of the help it can provide pupils to acquire the basic knowledge, skills, and work habits for pursuing the more rigorous and penetrating study that characterizes the senior high school. Brimm lists six functions of the junior high school, as follows:

1. Transition of the self-contained classroom of the elementary school to the highly departmentalized classes of the senior high school.

2. Transition from the emphasis on the basic skills of the elementary school to the content courses of the senior high school.
3. Transition from the program of all required courses of the elementary school to the elective program of the senior high school.
4. Transition from the childhood activities of the pre-adolescent to the accepted adult activities of the young adult.
5. Transition from the pre-adolescent set of values to the more serious adult values of our modern, complex economy.
6. Transition from the social patterns of childhood to the social life of the adult which draws a definite distinction between the activities of the sexes.

Some of the criticism directed against the junior high school is that it gives too much pupil freedom and responsibility and not enough adult supervision and guidance. It is also criticized because the curriculum is so full of activities which consume teacher time that teachers have little time left to prepare for classwork. Conant's[2] investigation of the junior high school, however, found many junior high schools patterned after the senior high school, and that the highly departmentalized content courses do not provide for a transition period. The most salient weakness of the junior high school is the difficulty of retaining faculty—more aspire to teach in senior high and move into senior high as soon as opportunities develop. The junior high school of today may be in a period of transition. It is proposed that New York City adopt a 4-4-4 plan, and a few other communities are adopting middle schools of grades 5, 6, 7, and 8, or some similar variation. These "middle schools" could develop along the lines of the elementary school with self-contained classrooms, or in the pattern of the junior high school with departmental organization, or in a new design which might represent a compromise between the two.

The Junior College

The junior college has as one of its functions that of providing a more gradual transition from secondary to higher education. In this respect it is similar to the junior high school. The idea of the junior college was developed at the turn of the century by William Rainey Harper, first president of the University of Chicago. The first junior college was organized at Joliet, Illinois, in 1901. Slow to get started, the junior college movement accelerated considerably in the latter part of the 1930's. The movement took hold particularly in Missouri, Illinois, the Midwestern states, and in California. In 1967 there were over 500 junior colleges operating throughout the nation. California passed the first law in the nation referring to junior colleges in 1907. California also opened the first public junior college at Fresno in 1910. Ever since, California has led the country in junior college education.

The reasons for establishing junior colleges are several. One that can be mentioned is the European analogy. The <u>Gymnasium</u> of Germany and the <u>lycée</u> of France have been for years giving secondary school students the equivalent of two years of college training, thus permitting the universities to devote full time to research and specialized training. A second reason for the junior college is to relieve the over-crowded four-year institutions of higher education. Since the turn of the century, college enrollments have experienced an increase of over thirty-fold. Collegiate appropriations, building space, and faculty members have not kept pace with the increased enrollment. Since many pre-professional occupations require only a year or two of collegiate training, the two-year junior college is much better suited to train these students. A third important reason for the junior college is the desire of many parents for additional education closer to home. Financial problems encountered by families in sending their offspring away to school, and the reluctance of some parents to send their children away from home to attend school until they have achieved greater maturity and self-reliance are powerful motivations for the establishment of local junior colleges.

There are five important functions of education that the junior college uniquely has come to serve. These are: (1) to offer courses in general education that have both terminal and transfer value; (2) to provide pre-professional and/or vocational training for the student who does not need a four-year college degree; (3) to offer the first two years of collegiate training for those who plan to pursue a full four-year college program; (4) to provide adult education, especially in evening and night courses; and (5) to remove matriculation deficiencies for those students who do not meet college entrance requirements.

The junior college is now generally accepted as a part of the educational structure of the United States, even though some criticisms have been made of it, chiefly on financial considerations. The escalation of the cost of public education in recent years has caused many taxpayer groups in many parts of the nation to revolt against bond issues for building new schools. There is also the feeling, widespread, that monies diverted into junior colleges rightfully should be used to help the high schools and four-year collegiate institutions. The two-year junior college, however, is probably here to stay, and will remain as an integral part of the educational system. More than half of the states now have enacted special legislation for the establishment of junior colleges.

Commission on the Reorganization of Secondary Education

Background. Culminating the effort to define the function and purpose of the American high school, an endeavor begun with the report of the Committee of Ten in 1893 was reached with the publication of the report in 1918 of the Commission on the Reorganization of Secondary Education and its statement of the Seven Cardinal Principles of Secondary Education. Brief mention must be made, however, of two other committee reports which preceded the Seven Cardinal Principles: The Committee on Economy of Time in Education, and the Committee of Nine on the Articulation of High School and College. The former committee was appointed in 1905 and made its report in 1911. Its work consisted of an endeavor to shorten the educational course, and it recommended a curtailment of two years. The Committee of Nine was appointed in 1910 to prepare a statement on the program of studies the high school should offer for college admission purposes. This committee, unlike its predecessors, was composed entirely of public school people, except for one professor of education, and one college dean. The committee which reported in 1911 argued against the rigid requirement of foreign languages and mathematics for college admission. The Committee defined a well-organized high school as one that required the completion of two major subjects and one minor subject. It proposed that fifteen units be required for high school graduation, and it further recommended three alternative plans of college admission. It held that of the fifteen units suggested for graduation and college entrance, at least eleven units should be devoted to English, foreign languages, mathematics, social science, and natural science.

HERBERT SPENCER (1820-1903) The Commission on the Reorganization of Secondary Education in issuing the Seven Cardinal

Principles of Education followed closely the idea of the English sociologist and philosopher Herbert Spencer, who declared that the goals of education should be based on the life activities of the individual. Spencer was born in Derby, England, and received the conventional public school education, which stressed the classical languages. Impressed by Darwin's theory of evolution, Spencer sought to apply the biological theory to the development of social institutions. He is the first of the Social Darwinists. He published four essays on education in 1860 as a book entitled: *What Knowledge is Most Worth?* He classified human activities and arranged them into five categories, then described the kind of knowledge that is related to each activity. His five categories of activities are: (1) activities which relate directly to self-preservation; (2) activities which indirectly relate to self-preservation; (3) activities which relate to the rearing and disciplining of children; (4) activities which relate to the maintenance of social and political relations; and (5) activities which relate to leisure and the qualification of tastes and feelings.

Science is the most important subject in education, according to Spencer. Mathematics is indispensable, he said. The applications of physics underlie our comforts and gratifications; chemistry bears on those activities by which men obtain the means of living; biology is fundamental to the processes of self-preservation; and finally, he says, there is the vital knowledge of the science of society. Spencer argued that what mattered in education was not so much method and drill, but the actual content of what is studied.

Previous to Spencer the analyses of the aims and objectives of education had been vague and general. Spencer's utilitarian and scientific doctrines made an impact on both sides of the Atlantic. His most articulate spokesman in America was Charles Eliot, a professor of chemistry at Harvard, who had risen to its presidency in 1869, and who in 1892 became chairman of the Committee of Ten. Clarence Kingsley, chairman of the committee that framed the Seven Cardinal Principles for the Commission, was the close friend of David Snedden of the Massachusetts state department of education. Snedden was an active Spencerian disciple.

Organization of the Commission on the Reorganization of Secondary Education. One of the recommendations of the Committee of Nine had been that committees be established to study the reorganization of the various high school subject fields. Twelve such committees were established by the National Education Association in 1912-1913. To oversee the work of the several committees, the Commission on the Reorganization of Secondary Education was appointed in 1913. In this way was thus established the most important group ever to give direction to secondary education in the United States. In 1918, fifty-eight years after the publication of Spencer's *What Knowledge is Most Worth?*, the famous report of the Commission, known as *Cardinal Principles of Secondary Education*, was issued.

The Seven Cardinal Principles. The 1918 report of the Commission is one of the most significant documents in the history of education in America, or elsewhere, as a matter of fact. The report said that, "Secondary education should be determined by the needs of the society to be served, the character of the individuals to be educated, and the knowledge of educational theory and practice available." The report held that education in the United States should be guided by a clear conception of the meaning of democracy:

> It is the ideal of democracy that the individual and society may find fulfillment in each other .... The purpose of democracy is so to organize society that each member may develop his personality primarily through activities designed for the well-being of his fellow members and of society as a whole .... Consequently education in a democracy ... should develop in each individual the knowledge, interests, ideals, habits, and powers whereby he will find his place and use that place to shape both himself and society toward ever nobler ends ....[3]

To determine the main objectives of education, the report states that an analysis of the activities of the individual must be made. This analysis led to the definition of the principal objectives of education known as the Seven Cardinal Principles: (1) health, (2) command of fundamental processes, (3) worthy home membership, (4) vocation, (5) citizenship, (6) worthy use of leisure, and (7) ethical character. These seven objectives are Spencer's five categories, transformed and rendered into specific goals for American secondary education. The Cardinal Principles received national attention, and during the decades since their enunciation they have guided the planning of the structure and program of secondary education in the United States.

Smith-Hughes Act.

The initiation of vocational education in secondary schools by the Smith-Hughes Act in 1917 is an important milestone in the development of secondary education in the United States in the twentieth century. During the first decade of the new century the nation continued its rapid pace of industrialization, and certain economic groups, such as the National Association of Manufacturers, the National Metal Trades Association, certain agricultural organizations, and the American Federation of Labor urged that facilities for vocational training be provided for in the public schools. On February 23, 1917, President Woodrow Wilson signed into law the Smith-Hughes Bill, which authorized federal grants to the states for vocational education below the college level. These funds are to be used to reimburse the states to the extent of, but not to exceed, one-half the salaries of teachers, supervisors, and directors of vocational education in agriculture, trades, and industries. For the purposes of the Act, home economics was also defined as a vocational subject. The Act as amended and supplemented is the basis of vocational education programs administered by the U.S. Office of Education. The most important changes made in the Smith-Hughes legislation are the George-Barden Act of 1946, which greatly expanded the grants to the states; the Health Amendments of 1956, which added a program of practical nurse training; a law of 1956, which provides funds for vocational training in the fisheries trades; and Title VIII of the National Defense Education Act of 1958, which authorizes expansion of existing state vocational education programs into inadequately served areas, and which authorizes enlargement to include training in scientific and technological skills useful for national defense purposes.

The Eight-Year Study

The Commission on the Relation of School and College of the Progressive Education Association was organized in 1930. This group was composed of ardent supporters of pragmatic education and critics of traditional educational practices. It was inevitable that college entrance requirements would be attacked by the Progressive Education Association. In 1933, with funds partially supplied by the Carnegie Corporation, the Commission launched the Eight-Year Study, which was designed to find a better basis for admitting high school graduates to college and which would also free high schools from the need to teach all college-preparatory pupils a prescribed set of courses for college entrance. Under the plan for the study, students in the thirty selected high schools in various parts of the country were all liberated from a college preparatory curriculum. These students were matched in college with their counterparts from high schools which had adhered to the conventional college preparatory program. More than 250 colleges and universities participated in the study.

During the eight years of the study the thirty schools were encouraged to develop the kind of curriculum that schoolmen felt would best achieve the basic objectives of secondary education, as per the Cardinal Principles, without necessarily requiring college preparatory pupils to pursue subjects usually prescribed for admission. The adolescents of the study were paired with students who had taken the conventional college preparatory program.

When the Commission reported in 1941, it was found that success in college did not depend upon the study in high school of certain subjects for certain periods of time. The Study indicated that there were many kinds of secondary school experience through which students develop the qualities of mind and character essential to success in college work. On the basis of the findings of the report, many educators advocated that the high schools be freed from the necessity of requiring their college-bound students to take prescribed subjects only for purposes of college admission, thus freeing the high school curriculum from domination and dictation by college and university academicians.

Educational Policies Commission

Nearly two decades had passed from the time of the National Education Association report on the Cardinal Principles before that association appointed another commission to study education in the United States. In 1935 the Educational Policies Commission was created to select various educational problems for study. The Commission was to be a continuing body composed of outstanding leaders in American education. The stature of the Commission is attested to by the fact that such prominent Americans as the following have served as members: Dwight D. Eisenhower, while President of Columbia University; James B. Conant, while President of Harvard University; and such outstanding city school superintendents as Alexander J. Stoddard of Philadelphia and Los Angeles, and William Jansen of New York City.

One of the important statements prepared by the Commission was issued in 1938 and is entitled *The Purposes of Education in*

American Democracy. This report divided the objectives of education into four broad categories as follows: (1) the objectives of self-realization; (2) the objectives of human relationship; (3) the objectives of economic efficiency; and (4) the objectives of civic responsibility.

In 1944 the Commission issued the report known as *Education for All American Youth.* A significant feature of this book is a statement of objectives for the American secondary school that is essentially a restatement in expanded form of the Cardinal Principles. This statement, called the Imperative Educational Needs of Youth, reads as follows:

1. All youth need to develop saleable skills . . . .
2. All youth need to develop and maintain good health and physical fitness . . . .
3. All youth need to understand the rights and duties of the citizen of a democratic society . . . .
4. All youth need to understand the significance of the family for the individual and society . . . .
5. All youth need to know how to purchase and use goods and services intelligently . . . .
6. All youth need to understand the methods of science . . . .
7. All youth need opportunities to develop their capacities to appreciate beauty . . . .
8. All youth need to be able to use their leisure time well . . . .
9. All youth need to develop respect for other persons . . . .
10. All youth need to grow in ability to think rationally . . . .[4]

Many high schools have adopted these ten imperative needs as their statement of objectives for curriculum planning. In 1952 the Commission published the book *Education for All American Youth: A Future Look.* Basically, this statement of the Commission is a plea for extending public secondary education upwards to include grades thirteen and fourteen through the establishment of junior colleges. Compulsory school attendance, the Commission thought, should be required until the eighteenth birthday. In 1961 the Commission reported in the volume *The Central Purpose of Education* that that which underlies the school's objectives as delineated by the 1918, 1938, and the 1944 reports, is the obligation to develop the rational powers of the individual. "The individual with developed rational powers," concluded the Commission, "can share deeply in the freedoms his society offers and can contribute most to the preservation of those freedoms."[5] During 1968 the activity of the Educational Policies Commission was allowed to lapse.

Commission on Life Adjustment Education

Throughout the depression years of the 1930's there was great concern expressed for the non-academic high school student. The curriculum was believed by many educators to be remote from the student's daily life outside the school. In 1945, Charles A. Prosser, at a national conference on vocational education, introduced a resolution calling upon the United States Office of Education to call a conference or a series of regional conferences to formulate plans for a program of "life adjustment" education in the schools. Regional conferences were held in New York City, Cheyenne, Sacramento, and Birmingham, and a national conference at Chicago in 1947. Following the Chicago meeting, nine educational organizations submitted nominees to John W. Studebaker, U.S. Commissioner of Education, for appointment to a National Commission on Life Adjustment Educations for Every Youth. This commission, with the aid of the U.S. Office of Education, has attempted to arouse interest in life-adjustment training in the schools.

Life adjustment education may be said to be education concerned with ethical and moral living and with physical, mental, and emotional health. It provides both general and specialized education. It has many patterns, and each school determines the best method of meeting the goals in each community.

The term "life-adjustment education" has come to be a most controversial one in and out of educational circles in recent years. One of its most enthusiastic spokesmen, Harl R. Douglass, wrote that during the depression thirties:

> ... *The life adjustment which our people needed ... was not the special need of any particular group; it was needed by all people. It has been pointed out also that when a pupil enters high school at thirteen or fourteen years of age, no one can tell whether he is going to college, into a skilled occupation, or into a semiskilled occupation. He must be dealt with as an individual and not as a member of a group.*[6]

Critics of American high school education such as Rear Admiral Hyman G. Rickover, Arthur E. Bestor, history professor at the University of Illinois, and Max Rafferty, California State Superintendent of Schools, blame the life-adjustment advocates for "watering down" the curriculum of the school. Rafferty has attacked life-adjustment education as follows:

> ... *What will History [sic] have to say of my generation of educators—the generation of the 30's, the 40's, and the 50's? We were so busy educating for "life adjustment" that we forgot that the first duty of a nation's schools is to preserve that nation............................*

The results [of this neglect] are plain for all to see: the worst of our youngsters growing up to become booted, sideburned, ducktailed, unwashed, leatherjacketed Slobs [sic], whose favorite sport is ravaging little girls and stomping polio victims to death; the best of our youth coming into maturity for all the world like young people fresh from a dizzying roller-coaster ride, with everything blurred, with nothing clear, with no positive standards, with everything in doubt. No wonder so many of them welsh out and squeal and turn traitor when confronted with grim reality of Red military force and the crafty cunning of Red psychological warfare.[7]

Arthur Bestor, one of the strongest supporters of an academic liberal arts curriculum, believes that certain intellectual disciplines are fundamental in the secondary school curriculum because they are basic in modern life. He believes English and foreign languages are essential because modern intellectual life is built upon these particular disciplines. Bestor avers that the curriculum in the latter part of the nineteenth century was closer to present needs than is life adjustment curricula.

Thus is the American high school attacked by two opposing forces: those educators and others who feel the school has strayed too far from the ancient and time-honored functions of disciplining the intellect and of transmitting the cultural heritage, and those who feel that the school has not fully accepted its commitment to develop a program of all-round education for the life-activities of the individual.

School Desegregation Decision

While the comprehensive secondary school seems best fitted to the American ideal of democracy, one exception to the general pattern of comprehensive schooling has been the rigid scheme of racial segregation of pupils in the southern states and of the de facto segregation in the North and West. With the historic decision of the United States Supreme Court in Brown vs. Board of Education in 1954, this situation is beginning to change.

Legal segregation of pupils on the basis of race did not begin in the South, but in that cradle of democracy, the City of Boston, in 1849. When a Negro by the name of Benjamin Roberts sought redress in the Massachusetts Supreme Court from Boston city's refusal to admit his five-year-old daughter in the white primary school of the district in which he lived, the justices found for the city. Six years later, however, Massachusetts became the first American state to outlaw separate schools for Negroes. After the Civil War, the 'reconstructed' southern states systematically reduced the Negroes' rights until, at the end of the nineteenth century, the best the black man could hope for educationally was schooling separate from his white brother. In 1896 the U.S. Supreme Court held in the case of Plessy vs. Ferguson that segregation of the races was not in violation of the U.S. Constitution provided the facilities, though separate, were equal. This theorem became known as the "separate but equal" doctrine. But in May, 1954, the nation's highest tribunal reversed itself and stamped segregation in public schools as unconstitutional. The Court spoke firmly with one voice — its decision, unanimous, no justice dissenting.

The 1954 decision of the Court rested on cases coming to it from the States of Kansas, South Carolina, Virginia, and Delaware. In each of the cases Negro children had been denied admission to schools attended by white children under laws requiring or permitting segregation according to race. The plaintiffs had contended that segregated public schools are not equal and cannot be made equal. The Court addressed itself to the question presented: Does segregation of children in public schools solely on the basis of race, even though the physical facilities and other tangible factors may be equal, deprive the children of the minority group of equal educational opportunities? "We believe it does," the Court answered. "We conclude that in the field of public education the doctrine of 'separate but equal' has no place. Separate facilities are inherently unequal."[8] The decision of the Court in this controversy is not based upon the federal government's authority to control the schools—for it has no such power—but upon its obligation to defend the individual citizen's rights by insuring everyone equal treatment under the law.

After the 1954 desegregation decision several attempts were made to bar federal aid from segregated school systems. Attempts to withhold aid from segregated schools were not successful until the enactment of the Civil Rights Act of 1964 by Congress, which provided several powerful, new incentives for increasing the pace of school desegregation. In addition to the ban on aid, the Act authorized the Attorney General of the United States to file suit for the desegregation of public schools, and authorized the U.S. Office of Education to give assistance to local public school systems in the process of desegregating.

Until the passage of the Civil Rights Act in 1964, federal authorities had no administrative powers to enforce desegregation. Since then, under the guidelines to implement the 1964 Act, Southern school systems have had to prove that they were taking steps to end dual systems if they wanted to receive federal aid.

The Southern Regional Council, a private biracial research agency financed by foundation grants, maintains that the federal government's weapon to force desegregation—termination of federal funds—has not worked. In a report issued in 1968 entitled *Lawlessness and Disorder,* the Council explains that most often the sufferers have been the Negro schools. Many Southern school authorities equate Negro and federal, and so they use federal funds to bring black schools up to the level afforded white schools by local finances. The Council says the nation has not seemed to be aware of the failure of desegregation, and there seems to be almost no hope that Southern schools will ever really desegregate. In another report, however, the Virginia State Advisory Committee to the U.S. Commission on Civil Rights concludes that all school desegregation in Virginia can be credited to the pressure applied by the enforcement office of the U.S. Department of Health, Education, and Welfare set up under the Civil Rights Act of 1964.

Officials of the Department of Health, Education, and Welfare have also reminded Northern school districts that discrimination is objectionable and illegal even if practiced within a school system that technically serves black and white students alike. New guidelines for the North require that there be no gerrymandering of students to keep some schools all-white and others all-black. School systems have to show they are not practicing racial discrimination in either the assignment of teachers or students.

In the summer of 1968 the U.S. Justice Department prosecuted the first school desegregation case in the North. A federal judge ordered a suburban Chicago school district to eliminate discrimination both in student bodies and the faculties of its six schools. In rendering his decision, District Judge Julius J. Hoffman said, "a school board may not consistently with the 14th Amendment [of the U.S. Constitution] purposefully tailor the components of a neighborhood school attendance policy so as to conform to the racial compositions of the neighborhoods in its school district; nor may it build upon private residential discrimination."[9]

In the spring of 1969, the federal government announced it was taking steps to withhold funds from the first Northern school district for alleged racial discrimination in public schools. The Ferndale, Michigan school district was told it was violating the 1964 Civil Rights Act. Leon E. Panetta, director of the civil rights agency in the U.S. Office of Education, said the action is identical to that taken against Southern school districts which have failed to correct discriminatory school programs.

White House Conference on Education, 1955

Continued public and professional controversy over the curriculum of the secondary school helped to bring about the calling of a White House Conference in 1955. In 1954 the Congress had enacted legislation authorizing the President of the United States to hold a conference on education. The purpose of the act was to encourage a nation-wide study of education and problems related to the development of the best programs of education possible. President Eisenhower appointed a committee of thirty-six prominent citizens, including some educators, to plan the national meeting. State conferences were held throughout most of 1955 which culminated in the White House meeting held from November 28 through December 1, 1955. Among the concepts emphasized in the White House Conference were: (1) responsibilities belonging exclusively to the schools, and (2) shared responsibilities with other agencies in society. The presidential committee then submitted a final report to the President, which included its own findings and recommendations. Under the title "What Should Our Schools Accomplish," authors of the final report, Adam Bennion and William G. Carr summarized the conclusions of the 2,000 persons attending the conference. They reported that it was the consensus that the schools should continue to develop the youth of the nation in the following areas:

1. A general education with increased emphasis on the physical and social sciences.
2. Programs designed to develop patriotism and good citizenship.
3. Programs designed to foster moral, ethical, and spiritual values.
4. Vocational education tailored to the abilities of each pupil and to the needs of the community and nation.
5. Courses designed to teach domestic skills.
6. Training in leisure-time activities.
7. A variety of health services for all children.
8. Special education for handicapped children.
9. Physical education.
10. Instruction to meet the needs of the abler students.
11. Education about other nations and international relations.
12. Programs designed to foster mental health.
13. Programs designed to foster wholesome family life.
14. Organized recreational and social activities.
15. Courses designed to promote safety, including instruction in driving automobiles, swimming, and civil defense.[10]

The National Defense Education Act, 1958

The largest federal commitment to the national general education program before 1965 is embodied in the National Defense Education Act of 1958. Designed to improve the teaching of science, mathematics, and foreign languages at all school levels, this originally one billion dollar federal effort was passed in reaction to Soviet achievements in space technology, symbolized by the 1957 orbiting of the first earth satellite—the Russian "sputnik." The 1955 White House Conference and the National Science Foundation reports helped to assist the Congress to accept the federal government's responsibility for education in the United States. Although the program was first presented as temporary and scheduled to expire in 1962, the Kennedy Administration in 1961 sought major amendments as well as a two-year extension of the Act.

Title III of NDEA provides matching grants to the states for public schools and ten-year loans to private schools for the purchase of equipment for use in teaching science, mathematics, and foreign languages. Title V authorizes grants to the state educational agencies to assist them in establishing and maintaining programs of testing and of guidance and counseling in secondary schools. In 1964 Congress again extended NDEA, this time to 1968, and included funds to aid as well the social sciences and the humanities.

The Public Prayer Decision of 1962

Decisions of the United States Supreme Court have had in recent years a profound effect on public education in this nation. The segregation of students in public schools on the basis of race and color was banned in 1954. Similarly, the Court has declared that certain laws, regulations, and practices relative to religious instruction in the schools abridge freedom of religion. The latest and most controversial of these decisions was rendered by the Court in 1962 and raised the question of the use of prayer in public schools.

The Board of Regents in the state of New York had composed a prayer which they recommended and published as a part of their statement on moral and spiritual training in the schools. After the practice of reciting the regents' prayer was adopted by certain school districts, the parents of ten pupils sought redress in the New York courts insisting that use of this official prayer in the public schools was contrary to their religious beliefs. Mr. Justice Black, speaking for the majority of the U.S. Supreme Court, agreed with the complainants. "We think," he said, "that by using its public school system to encourage recitation of the regents' prayer, the State of New York has adopted a practice wholly inconsistent with the establishment clause [of the First Amendment to the Constitution]." He went on to say:

> It is neither sacrilegious nor antireligious to say that each separate government in this country should stay out of the business of writing or sanctioning official prayers and leave that purely religious function to the people themselves and to those the people choose to look to for religious guidance.[11]

White House Conference on Education, 1965

A second White House Conference on Education was held on July 20-21, 1965. Its chairman was John W. Gardner, Secretary of Health, Education and Welfare, who formerly had been president of the Carnegie Corporation. The conference was attended by 650 delegates from throughout the nation. Among the major themes of the meeting were the need for better quality teaching in American schools, a change in traditional methods of instruction, and a closer link between educational programs and social problems.

President Johnson informed the delegates the purpose of the conference was "to stimulate some fresh thinking, not just talk about old ideas." He said the chief problem in American education was, "not merely more classrooms and more teachers, ...," but, "a fundamental improvement in the quality of American education.[12]

There was agreement among the delegates that education in the United States had failed to develop new methods and approaches to meet emerging social problems. The schools, both in the North and South, were said to have faltered in the task of providing leadership in racial integration. They felt schools lacked both money and techniques for educating under-privileged and culturally deprived children. They also felt that the schools needed to find new ways to train both gifted and handicapped pupils. While the purpose of the White House Conference was not to adopt policy resolutions, the net effect of the meeting was to assist implementation of the 1965 Elementary-Secondary Education Act signed by the President on April 11, 1965.

The 1965 Elementary-Secondary Education Act

In 1965 the Congress of the United States enacted legislation providing for comprehensive federal aid for elementary and secondary schools. Although federal aid to education had been a major issue in the post-World War II period, the specific provisions of the Johnson Administration's aid plan were new. They were drawn up in an effort to avoid the church-state controversy over aid to parochial schools which had prevented the enactment of similar legislation during the Eisenhower and Kennedy administrations. The "Great Society" approach of President Johnson was to provide aid to school children, not schools.

The specific provisions of the 1965 Act included: (1) a program of financial assistance to school districts having concentrations of children from low income families; (2) a program of grants for the acquisition of school library resources, textbooks, and other printed instructional materials for the use of pupils and teachers in public and private elementary and secondary schools; (3) a program of grants to the states for supplementary educational centers and services to provide vitally needed educational services not otherwise available, such as remedial instruction, vocational guidance, specialized instruction, and equipment for students studying advanced scientific subjects, foreign languages, and other courses; (4) a program of grants to universities, colleges, and other public or no-profit private agencies, institutions and organizations, and to individuals for research, surveys, and demonstrations in the field of education; and (5) a program of grants to stimulate and assist states to strengthen their state educational agencies.

On March 28, 1967, Commissioner of Education Harold Howe II submitted to Congress the first nation-wide report evaluating operations of the 1965 Act. Howe said programs were "soundly conceived and of tremendous benefit to the schools." The report states the one billion dollars spent in the fiscal year 1966 financed 22,173 projects, affected 8.3 million schoolchildren in 17,481 school districts, and created 200,000 new teaching jobs.[13]

Conclusion

The twentieth century began with the introduction of two new schools into the educational system, the junior high school and the junior college. The chief purpose of both institutions was to bring about better articulation between the various levels of the school system, to wit: elementary, secondary, and higher education.

The organization of the Commission on Secondary Education in 1913 represented a culminating effort to define the function and purpose of the high school in American democratic society. The report on the Seven Cardinal Principles issued by the Commission in 1918 have guided the planning of the structure of the program of secondary education in the United States into the final third of this century.

The initiation of vocational education in secondary school by the Smith-Hughes Act of 1917 was another important milestone in the development of American secondary education. The Eight Year Study begun in 1933 resulted in liberalization of college entrance requirements and was another step in freeing the high school from domination and dictation by college and university academicians.

From the time of its formation in 1935 until its demise in 1968, the Educational Policies Commission has produced a series of challenging reports which have helped to set the educational goals of the American people. The life-adjustment movement in American education grew out of the feeling of many educators during the depression years of the 1930's that the academically-oriented program of the high school was failing to meet the needs of large numbers of secondary school youth. The 1950's witnessed a reaction against the life-adjustment movement; and largely as a result of the technological achievements of the Soviet Union, conservative critics of the American high school have called for a return to what they consider the ancient and time-honored function of the school—that of rigorous, systematic, disciplined, intellectual training.

The historic decision of the U.S. Supreme Court in <u>Brown vs. Board of Education</u> in 1954 initiated the latest phase in the long struggle for equality of educational opportunity in this country. The public prayer decision of 1962 is the most recent effort of the high tribunal to maintain the impregnable wall between church and state with respect to educational matters. These important decisions of the Court are based, not upon the federal government's authority to control the schools—for it has no such power—but upon its obligation to defend the individual citizen's rights by insuring everyone equal treatment under the law.

The passage of the National Defense Education Act of 1958 and of the Elementary and Secondary Education Act of 1965 put the federal government irrevocably into the picture of financing the public schools of this country. With the passage of these measures the federal government has undertaken to live up fully to its historic commitment to public education as first exemplified in the Northwest Ordinance of 1787.

What changes the remaining decades of the twentieth century will bring to American secondary education cannot be known for sure. What is known, however, is that there will be change.

Chapter IX
Footnotes

[1] R. P. Brimm, *The Junior High School* (Washington, D.C.: The Center for Applied Research in Education, Inc., 1963), p. 9.

[2] See James B. Conant, *Education in the Junior High School Years* (Princeton, New Jersey: Educational Testing Service, 1960).

[3] Commission on the Reorganization of Secondary Education, National Education Association, *Cardinal Principles of Secondary Education* (Washington, D.C., Government Printing Office Bulletin, No. 35, 1918), pp. 7-8.

[4] Educational Policies Commission, *Education for All American Youth* (Washington, D.C.: National Education Association, 1944), pp. 225-226.

[5] Educational Policies Commission, *The Central Purpose of American Education* (Washington, D.C.: National Education Association, 1961), p. 12.

[6] Harl R. Douglass, *Education for Life Adjustment: Its Meaning and Implementation* (New York: The Ronald Press, 1950), p. 8.

[7] Excerpts from Freedoms Foundations George Washington Gold Medal Award Speech, "The Passing of a Patriot," by Max Rafferty.

[8] *Brown v. Board of Education of Topeka*, 347 U.S. 483. See also Henry Steele Commager, *Documents of American History,* Seventh Edition (New York: Appleton-Century-Crofts, 1963), II, 619-622; Tyrus Hillway, *American Education: An Introduction Through Readings* (Boston: Houghton Mifflin Company, 1964), pp. 116-119.

[9] *Los Angeles Times,* July 9, 1968.

[10] The Committee for the White House Conference on Education, *A Report to the President* (Washington, D.C.: Government Printing Office, 1956), pp. 8-9.

[11] *Steven I. Engel, et. al. vs. William J. Vitale, Jr., et. al.,* 370 U.S.; 421-460. See also Tyrus Hillway, *American Education: An Introduction Through Readings* (Boston: Houghton Mifflin Company, 1964), pp. 323-331.

[12] *Federal Role in Education* (Washington, D.C.: Congressional Quarterly Service, 1967), p. 9.

[13] *Ibid.,* p. 45.

Selected References

Alexander, William M., and J. Galen Saylor. *Modern Secondary Education.* New York: Holt, Rinehart and Winston, 1965.

Boque, Jesse P. *The Community College.* New York: McGraw-Hill Book Company, Inc., 1950.

Brimm, R. P. *The Junior High School.* Washington, D.C.: The Center for Applied Research in Education, Inc., 1963.

Conant, James B. *Education in the Junior High School Years.* Princeton, New Jersey: Educational Testing Service, 1960.

Douglass, Harl R. *Education for Life Adjustment: Its Meaning and Implementation.* New York: The Ronald Press, 1950.

French, William M. *American Secondary Education.* New York: The Odyssey Press, Inc., 1967.

Henry, Nelson B. (ed.). *The Public Junior College.* Chicago: The University of Chicago Press, 1956.

Reynolds, James W. *The Junior College.* New York: The Center for Applied Research in Education, Inc., 1965.

Chapter X

THE STRUCTURE OF SECONDARY EDUCATION IN THE UNITED STATES

The Graded System

The first graded school was Quincy Grammar School in Massachusetts, established in 1848, and predates scientific findings on child growth and development. Until the early part of the nineteenth century schools were small, and although there were levels of schooling, these schools were not organized by grades. A teacher was simply handed a group of pupils, and he assigned them lessons at their respective levels of achievement. The graded system was patterned after the German Volkschulen developed in Prussia by Fichte and others at the turn of the nineteenth century. The graded system allowed the teacher to work with a group of pupils of similar levels of attainment and to specialize in the work of that grade level.

Under the graded system the elementary school was divided into a primary, intermediate, and grammar division, each with a separate teacher. The divisions were poorly defined, and there were no standards for completion. The usual practice was to set the length of elementary schooling at eight years. Again American practice tended to follow German tradition. In Prussia and other German states schooling was compulsory for eight years, terminating with the attainment of puberty and with the rite of confirmation by the church.

The period of training at the American academy was indefinite in the beginning. Students attended until such time as they had accomplished their purposes. These purposes were for college preparation, teacher education, general culture, or vocational training. The curriculum was usually organized into a three-year period, but later this was changed to four years. The term of the first high school, the Boston Classical School (1821), was three years, but it was later changed to four. By the latter part of the nineteenth century the majority of elementary schools were organized into eight grades, and the high schools into four. The predominant system had come to be the 8-4, or eight years of elementary schooling followed by four years of secondary, or high school training.

Development of the Junior High School

The 8-4 plan had scarcely become well accepted throughout the nation before widespread criticism of it was voiced. Compulsory school laws required attendance at elementary schools, and such attendance was also a prerequisite for admission to the secondary school.

Dr. Charles W. Eliot, president of Harvard University for forty years, is usually credited first among the educational leaders who influenced reorganization of the school system. As early as 1873 he had pointed out in an annual report that provision might be made for students to enter college earlier and graduate younger. This he thought could be accomplished if all waste were eliminated from the elementary and secondary school curricula. He pointed out the average age of entering freshmen at Harvard was eighteen. He continued to agitate the matter and received considerable support from other college presidents. In 1888 he presented his thesis to the Department of Superintendents of the National Education Association.

Eliot presented cogent arguments for reorganization in an address to the NEA convention in 1892. He pointed out: (1) that two-fifths of all Harvard freshmen were over nineteen years of age at entrance; (2) that private and public educational programs should be shortened; and (3) that in French secondary schools the pupils were better prepared than in American schools at the same ages. The cause of this waste, Eliot said, was the duplication of studies and inferior instruction in the upper grades of the elementary school. To correct this situation he advocated that the secondary school be extended downwards to include grades seven and eight.

In 1892, the Committee of Ten with President Eliot as chairman recommended, among other things, that: (1) all secondary subjects, with the exception of Greek, be introduced into the last two years of the elementary school; (2) secondary education should begin two years earlier, leaving six rather than eight years in the elementary school; and (3) that high school methods of teaching should be introduced earlier. A parallel group organized by the NEA in 1893 concerned with elementary education, the Committee of Fifteen, recommended in 1895 that the elementary school retain its eight-year program and introduce some advanced courses; that the period of transition of the elementary to high school be eased by introducing a system of special teachers in grades seven and eight. President Nicholas Murray Butler of Columbia University in 1898 urged that six years were enough for the elementary school. When President William Rainey Harper of the University of Chicago initiated conferences in 1901-02 to study the problem of reorganization of the educational system, John Dewey voiced his opinion at one of these meetings that six years was sufficient for the elementary schools to accomplish their aims.

In reports submitted in 1907, 1908, and 1909, the Committee on Six Year Courses urged that the elementary school be shortened to six years and that the secondary school be extended to include grades seven and eight. The Committee on Economy of Time in Education that issued reports in 1909, 1911, and 1913 added to the growing demand for reorganization, and specifically recommended the organization of junior and senior high schools respectively.

The early proponents of reorganization were mostly advocates of a 6-6 plan of organization. They advanced these arguments to support the 6-6 system: (1) that economy of time could be effected by shortening the elementary school period; (2) that a six-year secondary school period would provide for a gradual transition from the elementary to the secondary school by providing two years of intermediate schooling for an orientation period; and (3) that pupils of grades seven to nine constitute a homogeneous group with respect to puberty.

During the first decade of the twentieth century the emphasis on reorganization shifted from proposals for a 6-6 system to one for a separate intermediate organization or junior high school idea. Several school systems prior to 1909 had introduced some features of the junior high school. But the first example of a school system organized on the 6-3-3 basis was Berkeley, California, in 1909. Columbus, Ohio, organized a junior high school in 1910, and Los Angeles did the same in 1911. These city school systems organized grades seven, eight, and nine into a separate school, and the programs of these systems became models for the development of this new secondary school. Once launched, the junior high school movement developed rapidly. By 1918 the U.S. Bureau of Education reported 557 junior high schools in cities of 25,000 population or over. The movement became even more widespread during the 1920-1930 decade.[1]

The orthodox educational functions of the junior high school may be summarized as follows: (1) to group together youngsters who are approaching adolescence or are in early adolescence; (2) to explore the interests and develop the aptitudes and capacities of young people in this age group; (3) to appraise the development of the pupil in order to ascertain if he is attaining desirable levels of growth in all aspects of personality and character; (4) to provide a program of guidance and counseling that will assist each pupil to make wise choices for his future educational, vocational, and social activities; (5) to provide a period of transition from the simpler learning activities of the elementary school to the more rigorous and exacting program of studies of the high school; and (6) to serve as a bridge between the self-contained classroom of the elementary and the departmentalized organization of the high school.

In recent years many junior high schools have been built that have consisted only of grades seven and eight. The purposes and functions of these two-year schools are the same as those of the regular three-year junior high school. It is claimed by some authorities that the two-year unit is even more advantageous because it provides for an even more homogeneous grouping; that it is a smaller school and so is able to develop closer pupil-teacher relationships; and that it permits pupils to have four years of senior high school.

Whether a school system develops a 6-3-3 plan, or 6-2-4 plan, or a 4-4-4 plan is often dictated by the realities of existing buildings, their potential for physical change, increasing enrollment, and shifts in neighborhood enrollments.

The Six Year High School

The six-year high school may be either a unified school of grades seven through twelve or a joint junior-senior high school. The six-year high school is found most frequently in smaller school systems and also in some larger city systems that serve fringe population areas.

In high school organization, it is important to have an enrollment large enough to graduate a minimum of 100 students to maintain efficiency, curricular variety, and economy. In smaller schools curriculum is limited, and some teachers are teaching subjects in which they are not academically prepared. Whether a Board of Education organizes the 3-3 plan or the 6 plan hinges on enrollment, existing buildings, etc. If, for example, a school district has only 600 students, the 6 plan is preferable; if the enrollment is 1400, the 3-3 plan is feasible.

The Eight-Year Secondary School Program

The junior college, or community college, is usually established and controlled by a local school district, although in many instances the junior college district is a separate entity and may include several high school districts within its boundaries. In a few instances it may be a part of the state system of higher education.

The concept that the thirteenth and fourteenth grades constitute a part of secondary education is widespread. The junior college has as one of its functions that of providing a more gradual transition from secondary to higher education.

In this respect it is comparable to the junior high school. The European secondary school, whether the British grammar school, the French lycée, or the German Gymnasium, is an institution whose curricular program of general education varies from six to nine years, the graduates then begin sepcialized training immediately upon entering the university. The student in a junior college in America would still be a secondary school student in Europe. The European secondary school has for years been giving students the equivalent of two years of American college training. In all probability the junior college will continue to remain organized as a separate institution apart from the secondary school, thus constituting a part of a 6-3-3-2, or an 8-4-2, or even a 6-6-2 school system.

Associations of Colleges and Secondary Schools

Background. In the latter half of the nineteenth century the system of admitting students to institutions of higher education on the basis of personal interviews and written examinations became too cumbersome. In 1871 the University of Michigan started the practice of admitting students without examinations from all high schools approved by the authorities of the university. The system soon spread to other schools, and within fifteen years the movement to organize associations of colleges and secondary schools was begun.

These associations formulate standards for accrediting high schools, and those which meet the standards are admitted to membership. While these associations do not have legal powers to accredit schools, membership in an association carries much prestige, and pupils graduating or transferring from member schools are accorded recognition by colleges within the association and by colleges in the other associations. A major purpose of the associations is to encourage better relationships between schools of the same regional association and between other associations.

The Associations. NEW ENGLAND ASSOCIATION OF COLLEGES AND SECONDARY SCHOOLS. The oldest of the regional associations is the New England Association of Colleges and Secondary Schools, founded in 1885. The Association has two different committees and three different sets of regulations. One committee heads the public secondary schools with one set of regulations; the other committee has two sets of regulations for institutions of higher learning. Public secondary schools must meet definite standards with respect to school philosophy and objectives, graduation requirements, guidance services, curriculum, faculty and administration, and physical plant facilities.[2]

MIDDLE STATES ASSOCIATION OF COLLEGES AND SECONDARY SCHOOLS. Founded in 1892 the Middle States Association embraces the states of New York, New Jersey, Delaware, and Pennsylvania. The basic program of the Association is to raise the educational standards of schools and colleges within its area. The Association is divided into two commissions: the Commission on Institutions of Higher Learning and the Commission on Secondary schools. Both are concerned with the transition from high school to college.[3]

NORTH CENTRAL ASSOCIATION OF COLLEGES AND SECONDARY SCHOOLS. The largest of the associations is the North Central Association, organized in 1895. It now comprises twenty states reaching from West Virginia to Arizona. The Association has as its goal the maintenance of excellence in all its member educational institutions and helps motivate their continuing improvement. These objectives are achieved in some degree through the process of accreditation.[4]

THE SOUTHERN ASSOCIATION OF COLLEGES AND SECONDARY SCHOOLS. Formed from the states of the old confederacy of Civil War days in 1895, the Association has a two-fold purpose: to identify and recognize good schools, and to encourage their continuous improvement. The Southern Association functions through four standing committees and has established well-defined procedures that must be followed by schools seeking accreditation.[5] Through the years, however, the Southern Association has maintained two sets of criteria: one for the white schools: the other for the Negroes.

THE NORTHWEST ASSOCIATION OF SECONDARY AND HIGHER SCHOOLS. Organized in 1918, the Association now includes the state of Alaska. The Northwest Association sets up minimum requirements that must be met for accreditation. However, schools are expected to exceed these basic requirements whenever possible.[6]

WESTERN ASSOCIATION OF SCHOOLS AND COLLEGES. The Western Association became an accrediting agency in 1948. The territory of the Association consists of the states of California and Hawaii, the Territory of Guam, and such other areas of the Pacific as may apply to it for service. The Association has taken a new approach to the accreditation of secondary schools by designing a plan for the improvement of instruction tailored specifically to each individual school. The accreditation certificate issued to the school signifies that the school is not only meeting minimal standards but is actively engaged in a continuous process of upgrading all aspects of its educational program.[7]

Cooperative Study of Secondary School Standards. In 1932 the officers of the respective regional associations recommended a cooperative study of standards for secondary schools be made. A national committee was organized which formulated a series of proposals and procedures whereby answers might be found to the following questions: (1) What are the characteristics of a good secondary school? (2) What means and methods may be employed to evaluate the effectiveness of a school in terms of its objectives? (3) By what means and processes does a good school develop into a better school? and (4) How can regional associations stimulate secondary schools to continuous growth?[8]

The formulated criteria were tried out in 200 school systems and then adopted by the regional associations as the basis for school evaluation. The Evaluative Criteria as revised in 1960 have proven of great assistance to the regional associations in perfecting their evaluation techniques.

A school to be accredited by an association is first asked to make a careful study of its own with special reference to: (1) its philosophy, (2) its pupil population, (3) the community it serves, (4) its educational program, (5) its instructional and administrative staffs, and (6) its physical plant. When the local school has completed its study, it then invites a committee of professionals from other schools and colleges to investigate and compare their judgments with those of the local school people. The results are then tabulated, and a report is made to show whether the school is to be judged superior, good, average, poor, or inferior in any way.

Carnegie Unit Rule. Accreditation remains largely based on such quantitative standards as the Carnegie unit rule. As previously noted, the Committee on College Entrance Requirements in 1899 proposed units of work as a basis for admission to college. In 1906, the Carnegie Foundation for the Advancement of Teaching defined a college as an institution that required fourteen units of high school work as a basis for admission. The Foundation formalized the unit rule for purposes of making grants to institutions that were true colleges. A unit was thus defined as the study of a subject in high school for one period a day for a school year consisting of from thirty-six to forty weeks. College admission practices and standards imposed by accrediting agencies have firmly implanted the Carnegie unit in American secondary education, and it has become almost the sole method of recording pupil progress through school and of determining graduation. Most high schools require now from 16 to 18 units for graduation. Many students graduate with 20-22.

The Conant Reports on the High School

Two former presidents of Harvard University have strongly affected the development of the American high school. The first was Dr. Charles W. Eliot, whose criticisms of American education resulted in the formation of the Committee of Ten under his chairmanship, the first of the influential committees on the reorganization of secondary education. The second is James Bryant Conant. A member of the Educational Policies Commission while still president at Harvard, Conant's major contributions were made after his regime there, and after his services to the U.S. government as United States High Commissioner to the West German government and Ambassador to the Federal Republic of Germany. Known as the Conant reports, his publications on American secondary education have been given widespread circulation and have become the most widely discussed books in education in recent history. They are: *The*

American High School Today (1959); *Education in the Junior High School Years* (1960); *Slums and Suburbs, A Commentary on Schools in Metropolitan Areas* (1961); *The Education of American Teachers* (1963); and the most recently published *The American High School Revisited* (1966).

The Conant book, *The American High School Today* contains his basic recommendations. It is divided into four sections: (1) the characteristics of American education; (2) the comprehensive high school as a uniquely American institution; (3) recommendations for improving public secondary education; and (4) a treatment of high schools with only a limited degree of comprehensiveness.

The book is an overall proposal for reform of the high school. In the first section of the work Conant discusses the American tradition of local control, the uniqueness of American schools, and education as a means of achieving equality of opportunity:

> *I think it safe to say that the comprehensive high school is characteristic of our society and further that it has come into being because of our economic history and our devotion to the ideals of equality of opportunity and equality of status.*[9]

In Europe he finds on the other hand a system of secondary education available to only fifteen to twenty per cent of an age group: "It is true that something like a third of our young people are 'going to college,' and only about a fifteenth or twentieth of the boys and girls in a European country are university students."[10] He says, however, no one can estimate how much potential talent in Europe remains undeveloped because of early selection of pre-university students.

In the second section Conant concentrates his attention on the comprehensive high school and makes only incidental reference to vocational, commercial, and technical high schools. What Conant and his co-workers did was to visit 103 comprehensive high schools in twenty-six states and discuss problems with administrators, teachers, and students related to the three main objectives of a comprehensive high school Conant defines such a school in the following manner: (1) to provide a general education for all the future citizens; (2) to provide good elective programs for those who wish to use their acquired skills immediately upon graduation; and (3) to provide satisfactory programs for those whose vocations will depend on their subsequent education in a college or university.[11]

The most significant part of Conant's report on the high school is the third section which lists his recommendations for improving secondary education. These recommendations are limited to sound

practices which he had observed in some of the schools he visited. In summary, the recommendations are:
1. Counseling should start in the elementary school, and there should be good articulation between the counseling in the junior and senior high schools.
2. Every student should have an individualized program; there should be no classification of students according to tracks such as 'college-preparatory,' 'vocational,' and 'commercial.'
3. All students should be required to take four years of English, three to four years of social studies, one year of mathematics, and one year of science.
4. In required subjects, excepting a course in American problems, students should be grouped according to ability, subject by subject.
5. A diploma should certify only that the student has completed the required work in general education and has completed a sequence of elective courses.
6. English composition should occupy about half of the total time devoted to the study of English.
7. Schools should offer diversified programs for the development of marketable skills in such areas as typing, stenography, home economics, and distributive education.
8. There should be special consideration given to slow readers, and these students should be instructed in English, social studies, and remedial reading by special teachers who are sympathetic to their problems.
9. There should be an enriched program of studies for the academically talented.
10. A special guidance officer should be assigned to the highly gifted to see they are challenged not only by course work but by the development of their special interests as well.
11. The school should publish an academic inventory each year summarizing the programs of the academically talented students and what their achievements were in higher education.
12. The school day should include at least six periods in addition to physical education and driver training.
13. At least the grade of a 'C' should be required for entrance into advanced academic courses.
14. Students should not be given a rank in class according to their grades in all subjects.
15. There should be an academic honors list and a special recognition to provide an incentive for those who elect a nonacademic sequence of courses.

16. There should be a developmental reading program.
17. There should be a tuition-free summer school both for bright students and those who have to repeat a subject.
18. The third and fourth year of a foreign language should be offered.
19. All students should obtain some understanding of the nature of science and the scientific method.
20. Homerooms should be organized in such a way as to make them significant social units in the school.
21. American problems or American government should be required in the twelfth grade.[12]

Conclusion

It has been the purpose of this chapter to describe various aspects of the organization and structure of secondary schools in the United States. As defined in American terms, secondary education consists of the schooling of all adolescents conducted primarily within the comprehensive high school framework that has evolved from out of the nation's history and its ideals. Other societies have found other schemes for satisfying the educational needs of its adolescents and of society's need for educating adolescents. Perhaps today the time has arrived for all peoples to begin to work for the development of a world-wide social order and an educational framework satisfactory for that type of world community. Certainly patterns of education have been influenced by the degree of interaction of beliefs and institutions of other cultures. Today the velocity of this interaction increases as the world grows progressively smaller in the modern technological sense and differing cultures become less isolated from each other. As this trend continues, educational needs become less individual in the cultural sense and more common to all men everywhere.

Chapter X
Footnotes

[1] Rudyard K. Bent, and Henry H. Kronenberg, *Principles of Secondary Education* (New York: McGraw-Hill Book Company, Inc., 1955), p. 114.

[2] Stanley W. Williams, *Educational Administration in Secondary Schools* (New York: Holt, Rinehart and Winston, 1964), pp. 484-485.

[3] *Ibid.*, p. 484.

[4] *Ibid.*, p. 485.

[5] *Ibid.*, p. 486.

[6] *Ibid.*, p. 485.

[7] *Ibid.*, p. 486.

[8] Cooperative Study of Secondary School Standards, *How to Evaluate a Secondary School* (Washington, D.C.: The Cooperative Study, 1938), p. 11.

[9] James B. Conant, *The American High School Today* (New York: McGraw-Hill Book Company, Inc., 1959), p. 8.

[10] *Ibid.*, p. 3.

[11] *Ibid.*, p. 17.

[12] *Ibid.*, pp. 44-76.

Selected References

Alexander, William, and J. Galen Saylor. *Modern Secondary Education.* New York: Holt, Rinehart and Winston, 1965.

Bent, Rudyard K., and Henry H. Kronenberg. *Principles of Secondary Education.* New York: McGraw-Hill Book Company, Inc., 1955.

Conant, James B. *The American High School Today.* New York: McGraw-Hill Book Company, Inc., 1959.

De Young, Chris A. *Introduction to American Public Education.* New York: McGraw-Hill Book Company, Inc., 1968.

French, William Marshall. *American Secondary Education.* New York: The Odyssey Press, Inc., 1967.

Rollins, Sidney P., and Adolph Unruh. *Introduction to Secondary Education.* Chicago: Rand McNally and Company, n.d.

Tanner, Daniel. *Schools for Youth.* New York: The Macmillan Company, 1965.

Taylor, L. O., Don R. McMahill, and Bob L. Taylor. *The American Secondary School.* New York: Appleton-Century-Crofts, Inc., 1960.

Chapter XI

ADMINISTRATION OF SECONDARY EDUCATION: ROLE OF THE FEDERAL GOVERNMENT

Growth of Federal Aid to Education

The federal government is deeply involved in American education. From the nursery school to the university, it would be difficult to find a single pupil, teacher, or classroom in the nation not in some way affected by the national government's expanding interest and assistance.

The commitment of the federal government to education is historic. Early interest was documented in ordinances in the post-Revolutionary era. In 1785 the Congress of the Confederation adopted a system of rectangular surveys for its new western territories, by which the land was divided into townships, six miles square, to be further subdivided into thirty-six sections, one mile square. This ordinance included the significant words: "There shall be reserved the lot number sixteen of every township for the maintenance of public schools within the said township."[1]

The Congress adopted on July 13, 1787, the famous "Ordinance for the Government of the Territory of the United States Northwest of the River Ohio," which postulated that the following principle should be applied to states organized from the territory: "Religion, morality, and knowledge being necessary to good government and the happiness of mankind, schools and the means of education shall be forever encouraged."[2] Lot number sixteen of each township was assigned to the states to be created out of the territories for the maintenance of public schools as directed by the earlier Ordinance of 1785.

Despite the fact that education is not mentioned in the Federal Constitution ratified in 1789, indirect justification for a national program of education may be found in several of its provisions. The general welfare clauses, in the preamble and in the section on taxation (section 8, Art. I), are the closest approach to an authorization. Certainly the promotion of "general welfare" entails the federal obligation to advance public education.

With the admission of the state of Ohio to the Union in 1803, the federal government inaugurated its practice of giving land for general educational purposes. In the enabling act for the admission of Ohio, Congress gave the sixteenth section of land in each township to the inhabitants thereof for schools. With few exceptions and variations, this practice was continued with each new state admitted.

The passage of the first Morrill Act in 1862 by the Congress marked the next significant step in the history of federal aid to education. Under the terms of this act, each state was to receive 30,000 acres of land for each senator and representative in Congress. All proceeds from the sale of these lands were to be invested at five per cent, and the proceeds in each state to be used for "the endowment, maintenance, and support of at least one college where the leading object shall be, without excluding other scientific and classical studies and including military tactics, to teach such branches of learning as are related to agriculture and the mechanic arts."[3] In the second Morrill Act passed in 1890, the Congress authorized annual federal grants to the states for the operation of the 'land-grant' colleges. The purpose of the Morrill Acts was to provide both liberal and practical education for the working classes.

Changes in the Morrill Acts made by the 1907 Nelson Amendment, the 1935 Bankhead-Jones Act, and other legislation raised the annual grants to the colleges to over $5,000,000 a year. Legislation passed in 1960 increased the annual authorization to $14.5 million dollars, starting in the fiscal year 1962. The funds could be used by the colleges for any educational expense, but not for construction facilities. At the end of 1964 there were sixty-seven land-grant colleges in the fifty states and Puerto Rico.

The dire effects of the Civil War (1861-1865) and the reunion of the states gave rise to a new interest in national education. The Freeman's Bureau established in 1865 aided schools in the South for Negro children, providing more than $5,000,000 in four years. In 1864 a proposal of the National Association of State and City School Superintendents (now the American Association of School Administrators) for a federal bureau of education was presented to the Congress, and the "Department of Education" bill was approved by President Andrew Johnson on March 2, 1867. The department was made an "Office of Education" in the Department of Interior in 1869. The title changed to "Bureau of Education" in 1870, but it was restored to "Office of Education" in 1929. The U.S. Office of Education in 1939 was assigned to the Federal Security Agency. The federal Department of Health, Education and Welfare, whose head is a cabinet member, was created in 1953, and the Office of Education is now an integral part of that Department.

The Hatch Act of 1887 established Agricultural Experiment Stations. The Congress was authorized to appropriate $15,000 annually to each state and territory having an agricultural college. The purpose of the law was to promote scientific investigation with respect to the principles and applications of agriculture science. Among the federal grants which, in part or whole, have gone to schools is the Forest Reserve Income Act of 1908, according to which twenty-five per cent of the money received from each forest reserve goes to schools or roads of the county containing the reserve.

The movement for federal aid to vocational education at the secondary school level did not develop until the twentieth century. President Wilson signed into law the Smith-Hughes Act on February 23, 1917. This bill authorizes federal grants to the states for vocational education below the college level. The program was to be administered by a Federal Board for Vocational Education. In 1933 such administration was transferred to the U.S. Commissioner of Education. Under the Smith-Hughes law certain permanent appropriations were made to finance the grants to the states. They required no further congressional action inasmuch as the money thereafter was to be automatically available from the Treasury. Several additional laws supplementing the 1917 Act were passed, and these were the George-Reed Act of 1929, the George-Ellzey Act of 1934, and the George-Dean Act of 1936. These acts all provided either temporary or permanent additional fund provisions for vocational education.

Various federal emergency agencies set up during the depression years of the 1930's engaged in educational activities as part of the relief program. The Public Works Administration (PWA) made loans and grants for school construction, and the Federal Emergency Relief Administration developed adult education and nursery school programs. Under the Fitzgerald Act of 1937 Congress authorized the Secretary of Labor to carry on a program of promoting apprenticeship schemes designed to train journeymen workers in skilled occupations. These activities were transferred to the Federal Security Agency in 1942, then to the War Manpower Commission, and subsequently, in 1945, returned to the Labor Department. In 1940 the U.S. Office of Education was allotted several million dollars for a program under which state boards of vocational education and local school officials offered vocational training facilities through the National Youth Administration (NYA).

The Lantham Act in 1940 authorized federal aid to local governments for construction, maintenance, and operation of facilities, including schools. Aid was given to communities with populations swollen by increased military personnel and defense workers. This piece of legislation was the forerunner of temporary legislation between 1946 and 1950 for "emergency" school aid and, beginning in 1950, with "impacted" areas aid.

The Servicemen's Readjustment Act (G.I. Bill of Rights) of 1944 was the greatest single venture of the federal government in education in the history of the republic up to the end of World War II. The G.I. Bill has enabled millions of young men and women to attend high schools, colleges, universities, specialized schools, and adult education facilities throughout the land, and even some have studied abroad. A program of educational benefits has also been provided for veterans of the Korean war and the Viet Nam fighting.

Major Programs of Federal Aid Since World War II

Federal aid to education has taken many forms in the post-World War II era, from funds for science equipment to milk for school lunches. Major programs of school aid are summarized below.

Impacted Areas School Aid. Aid to impacted areas programs were begun as the outgrowths of federal commitments in the Lantham Act of 1940 (see above) and subsequent year-by-year legislation from 1946 to 1950 to provide school aid in areas where federal activities brought in more families and non-taxable property. Two laws passed by the Congress in 1950 authorized federal grants to areas "impacted" by tax-free federal property and installations, Indian reservations, or government contractors. One act authorized federal payments for building maintenance and teachers' salaries. The other act authorized federal payments for school construction. From 1951 through 1965 Congress appropriated $4,799,352,788 under the provisions of these two acts. School districts receiving the aid accounted for more than thirty per cent of all public elementary and secondary school pupils or over 12.5 million school children.[4]

In 1965 President Johnson tied his general aid to education proposal to the impacted areas concept. The Elementary-Secondary Act of 1965, in effect, extended the impacted areas programs to include areas impacted by the presence of large numbers of children from low-income families. The bill also extended the old provisions for federally impacted areas beyond the 1966 expiration date earlier set.

National Science Foundation. The Congress, in 1950, established the National Science Foundation to promote scientific research and education of future scientists. The National Science Foundation Act authorized the Foundation to: (1) make grants and loans for research in the mathematical, physical, medical, biological sciences, engineering, and other fields; (2) undertake military research for national defense; (3) award scholarships and graduate fellowships; (4) aid the interchange of information among scientists in the United States and other countries; (5) correlate its program with private and other public research projects; and (6) maintain a roster of scientific and technical personnel, and act as a clearinghouse for scientific information. The Act was amended in 1942, 1953, 1958, and 1959, broadening NSF's functions, particularly in the field of education. The Foundation's budget for 1965 was $420 million.[5]

At the present time the Foundation carries out such educational programs as the following: (1) support of students of science, mathematics, and engineering at the graduate level; (2) support of programs for students at the undergraduate level and below, and support of training institutes for science teachers at all grade levels; (3) aid to teachers of science, mathematics, and engineering at all levels; (4) aid to improve and update the content of science courses; and (5) promotion of public understanding of science through support of lectures, etc. The sciences now supported include the social sciences.[6]

National Defense Education Act. This original one billion dollar federal commitment to education was made by the Congress in 1958. A program designed to improve the teaching of science, mathematics, and foreign languages at all school levels, the measure consists of ten titles summarized as follows:

TITLE I — Contains a declaration of purpose, prohibits federal control of education, and defines terms used in the bill.

TITLE II — Authorizes the U.S. Commissioner of Education to lend money to university and college student loan funds to enable needy students to continue their education.

TITLE III — Provides matching grants to the states for public schools and ten-year loans to private schools for the purchase of equipment for use in teaching science, mathematics, and foreign languages.

TITLE IV — Authorizes a program of graduate fellowships to those interested in college teaching.

TITLE V — Provides grants to state educational agencies to assist them in establishing and maintaining programs of testing and of guidance and counseling in secondary schools.

TITLE VI — Authorizes grants to colleges for establishing advanced institutes for the teaching of modern foreign languages, science, mathematics, and guidance to train public school teachers.

TITLE VII — Provides for federal grants to public or non-profit groups and individuals to conduct research into modern teaching aids.

TITLE VIII— Authorizes grants to the states to assist them in training persons for employment as highly skilled technicians in occupations requiring scientific knowledge.

TITLE IX — Authorizes the National Science Foundation to establish a Science Information Service to disseminate scientific information and develop new programs for making the information available.

TITLE X — Contains miscellaneous provisions relating to other provisions of the Act, including administration, advisory committees, etc. This section also included the subsequently controversial requirement that loan recipients swear an oath of loyalty to the United States and sign an affidavit disclaiming belief in, or membership in, or support of, any organization that believes in or teaches the overthrow of the Government. The loyalty oath requirement was removed by amendments to the Act in 1962.[7]

In 1964 the Congress extended NDEA to 1968 and included the social sciences and English as subjects covered under the terms of the Act.

In its first decade N.D.E.A. has provided a federal investment of nearly 3 billion dollars to buttress American education from kindergarten through graduate school. More than 500 million dollars has been paid to the states for strengthening instruction in "critical" subjects taught in the public schools. Language laboratories in high schools have increased from forty-six in 1958 to at least 10,000. More than 479,000 local public school projects have been approved for buying or remodeling equipment. Grants to the states have helped increase the number of counselors from 12,000 in high schools to 44,000 full-time equivalent counselors in public schools from kindergarten through junior college. More than 100,000 teachers have attended almost 2,500 institutes for advanced study to improve their qualifications.

Education in Other Federal Programs. In 1963 the Congress enacted an extensive vocational education measure which updated and expanded old programs dating back to the 1917 Smith-Hughes Act. President Johnson's antipoverty bill, enacted in 1964, authorized creation of three new education programs summarized below:

- **JOB CORPS**—Creation of a Job Corps in which young men and women aged sixteen to twenty-one could enroll for two years. The Corps, similar in character to the Civilian Conservation Corps of the 1930's, would provide work and training in rural and urban centers. This program is aimed at helping unemployed and untrained youths.
- **WORK-TRAINING PROGRAMS**—Authorizes federal assistance to state and local programs which provide work experience and training for youths aged sixteen to twenty-one, designed to enhance their chances of employment or to enable them to continue their education.
- **VISTA**—Provides funds for creation of a group called Volunteers in Service to America (VISTA), in which trained persons are enrolled to assist community service projects in various parts of the nation. VISTA is designed to do for this country what President Kennedy's Peace Corps was authorized to do in other parts of the world.[8]

One of the most popular antipoverty efforts is Project Head Start, begun in 1965. Designed to provide training, free lunches and medical checkups for impoverished school children, the program today is one of the most successful war-on-poverty measures. Also in 1965 a National Teachers Corps was established to operate in poverty areas, and was provided for by the Higher Education Act of that year. Actuated by the spreading fighting in Viet Nam, the Congress, in 1966, voted legislation that provided a permanent program of educational and vocational training assistance for all veterans who have served in the armed forces any time after January 31, 1955, when eligibility for benefits under Korean War legislation was terminated.

The federal government, under the National School Lunch Act of 1946, subsidizes the states for purchases of food for nonprofit school lunches in public and private schools. This program is operated by the Department of Agriculture through state departments of education. The Agriculture Act of 1954 authorizes the Commodity Credit Corporation to supply school milk, and in 1966 the Child Nutrition Act expanded the school food program to include, among other things, a new pilot school breakfast program.

The 1965 Elementary-Secondary and Higher Education Acts

Elementary-Secondary Education Act. Congress, in 1965, for the first time passed a bill providing comprehensive aid for elementary and secondary schools. The measure included aid to private school children through special programs and loan of federally financed teaching materials. The Act consists of six titles summarized as follows:

TITLE I — Declares it the policy of the U.S. government to provide financial assistance to local educational agencies serving areas with concentrations of children from low-income families.

TITLE II — Authorizes a program of federal grants for the acquisition of school library resources, textbooks, and other printed instructional materials for use in public and private elementary and secondary schools.

TITLE III — Provides a program of federal grants to the states for supplementary educational centers and services to provide for educational needs not otherwise being met.

TITLE IV — Authorizes the U.S. Commissioner of Education to make grants or enter into contracts or jointly finance cooperative arrangements with colleges and other research institutions for research in the field of education, and to disseminate information derived from such research.

TITLE V — Provides for a program of federal grants to stimulate and assist states to strengthen their state educational agencies.

TITLE VI — Contains miscellaneous provisions relating to other provisions of the Act, including administration, advisory committees, etc.

The Nixon administration has indicated it favors a modest boost in appropriations for Title I but recommends cuts in the other programs. Secretary of Health, Education, and Welfare Robert Finch has sought only a two-year extension of the Act instead of the five years sought by the House Education and Labor Committee of the 91st Congress.

The Higher Education Act. In 1965 Congress also enacted a law to provide for a wide variety of major new programs to aid students and colleges. The bill contains eight titles, summarized as follows:

TITLE I — Authorizes federal matching funds to the states to develop university extension courses related to community problems.

TITLE II — Provides for federal grants to enable institutions of higher education to improve their library resources.

TITLE III — Authorizes federal funds to raise the academic quality of impoverished small colleges.

TITLE IV — Approves federal scholarships for undergraduate students.

TITLE V — Authorizes the establishment of a National Teachers Corps to work in areas of concentrations of children from low-income families.

TITLE VI — Provides matching federal grants to colleges for laboratory, audiovisual equipment, and printed material, other than textbooks, for courses in science, the humanities, art, and education.

TITLE VII — Increases federal funds for college classroom construction originally approved in 1963.

TITLE VIII— Contains miscellaneous provisions defining terms and outlawing any federal control over higher education.[10]

Important amendments to the Higher Education Act were made by the Congress in 1966 that extends and expands the provisions of the law.

1967 Presidential Message on Education. President Lyndon B. Johnson, on February 28, 1967, sent the Congress a message emphasizing the need for an evaluation and development of existing federal programs in education. He estimated the total cost of education and related programs for 1968 at eleven billion dollars, a one-billion dollar increase over 1967. In summary, his major recommendations to the Congress were as follows:

EXPIRING LEGISLATION—Extension of such major education measures due to expire as the National Defense Education

Act and the Higher Education Act.

EDUCATIONAL TELEVISION—Creation of a Corporation for Public Television to channel public and private funds to noncommercial radio and television facilities and programs.

EDUCATION PROFESSIONS ACT—Enactment of a measure to combine many of the scattered statutory provisions for teacher training assistance, and to provide new authority to train school administrators, teacher aides, and other education workers.

TEACHER CORPS—Expansion of the Corps and enhancement of the role of the states in training and assigning Corps members.

DISCRIMINATION—An appropriation to help states and communities in coping with desegregation problems.

EDUCATING THE HANDICAPPED—Legislation to establish regional resource centers to help parents and teachers educate handicapped children.

INTERNATIONAL EDUCATION—An appropriation for improving graduate and undergraduate programs of international studies.

VOCATIONAL EDUCATION—Legislation to aid secondary schools and colleges to develop new programs.

NATIONAL SCIENCE FOUNDATION—Establishment of an experimental program for developing the potential of computors in education.[11]

The United States Office of Education

The agency of the United States government most directly concerned with public education is the U.S. Office of Education, one of the three divisions of the Department of Health, Education and Welfare. The Act creating the agency was approved by President Andrew Johnson on March 2, 1867, and it reads in part as follows:

... that there shall be established ... a department of education, for the purpose of collecting such statistics and facts as shall show the condition and progress of education in the several states and territories, and of diffusing such information respecting the organization and management of schools and school systems and methods of teaching as shall aid the people of the United States in the establishment and maintenance of efficient school systems, and otherwise promote the cause of education throughout the country.[12]

A Commissioner of Education appointed by the President directs the agency. It was appropriate that Henry Barnard who, for thirty years, led the movement for a federal fact-finding agency should be selected as the first U.S. Commissioner. It was he who established the basic policy guidelines of that office. The three main functions of the Office are: (1) collecting statistics and facts, (2) diffusing information about schools, and (3) promoting the cause of education. In carrying out these functions, the Office has these principal duties summarized below:

Collecting and Providing Data on Education. Statistical data on enrollment, attendance, finances, administrative organization, and related information are collected and published in bulletins, circulars, the *Biennial Survey of Education,* and the magazine *School Life.*

Conducting Research. The Office employs a large staff of educational experts and research workers for the purpose of conducting or sharing in the conduct of surveys of various aspects of education. The Office is also authorized by the Congress to enter into agreements with educational institutions to carry out research projects subsidized from federal funds.

Administering Federal Grants-in Aid. A major duty of the Office is to administer certain grants made to the states or to public school systems for educational purposes, such as those for vocational education, building and maintenance of schools in federally impacted areas, and those grants authorized under the terms of the National Defense Education Act of 1958, and the 1965 Elementary-Secondary Education and Higher Education Acts.

Administering Exchange Programs. The Office has some responsibilities in the administration of the exchange of students and educators with foreign countries. The Office maintains a Division of International Educational Relations to assist students and educators of this country who wish to study and teach abroad.

Consultative Services. Education specialists of the Office may serve as consultants to state and local school systems on problems within their respective fields of specialization. The views of the experts are also published in the official publications of the Office. The Agency also advises the President and the Congress on policy and legislative matters relating to education, and it counsels as well other governmental agencies concerned with educational matters.

Federal Operation of Educational Institutions

The federal government itself is responsible for the establishment, maintenance, and operation of a number of schools and other educational institutions.

Operation of School Systems. The Congress of the United States has authority over the schools in the federal areas of Washington, D.C. and the Canal Zone in Panama. The armed services also operate overseas schools for dependents of governmental personnel. The Atomic Energy Commission is also responsible for maintaining schools for the children of personnel employed at its three major installations. The federal government has responsibility for providing schools for its wards, such as for Indian children. And the U.S. government has final responsibility for schools established in the federal territories until they achieve statehood.

Federal Educational Institutions. The national government maintains a number of post-secondary level educational institutions. These include the three academies of the armed services at West Point, Annapolis, and Colorado Springs, and the Federal Merchant Marine Schools. The armed forces also provide extensive technical training programs for their members. Other federal agencies also provide facilities and opportunities for research, including graduate study.

Education and Constitutional Rights

The Supreme Court of the United States has notably affected the development of American public education through a number of its decisions protecting the rights of citizens under the Constitution of the United States. A summary of a few of these significant cases follows:

The Oregon Case Decision (1925). In this decision the U.S. Supreme Court sustained the right of private schools to exist alongside of public schools. The state of Oregon, in 1922, had enacted a compulsory education law that required every child between the ages of eight and sixteen to be sent to a public school in the district where he lived. The Court held that this was an unreasonable interference with the liberty of the parents to direct the upbringing of the children; and furthermore, that private schools were threatened with extinction through the improper compulsion exercised by this statute upon parents. The Court, in rendering this decision, did not question the right of the state reasonably to regulate all schools and to inspect, supervise, and examine them to be sure nothing is taught which is manifestly inimical to the public welfare.[13]

The Everson Case Decision (1947). The issue at stake in this decision was over the question of whether or not a state could provide free bus transportation for all pupils to public and parochial schools alike. A New Jersey law had authorized its local school districts to make contracts for the transportation of children to and from public and parochial schools. Complainants alleged the statute forced citizens to pay taxes to help support schools which teach a religious faith, and that such state power to support church schools is contrary to the religious establishment clause of the First Amendment of the Constitution. While the High Court agreed that the wall between church and state had to be kept high and impregnable, the Justices did not agree that the state of New Jersey had breached it with this law. The Court held that the First Amendment did not prohibit New Jersey from spending tax-raised funds to pay the bus fares of parochial school children as a part of a general program under which it pays the fares of pupils attending public and other schools.[14]

The Decision of the Use of Public Schools for Religious Instruction (1948). The High Tribunal held, in 1948, that the giving of religious instruction in the public schools under a released time arrangement is in violation of the constitutional principle of separation of church and state, as expressed in the First Amendment of the Federal Constitution. The background for this decision is as follows: A local school board in Illinois agreed to the giving of religious instruction in the schools under a "released time" arrangement whereby pupils whose parents signed "request cards" were permitted to attend religious-instruction classes conducted during regular school hours in the school building by outside teachers furnished by an interfaith religious council. The Court held that tax-supported public school buildings cannot be used for the dissemination of religious doctrines, and that to provide pupils their religious classes through use of the state's compulsory public school machinery violates the constitutional principle of separation of church and state.[15]

The Feinberg Law Decision (1951). The Supreme Court, in 1951, answered the question as to whether or not public employment, such as in the public schools, is a privilege, or right, of citizenship. The Justices answered that public employment is a privilege, and not a right, of a citizen. The Feinberg Law, in the state of New York, had provided for the disqualification and removal of persons employed by the public schools who advocate the overthrow of the Government by unlawful means, or who are members of organizations which have like purpose. It was argued that the Feinberg statute constituted an abridgment of the freedom of speech and assembly of persons employed in the public schools. But the Court held that while such persons have the right under law to assemble, speak, think, and believe as they will, it is equally clear that they have no right to work for the state in the school system on their own terms.[16]

The Oklahoma Loyalty Oath Case Decision (1952). In recent years the U.S. Supreme Court has outlawed a half dozen state loyalty oaths. The Oklahoma case is the first of many over the question that continues to plague the High Tribunal—i.e., the validity of state loyalty oaths for teachers and other public employees. The Court has, in certain instances, upheld such oaths, and in others, as in the Oklahoma case, it has struck down the oath. The facts in the Oklahoma case are as follows: It was alleged that the purpose of the loyalty oath prescribed by Oklahoma statute for all state employees was to make loyalty a qualification for employment by the state. The Court held, under the Oklahoma Act, that the attempt to exclude persons from public employment solely on the basis of organizational membership, regardless of their knowledge concerning the organizations to which they had belonged, was an indiscriminate classification of innocent with knowing activity, and was an assertion of unlawful arbitrary power.[17]

Since Oklahoma. Loyalty oaths are still possible, but they are likely to meet the test of constitutionality only if they are a positive affirmation of loyalty rather than a disclaimer of subversive affiliation or advocacy. Since 1960 the high court has struck down loyalty legislation in the states of Florida, Washington, Arizona, and New York. It has not upheld such a law since 1951 when the Feinberg law was ruled valid. The high tribunal in ruling against Arizona's law in 1966 held that even if a member of a subversive organization knew about the organization's purposes, he himself might not subscribe to them.

The Nonsegregation Decision (1954). The historic decision of the U.S. Supreme Court handed down on May 17, 1954, has been discussed on pages 161-163. At this point it needs to be reviewed only briefly. The High Court, in 1954, reversed its earlier decision in

Plessy vs. Ferguson (1896) that established the "separate but equal" doctrine with respect to racial practices. The Court now held that separate educational facilities are inherently unequal and therefore unconstitutional.[18]

The Public Prayer Decision (1962). This decision also has been considered earlier on pages 165-166 and now needs only brief mention. In this case, which involved the use of the New York Regents' prayer in the public schools, the High Court held the practice to be in violation of the religious establishment clause of the First Amendment of the Federal Constitution.[19]

The U.S. Supreme Court has, in these decisions, and in others not here mentioned, exercised the power of the federal government to change educational practices. These decisions have profoundly influenced the course of public education in this country within recent years. These decisions also indicate how the federal government can, and does, exercise influence over educational policies within the states when the basic rights of citizens, as defined in the Federal Constitution, are involved.

Conclusion

This chapter has presented the role of the federal government in education. It has been pointed out that the Constitution of the United States did not reserve unto the federal government powers to establish schools and provide education; yet the federal government, in a very real way does, in fact, influence and assist the educational development of the American people. The following chapter will discuss the role of the states and local communities in the administration of public education in the American nation.

Chapter XI
Footnotes

[1] As quoted by Henry Steele Commager (ed.), *Documents of American History*, Vol. I (New York: Appleton-Century-Crofts, Inc., 1949), p. 124.

[2] *Ibid.*, p. 131.

[3] *Ibid.*, p. 413.

[4] *Federal Role in Education* (Washington, D.C.: Congressional Quarterly Service, n.d.), p. 6.

[5] *Ibid.*, p. 7.

[6] *Ibid.*

[7] *Ibid.*, pp. 8-9.

[8] *Ibid.*, p. 13.

[9] *Ibid.*, pp. 46-48.

[10] *Ibid.*, pp. 50-53.

[11] *Ibid.*, p. 33.

[12] Chris A. De Young, *Introduction to American Public Education* (New York: McGraw-Hill Book Company, Inc., 1950), p. 23.

[13] See: *Pierce, Governor of Oregon, et al. vs. Society of Sisters; Pierce, Governor of Oregon, et al. vs. Hill Military Academy*, 286, U.S., 510 (1925).

[14] See: *Everson vs. Board of Education*, 330 U.S. 1 (1947).

[15] See: *People of the State of Illinois ex rel. Vashti McCullum vs. Board of Education of School District No. 71, Champaign County, Illinois, et al.* 333 U.S., 203 (1948).

[16] See: *Irving Adler, George Friedlander, Mark Friedlander, et al. vs. Board of Education of the City of New York*, 342 U.S., 485 (1951).

[17] See: *Robert M. Wieman et al. vs. Paul Updegraff et al.*, 344 U.S., 184 (1952).

[18] See: *Brown vs. Board of Education*, 347 U.S., 483 (1954).

[19] See: *Steven I. Engle et al. vs. William J. Vitale, Jr., et al.*, 370 U.S., 460 (1962).

Selected References

Alexander, William M., and J. Galen Saylor. *Modern Secondary Education.* New York: Holt, Rinehart and Winston, 1965.

Allen, Hollis P. *The Federal Government and Education.* New York: McGraw-Hill Book Company, 1950.

Commager, Henry Steele (ed.). *Documents of American History.* 2 vols. New York: Appleton-Century-Crofts, Inc., 1964.

DeYoung, Chris A. *Introduction to Public Education.* New York: McGraw-Hill Book Company, Inc., 1950.

Federal Role in Education. 2nd edition. Washington, D.C.: Congressional Quarterly Service, n.d.

Freeman, Roger A. *Federal Aid to Education—Boon or Bane?* Washington, D.C.: American Enterprise Association, Inc., 1955.

Hales, Dawson W. *Federal Control of Public Education: A Critical Appraisal.* New York: Bureau of Publications, Teachers College, Columbia University, 1954.

Quattlebaum, Charles A. *Federal Educational Activities and Educational Issues Before Congress.* Washington, D.C.: Government Printing Office, 1951.

United States House of Representatives, Committee on Government Operation. *Federal-State-Local Relations: Federal Grants-in-Aid.* 85th Congress, 2nd Session, House Report No. 2,533, August 8, 1958. Washington, D.C.: Government Printing Office, 1958.

Chapter XII

ADMINISTRATION OF SECONDARY EDUCATION: ROLE OF THE STATES AND LOCAL COMMUNITIES

Role of the States

Responsibilities Exercised by the States

The primary responsibility for education in the United States rests with the states, not with the federal government. The source of this authority is the Tenth Amendment to the Constitution, ratified in 1791, which states: "The powers not delegated to the United States by the Constitution, nor prohibited by it to the states, are reserved to the states respectively, or to the people." By implication therefore, education, one of the unmentioned powers so reserved, is a state function. Numerous court decisions support this inference.

Most states have general constitutional provisions for the establishment of a state-supported public school system. Some state constitutions contain very specific sections on education. Usually, however, the legislature, under a general mandate, reinforced by the courts, determines the organization and administration of the public schools. The legislature, in addition to determining the structure and organization of the state's educational system, delegates powers to various agencies created, such as local school districts, intermediate units of control, and state departments.

One of the most important powers of the state is determining the methods of financing schools. The state through its control of the taxing power can prescribe the methods to be used in raising taxes for school purposes and by imposing limitations on the taxing power of local school districts, it possesses strong control over the public education system.

All but five states specify subjects required for graduation from high school. In many states laws require that pupils receive instruction in certain courses. The California Education Code until recently, for example, required twenty-three courses in high schools, including instruction in the Constitution of the United States, in American history, in state and local government, in foreign languages, in manners and morals, in the dangers of the use of alcohol and narcotics, in fire prevention, in first aid, in physical education, and in driver education.

State Departments of Education

In order to develop a broad program of education, each state had to create an agency through which it could act. The typical state department of education consists of (1) the state board of education, which is the policy-making body; (2) the state superintendent or state commissioner of schools, who is the chief state school officer; and (3) the professional staff of the state department who carry out the policies of the board of education under the immediate direction of the superintendent or commissioner.

The State Board of Education. The earliest example of a state board of education is the Board of Regents for the state of New York, established in 1784. This body was given supervision over collegiate and academic education throughout the state, and the schools under its control have ever since been jointly known as the University of the State of New York. No other state board was organized until 1825 when North Carolina created a group known as the President and Directors of the Literary Fund. It was not, however, until 1837 when Massachusetts established its State Board of Education that the pattern was developed which has been followed throughout the nation. The Massachusetts Act of 1837 called for a board of ten members. This board was empowered to appoint a secretary, and Horace Mann was selected as the first secretary. The pioneering efforts of Mann as secretary of the board earned him the title "father of public-school education." Today, all states have the equivalent of a state board of education. This board, as the chief educational authority for the state, helps to develop policies and programs for the state department of education.

The major ways of determining membership on the state board are by (1) *ex officio* status; (2) election; and (3) appointment. Ex officio board members are persons who hold other state offices, and because of that status are automatically members of the state board of education. In the state of Florida, for example, the state superintendent, the governor, the attorney general, the secretary of state, and the state treasurer are the members of the board, and the terms of their regular offices determine the length of their membership. The trend over the past half century has been away from boards wholly or chiefly *ex officio*.

In some states the state board is elected. Members may be elected at large, or from some type of district. In the states of Utah and Washington, local school board members in convention elect the members of the state board. The state superintendent or state commissioner is the only *ex officio* member of an elected state board of education. In most states of the Union, the members of the state board of education are now appointed by the governor. In Wyoming they are appointed by the state superintendent with the approval of the governor. The number of members on a state board ranges from seven to fourteen; terms of office vary from state to state from two to ten years' duration. The typical state board is made up of lay people. Only a few states require that membership include professional educators.

Duties generally performed by state boards of education include the following: (1) formulating policies and regulations for carrying out its responsibilities as stipulated in the constitution and statutes of the state; (2) appointing the professional staff of the state education department upon recommendation of the chief state school officer; (3) establishing standards for teacher certification; (4) establishing standards for the classification, approval, and accreditation of public and private schools; (5) prescribing a uniform system of educational data on such matters as enrollment, finance, and evaluation of educational progress; (6) providing an annual report to the governor and legislature on educational progress and problems; (7) publishing the laws on education; (8) providing for supervisory and consultative services through the state education department; (9) distributing funds and commodities from the state and federal governments to the various school districts; and (10) defining its supervisory responsibilities over education, public and private, in accordance with the law.[1]

The Chief State School Officer. In New York in 1813, Gideon Hawley became the first state school superintendent. But it was not until 1837, when the Massachusetts State Board of Education engaged Horace Mann, that the evolution of the office of the chief state school officer began in earnest. Before the outbreak of the Civil War, each state employed a chief school officer.

The superintendent of public instruction or commissioner of education, as he is sometimes entitled, is the chief administrative officer on educational matters in the state. In some states he is elected by the people; in others he is appointed either by the state board or by the governor. The state of Wyoming has both a state superintendent of schools and a commissioner of education. The former is elected and is entrusted with the general supervision of the public schools, and the latter is appointed by the state board of education and is charged with enforcing the educational policies of the state board under the general supervision of the superintendent. Most authorities agree that the chief state school officer should be appointed by the state board of education.

The state superintendent or state commissioner usually serves as the executive officer of the state board of education. He is responsible for administering the state department of education; advising the board on educational policies, operations, and standards; interpreting the school laws and rulings of the state board; preparing the budget for the education program of the state; and reporting to the state board, the governor, the legislature, and the public on the state of the schools. His duties fall into a few main categories such as the following: (1) statistical—compiling data on the schools of the state; (2) advisory and judicial; (3) supervisory and administrative; and (4) integrative—attending meetings and coalescing the various educational interests in the state. In most states the superintendent or commissioner exercises leadership necessary to improve the schools through budgetary recommendations, through establishing high minimum standards of academic and professional preparation for the certification of teachers and administrators, and by working with local districts in improving their programs and salary schedules.

The State Department of Education. The state department of education has the responsibility for carrying out the programs formulated by the state board and the state superintendent or commissioner of education. In the days when Horace Mann was the secretary of the state board of education in Massachusetts, he was his own state department of education. As the concept of the state's function in education broadened, no single official could handle all the work. After 1917 there was a rapid growth of personnel in state departments of education in numerous states largely as the result of the following factors: (1) new duties devolving on state departments as a result of the passage of the Smith-Hughes vocational training law; (2) the shocking revelations from the physical, mental, and literacy tests administered during World War I; and (3) the growing appreciation on the part of the public of the need for a strong program of education to meet modern conditions. Today most state departments of education are divided into specialized areas such as instruction, certification, finance, school buildings, research and guidance, etc. with a professionally qualified person in charge of each division. These persons are appointed by the state superintendent or commissioner subject to the approval of the state board of education, and are accountable to him.

The functions of state education departments fall into several categories, such as the following: (1) regulatory functions; (2) operational functions; (3) administrative functions; and (4) leadership functions.

Regulatory functions consist of the following duties:

1. Protection of the life and health of pupils through the enforcement of minimum standards for buildings, regulations about the operation of busses, safety requirements, and health examinations of pupils and teachers.
2. Enforcement of compulsory attendance laws.
3. Enforcement of the laws and regulations established by the state to assure all pupils at least a minimum program of education. Examples of the exercise of such powers include the certification of teachers; regulation of tenure for teachers; prescription of textbooks to be used; issuance of courses of study and curriculum guides; accreditation of schools on the basis of predetermined standards; reorganization of school districts; establishment of requirements for graduation from high school; prescription of certain subjects that must be taught, etc.
4. Expenditure and safekeeping of school district funds. Each state has enacted a body of laws with respect to the expenditure and safekeeping of school district funds. Methods of accounting are determined by the state department and bonds are required of certain school officials.[2]

Operational functions of the state departments of education include the direct operation of some educational institutions or classes such as state vocational or trade schools, schools for the handicapped, state libraries and museums. In the field of higher education, the state department of education may have control over teacher colleges, state colleges, technical institutes, and junior colleges.

Administrative functions of state departments of education include record keeping, dispensing of state and federal educational funds, and interpreting school law. The state department collects data from local school systems, compiles it, and may also publish the data. In turn, it provides information to the U.S. Office of Education so that national statistics on education can be made available. With the substantial increase in state and federal support for education in recent years, state departments must devote increasingly greater amounts of staff time to the distribution of these funds to local school districts.

Leadership functions of state departments of education in recent times have emerged as perhaps their most significant responsibilities. Aspects of these leadership functions include the following:

1. Planning. Not only planning state-wide is important, but also the guidance offered to local school districts in clarifying major issues, defining problems, and suggesting possible courses of action are of considerable value.
2. Research. There is no substitute for knowledge. Research is, therefore, a vital function of the state department. It may also publish and disseminate the results of research conducted by school systems, individual scholars, or by other agencies.
3. Consultation. Most state departments make periodic visitations to local school systems, and such occasions provide excellent opportunities for personal consultation with local school administrators, boards of education, and school staffs.

Some state departments of education are weak. They are inadequately staffed and inadequately financed. Salaries of professional personnel are too low to obtain superior educational leadership. Title V of the Elementary and Secondary Education Act of 1965 represents an effort on the part of the federal government to assist state departments of education to upgrade their services.

Role of the Local School Districts

Responsibilities Exercised by the Local School District

Even though the state is the final authority, general and enabling powers for the establishment and control of schools are delegated traditionally by the state to the communities in which the schools are located. The local school district is usually administered by a board of education ranging from three to twelve members, and a superintendent of schools with his staff. Some boards are appointed by the chief executive officer of the city. The pattern of having a local board responsible for the schools originated in New England and has since spread over the nation. In the middle of the nineteenth century the boards actually assumed the responsibility of running the schools. In time, as the schools grew in number and in complexity, it became necessary for boards to employ a professional educator who would devote full time to the job of operating a school system.

Today, the most important task of the local school board is selecting a competent superintendent who, together with his teachers, will in reality run the schools.

Types of Local School Districts

The autonomous school district, organized as a separate and distinct unit of government, is essentially an American innovation. In the beginning the unit for school administration grew out of the arrangements made by the settlers in the colonies themselves or by the company or group settling the colony. In New England the unit was the town; in the southern colonies it was the county, and the middle colonies made adaptations of both patterns. As school systems developed in the new western states after the Revolutionary War, three basic kinds of local school control emerged: the common school district, the township district, and the county district.

The Common School District. Over half of the American states have the common school district. This basic type of school district is usually independent of other units of local government. Its boundaries may be coterminous with, or overlap, other local governmental lines. The common school district includes a variety of district types, such as: rural (population under 2,500 persons); village (2,500 to 5,000 population); city (5,000 to 100,000); and metropolitan (population over 100,000) districts; also consolidated, union, and separate high school districts.

The Township School District. This type of district is usually coterminous with the town in the New England States or with the township in the midwestern states. In reality, it is a common school district. Historically, the New England town included, in addition to the settlement of colonists, a considerable amount of land surrounding the settlement. New settlements might therefore locate within the territory of the town, yet be physically separated from the original village. In this way the town became a geographical unit of local government that had authority for the establishment of schools. This is the unit of school administration that has been retained in the New England states to the present time.

In the Northwest Territory pioneers from New England found the township, usually consisting of an area six miles square, or thirty-six sections of land, to be a familiar and satisfactory unit for governmental purposes. The township also became the school district. These units of local school administration continue to be the basic structure in such states as Indiana, Illinois, New Jersey, and Pennsylvania.

The County Unit District. The county as a unit of local government became well established in the South, and it was also the unit for school control as well. This unit of school administration is found in the twelve states of Alabama, Florida, Georgia, Kentucky, Louisiana, Maryland, New Mexico, North Carolina, Tennessee, Utah, Virginia, and West Virginia. The county unit school district is nearly always coterminous with county jurisdiction. The county unit district is not to be confused with the county serving as an intermediate type of state administration—that will be discussed later.

The Junior College District. The Junior College is now frequently looked upon as an extension of secondary education, and many people believe it to be essentially a part of the free public school system. Thirty-two states have enacted laws authorizing public junior colleges, and this legislation usually provides for the creation of junior college districts. In certain states the common school district also serves as the junior college district; whereas in others, the junior college district is a separate corporate entity. It may be coterminous with a common school district, and even have the same governing board, yet still be a separate unit of school administration. In most situations, however, it will embrace several school districts.

Functions of the Local School District

The basic function of the local school district is to establish, maintain, and operate schools within the framework of authority delegated to the district by the state constitution and/or by the legislature through statutory law. In carrying out this duty the local school district, through its governing body, the board of education, and the professional staff headed by the superintendent of schools have responsibilities within limitations imposed by state law or regulation.

The Board of Education. The local school board is the policy-making and appraisal-determining group, and its chief task is to select a competent superintendent of schools who will act as its chief administrative officer. Historically, the school board evolved as follows: During the colonial period in New England, every item of school business was brought before the town meeting in which every citizen took a direct part. As towns grew larger, most of the business of the town meeting, including the managing of schools, was delegated to officials known as selectmen. As towns continued to grow, the selectmen were unable to keep up on school affairs, and so special school committees were then created, and with that practice the school board *per se* came into being. Colonial practice provided the background for early state legislation.

The local school board is usually granted such broad powers by the state legislature as the following: (1) to appoint administrators, supervisors, teachers, and other employees; (2) adopt courses of study; (3) to purchase supplies; (4) to acquire school sites; (5) to erect school buildings; (6) to levy taxes or to submit estimates to some other body; (7) to make rules and regulations for the management of the schools; (8) to enforce the compulsory school attendance legislation; and (9) to perform such duties as are necessary for the attainment of the ends for which the school districts are organized.

The Superintendent of Schools. The board of education places the responsibility for the administration of the schools upon the superintendent of schools, who, in metropolitan districts, may delegate powers to assistant superintendents and others subordinate to him. The cities of Buffalo, New York, and Louisville, Kentucky, each created the position of superintendent of schools in the year 1837. Until 1870, less than thirty cities of the nation had school superintendents. When after 1870 cities began to grow and educational problems became increasingly complex, and boards of education could no longer exercise direct supervision over the schools, responsibilities for running them were placed in the hands of a superintendent of schools.

The following are some of the powers and duties usually assigned to the superintendent of schools: (1) to serve as the chief executive officer of the board of education; (2) to nominate the professional staff of the schools and all other employees authorized by the school board; (3) to select, after due consultation, texts and all other supplies and equipment needed by the schools; (4) to direct the supervision of the schools; (5) to assign the professional staff and all other employees to the schools; (6) to prepare the school budget and submit it to the board for action; (7) to direct all purchases and expenditures; (8) to keep the board informed as to school building needs; and (9) to prepare for the approval of the board rules and regulations needed for the governing of the schools.

The School Principal. The principal is the educational leader of the individual school. He is selected by the superintendent, and the appointment is confirmed by a vote of the board of education. The principal has the most delicate and exacting job in the whole school system. Both by tradition and training he remains close to the teaching process, and the supervision of the instructional program is considered his primary responsibility. He also has these additional responsibilities: (1) implementation of the adopted course of study; (2) preparation of the schedule of instruction and assignment of teachers; (3) supervision of the noncertified personnel assigned to the school; (4) coordination of the work of special service personnel such as doctors, nurses, psychologists, and consultants who have been assigned by the district and/or county office; (5) student discipline; (6) overseeing the operation of the school cafeteria, the library, and the extracurricular program; and (7) preparation of a budget for the school.

Role of the Counties

Responsibilities Exercised by the Counties

In the majority of states the county serves as an intermediate unit of school administration. The county as an intermediate unit should not be confused with the county as a local school district, although the distinction between the two is vague in some states.

The county, as an intermediate unit of school administration, stands between the state and the local school district. The chief administrative officer of the county unit is the county superintendent of schools. In some states there is a county board of education, which serves as a policy-making or advisory group for the county superintendent. Historically, the county superintendency evolved as follows: As state interest in public education began to grow in this country, the need to develop some subordinate form of state control became evident. A county school officer known as a county superintendent of schools was provided for. At first his tasks were only clerical and statistical and required only a modicum, if any, of professional training. In the majority of states that still maintain the county education office, the county superintendent is elected by the people. Most states require him to have some professional experience, and his term of office is usually the same as for other elected county officials.

Functions of the County Intermediate Unit

The county school office is usually the channel through which flows much of the school money expended by the local districts. The county superintendent is often the certificating officer for the state, and no one in the county is legally qualified to teach without his sanction. As the legal representative of the state, he interprets school laws. His duties vary widely from state to state. Examples of services provided by the country office include: school bussing, curriculum consultant services, guidance and personnel services, health services, programs for exceptional children, provision of teaching resources, and programs for in-service education of teachers.

Public School Systems of the United States (Statistics)

It has been suggested that at least sixty per cent of the school districts of the United States are inefficient and uneconomical. The biggest problem facing rural educators is the consolidation and reorganization of small school districts. Using a local community or a group of interrelated communities as the basis for a school district is now obsolete and indefensible. There is little hope for small rural communities to survive as dynamic social and economic entities, and leading educators now recommend that school districts be organized around "city centers" of at least 5,000 people or 2,500 in special cases.[3] Nearly all educators agree that small schools are inferior. Studies have shown that although the unique atmosphere of small schools offers subtle benefits for students, the possible advantages are purchased at the price of poorer quality in academic programs.

In the United States in 1966 there were a total of 23,464 school districts. The eleven North Atlantic states, including the District of Columbia, accounted for 3,667 of this number, including 986 for the state of New York. The twelve states of the Great Lakes and Plains region accounted for 11,935, including 2,388 for the state of Nebraska. The twelve states of the Southeast accounted for 1809, including 398 for the state of Florida. The fifteen states of the West and Southwest accounted for 6,053, including 1,303 in the state of Texas. California, the most populous state in the Union, had 1,187. The outlying areas of the United States accounted for 6 school districts.[4]

The average enrollment (1965-1966) per district throughout the United States was 1,562. By regions, the respective figures were as follows: North Atlantic, 2,463; Great Lakes and Plains, 804; Southeast, 5,336; and West and Southwest, 1,669.[5]

In the fifty states (1965-1966), 1,745 bond elections for public school purposes were held to raise $3,559,979,000. Bonds totaling $2,651,979,000 were approved in 1,265 of these elections—roughly, three-quarters of what was asked for.[6]

Total expenditures (1966-1967) by school districts throughout the nation was $27,945,843,000. The districts of the eleven North Atlantic states, including the District of Columbia, spent $7,873,524,000, including $3,173,000,000 in the state of New York. Districts in the twelve states of the Great Lakes and Plains region spent $7,578,439,000, including $1,412,000,000 in the state of Illinois. Districts in the twelve states of the Southeast spent $4,942,721,000, including $813,952,000 in the state of Florida. Districts in the fifteen states of the West and Southwest spent $7,551,159,000, including $3,610,000,000 in the state of California.[7]

The nation-wide annual (1966-1967) current expenditure per pupil in average daily attendance was $549. In the twelve states of the North Atlantic, including the District of Columbia, the figure was $717, including $912 for the state of New York. In the twelve states of the Great Lakes and Plains, the figure was $556, including $634 for the state of Minnesota. In the twelve states of the Southeast, the figure was $438, including $567 for the state of Louisiana. In the fifteen states of the West and Southwest, the figure was $565, including $877 for the state of Alaska.[8]

The nation-wide average annual (1966-1967) salary for classroom teachers was $6,820. In the twelve North Atlantic states, including the District of Columbia, the sum was $7,360, including $7,800 for the District of Columbia. In the twelve Great Lakes and Plains states, the sum was $6,770, including $7,400 for the state of Illinois. In the twelve states of the Southeast, the sum was $5,790, including $6,530 for the state of Florida. In the fifteen states of the West and Southwest, the sum was $7,230, including $8,923 for the state of Alaska.[9]

In the 1965-1966 fiscal year, local school districts raised $13.4 billion in revenues for public elementary and secondary schools, or 53.8 per cent of the total revenue receipts. State governments contributed $9.6 billion or 38.6 per cent, and the federal government allocated $1.9 billion or 7.6 per cent.[10]

Conclusion

It has been shown in this chapter that education is a state responsibility, but that the task of establishing and maintaining schools has been delegated to local school districts. There has been a positive trend in recent years toward the consolidation of small school districts into larger units. Many feel that further consolidation is necessary for the economical and efficient operation of the nation's schools. There is no one answer as to what is the most satisfactory local school administrative unit. The answer must be sought in the light of local, state, and nation-wide planning on sound educational, economical, and sociological bases.

Chapter XII
Footnotes

[1] See: National Council of Chief State School Officers, *The State Department of Education* (Washington, D.C.: The Council, 1952), pp. 14-16.

[2] Fred F. Beach, *The Functions of State Departments of Education* (U.S. Office of Education, Miscellaneous No. 12; Washington, D.C.: Government Printing Office, 1950), Chap. III.

[3] This is the opinion of officials in four states—Iowa, Missouri, Nebraska, and South Dakota—who have formed the Great Plains School District Organization Project to study reorganization. The project is funded by the U.S. Office of Education under the provisions of the Elementary and Secondary Education Act.

[4] U.S. Office of Education, *Fall 1966 Statistics of Public Schools,* as quoted by *Standard Education Almanac,* 1968 (Los Angeles: Academic Media, Inc., 1968), p. 186.

[5] U.S. Office of Education, *Digest of Educational Statistics,* 1966, as quoted by *op. cit.,* p. 185.

[6] U.S. Office of Education, *Bond Sales for Public School Purpose, July 1, 1965,* as quoted by *op. cit.,* p. 184.

[7] U.S. Office of Education, *Fall 1966 Statistics of Public Schools,* as quoted by *op. cit.,* pp. 175-176.

[8] *Ibid.*

[9] *Ibid.*

[10] U.S. Office of Education, *Progress of Public Education in the United States of America, 1966-67,* as quoted by *op. cit.,* p. 174.

Selected References

Alexander, William M., and J. Galen Saylor. *Modern Secondary Education.* New York: Holt, Rinehart and Winston, 1965.

Beach, Fred F. *The Functions of State Departments of Education.* U.S. Office of Education, Miscellaneous No. 12. Washington, D.C.: Government Printing Office, 1950.

Beach, Fred F., and Robert F. Will. *The State and Education.* U.S. Office of Education, Miscellaneous No. 23. Washington, D.C.: Government Printing Office, 1955.

Committee on Education. *Responsibility of the States in Education—the Fourth R.* Washington, D.C.: United States Chamber of Commerce, 1947.

Cubberley, Ellwood P. *State School Administration.* Boston: Houghton Mifflin Company, 1927.

De Young, Chris A. *Introduction to American Public Education.* New York: McGraw-Hill Book Company, Inc., 1968.

Dutton, S. T., and D. Snedden. *The Administration of Public Education in the United States.* New York: The Macmillan Company, 1908.

Graves, F. P. *The Administration of American Education.* New York: The Macmillan Company, 1932.

National Council of Chief State School Officers. *The State Department of Education.* Washington, D.C.: The Council, 1952.

National Scoiety for the Study of Education. *American Education in the Post-War Period* (Forty-fourth Yearbook). Chicago: University of Chicago Press, 1945.

Chapter XIII
DEVELOPMENT OF THE SECONDARY SCHOOL CURRICULUM

Origin of the Curriculum

Greek civilization is the culture responsible for originating the formal school curriculum of modern Western societies. This curriculum combined the intellectual, physical, and aesthetic aspects of life.

On the intellectual side the ancient Hellenes were responsible for developing what, ever since, has been known in curricular terms as the seven liberal arts. What the medievalists called the trivium consisted of the subjects of grammar, rhetoric, and logic (or dialectic). Teachers like the Sophists created the science of grammar; and what the sophist Protagoras did for grammar, Plato and Aristotle did for logic, and still others for rhetoric. The quadrivium, a term also used by medievalists, composed the remaining subjects of the liberal arts; they were: arithmetic, geometry, astronomy, and music. To the Greeks the so-called scientific studies of the quadrivium did not seem as important as the linguistic studies of the trivium. The pursuit of science involved concrete things, whereas their main preoccupation was with ideas.

Physical exercise was viewed by the Greeks as an important aspect of character building. Greek physical education included such sports as running, jumping, boxing, wrestling, throwing the discus and the javelin. Originally these activities had a military significance. In time, however, the Greeks came to play these games more for moral and aesthetic goals. The games reached their highest point of development in the Panhellenic Olympic festival, a sports event still celebrated in the modern world. So strongly did the Greeks believe that athletic sports strengthened resolution of character and will power that they were largely convinced that physical beauty was an indication of moral perfection.[1]

The Greek curriculum neglected vocational education. To the ancient Hellenes the industrial arts were too closely associated with the institution of slavery. Physical exercise and the performance of the duties of citizenship were the pursuits of the Greek freeman of leisure. However, despite the dislike of the Greeks for vocational education, such training was provided informally by apprenticeship for those Greeks who had to earn a living with their hands.

Roman education was essentially an adaptation of the Hellenistic curriculum to the imperatives of Roman civilization—law, government, and engineering. The Greek studies of the trivium found especial favor in Rome. The preoccupation of the Romans with grammar, rhetoric, and logic, however, did not render them insensitive to the more scientific subjects of the quadrivium. It was the Romans, also, who arranged the educational system into lower, middle, and higher schools.

Graeco-Roman institutions, thought, and culture were carried over into the period of the Middle Ages by the emergence of the Roman Catholic Church as the major force for social order of the times. With the Church paramount in the lives of men, religious and moral considerations became the foremost concern of the curriculum. Physical education, for example, gave way to asceticism, and the Graeco-Roman subject of logic became Christian philosophy.[2]

Evolution of the Humanities

In the fourteenth century the scholasticism of the Middle Ages gave way to a new spirit of inquiry. With the advent of the Renaissance such scholars as Petrarch and Battista Guarino restored the balance among the intellectual, physical, and aesthetic aspects of the curriculum. The focus of the Renaissance curriculum was on the classical languages and literature, and Latin was the language of instruction. Renaissance man thought the classic languages and literature had particular value in forming the mind of man, and therefore were called the humanitas, the pursuits proper to mankind.[3] The intent of the humanistic curriculum was to provide the same well-rounded and harmonious education as the ancient classics prescribed for Graeco-Roman youth. The linguistic studies of the trivium were still preeminent during the Renaissance. Rhetoric was especially restored to the importance it had enjoyed in the ancient world. The aesthetic qualities sought for in speech and writing were also a goal of physical education.

North of the Alpine Mountains in Europe, the humanistic curriculum became a means of achieving religious and social reform. Critical minds throughout northern Europe grew impatient with the wealth, power, and corruption of the Roman Church, and demanded reform. While the Reformation was basically a religious movement, Protestant educators were interested in the general instruction of the masses, and the classic languages were considered important, as knowledge of them meant that the Bible might be read in its original languages.

In the post-Renaissance world, the study of ancient languages began to decline. Although Latin remained the language of scholarship, diplomacy, the church, and the courts of law, it was not holding its own in competition with vernacular languages. The theory for justifying the continued inclusion of the ancient tongues in the curriculum was based on the ground of their disciplinary value. The concept of formal discipline held that a subject was important if it was difficult enough to develop habits of persistence, industry, and reasoning.

The Progress of Science in the Curriculum

The sixteenth and seventeenth centuries comprised the age of the beginnings of experimental and natural sciences. During the seventeenth and eighteenth centuries, curricular knowledge began more and more to be based on sense observation rather than on ideas from the ancients. The English scholar Francis Bacon (1561-1626) and the Moravian cleric-educator Johann Amos Comenius (1592-1670) envisaged a new, encyclopedic curriculum heavily based on science. The English essayist John Locke (1632-1704) claimed that the study of mathematics had greater disciplinary power than Latin. The Realschule of Julius Hecker (1707-1768) led the way in incorporating scientific studies into the curriculum.

The Industrial Revolution, beginning late in the eighteenth century, greatly helped to increase interest in science. In England, the home of the Industrial Revolution, the commercial and industrial greatness of the nation was largely dependent upon the development of the scientific disciplines of physics and chemistry. The outstanding proponent of putting science in the English schools was Thomas Henry Huxley (1825-1895), and Herbert Spencer (1820-1903) insisted that science not only equalled, but excelled, language as a discipline of the mind.

Introduction of Modern Languages and History into the Curriculum

The introduction of modern languages and history in the curriculum is closely associated with the forces of nationalism and democracy unleashed upon the world by the American and French Revolutions. Schools in which the vernacular tongue was used as the language of instruction had been established in the late Middle Ages, but it was some time before vernacular literatures were accepted as objects of instruction. The concept of politico-religious unity, as exemplified by the Holy Roman Empire and the Roman Catholic Church, had achieved for Latin the status of a near-universal language. When Napoleon finally destroyed the crumbling Holy Roman Empire, the modern nation-state had arrived at center stage in world history as the force for unity in modern society. To help capture the feeling of a country's nationalism, folk literature and native classics were incorporated into the curriculum of the schools.

At the time when vernacular tongues were forcing the ancient languages and literatures into a position of secondary importance, history also achieved an independent status in the curriculum. Earlier, history had been regarded as only important for the knowledge it gave of the Greeks and Romans, and that type of knowledge was only incidentally acquired through reading of the classics. When the American and French Revolutions released the movements of modern nationalism and democracy, history was separated from literature and acquired its independent status in the curriculum. It was the German historian Karl Friedrich Eichhorn (1781-1854) who, when aroused by the French Revolution, resolved to dedicate himself to the salvation of Germany by teaching his students to love their country and its history.[4] Herbart added that literature and history were the two chief sources of a knowledge of man, which, together with a knowledge of things, composed his curriculum.[5] Courses in American history were included in the curriculum of the academies shortly after the American Revolution. American history came of age with George Bancroft (1800-1891), who possessed the first and best claim to the title of national historian.[6]

Reappearance of Physical Education in the Curriculum

The forces of nationalism and democracy in the modern world also helped to heighten curricular interest in physical education. Physical fitness and national fitness have been closely identified in the mind of such gymnasts as Friedrich Ludwig Jahn (1778-1852), who tried to harness gymnastics to the cause of patriotism.[7] Earlier, John Locke had advocated in his essay Some Thoughts Concerning Education the hardening of the body to achieve his educational ideal of a sound mind in a sound body.

Sweden was the nation where gymnastics and calisthenics in physical education were first worked out. It was not until after the American Civil War that gymnastics was introduced into the schools of the United States. Calisthenics was presented in America by Diocletion Lewis (1823-1886). The kind of physical training advocated by Lewis consisted of a program of systematic and balanced exercise for every part of the body.[8]

In America, however, as in England, the love of sports overshadowed formal gymnastics in the physical education curriculum. Concurrent with the addition of school games to the curriculum of physical education was the development of a program of health education. Both physiology and hygiene entered the school curriculum in the post-Civil War period. The health education program was further expanded after the statistics of the First World War revealed a distressing amount of physical disability among the youth of the nation. While statistics of the Second World War disclosed some improvement, there has been expressed continuing national concern over the physical health of the young.[9]

Introduction of Vocational Education into the Curriculum

The coming of the Industrial Revolution in the mid-eighteenth century resulted in the shift of the center of work output from the home to the factory and the mechanization of handwork. Inasmuch as technology was dependent upon the development of a body of scientific principles, vocational training was elevated to the status of a formal school subject. Philipp Emanual von Fellenberg (1771-1844), the Swiss nobleman and educator, was among the first to incorporate manual labor into the school curriculum. Fellenberg's idea was transplanted in the United States chiefly in terms of the manual training institute. During the latter part of the nineteenth century this institution helped to solve not only difficult problems created by the Industrial Revolution. It also assisted in racial adjustment. Hampton and Tuskegee Institutes for Afro-Americans, and Haskell for Indians, were excellent examples of schools dedicated to the training of minority groups.[10]

In spite of the advances made by incorporating vocational training into the curriculum through the establishment of technical institutes, a federal commission revealed, just prior to America's entry into World War I, that less than one per cent of the workers of the nation had technical training for their occupations.[11] These findings helped to secure passage of the Smith-Hughes Act of 1917, which provided federal aid to secondary schools for vocational education.

Role of the Fine Arts in the Curriculum

The history of the fine arts in the curriculum can be traced back to the ancient period. The Greeks included music as one of the seven liberal arts. Greek interest in the fine arts did not fare well in the curricula of subsequent ages. The music that continued to be taught during the Middle Ages was to be found in special song schools established by the church to recruit its choirs.

During the course of the nineteenth century the singing of folk songs and studies in the field of industrial design helped to forge the bonds of patriotism and assist industrial development. In the twentieth century the dance and instrumental music were added to the music curriculum of the schools. The graphic arts, distinct from industrial design, also gained recognized social value in the schools.[12]

Building the Modern Curriculum

What Knowledge is Most Worth?

By the mid-point of the nineteenth century the complexity of modern industrialized and civilized living was so burdening the capacity of the school curriculum to meet all the demands being placed on it that concern was expressed that curricular reorganization was badly needed. It was Herbert Spencer, the English sociologist-philosopher, who in an essay written in 1865, asked the basic question: *What Knowledge is Most Worth?* It was not, however, until the last decade of the nineteenth century that Spencer's question began to bear answers in the United States. Among those who sought more than a piecemeal revision of the curriculum was Franklin Bobbitt (1876-1952). To arrive at sound educational objectives, Bobbitt made an activity analysis of the range of human experience and developed ten major categories which bore obvious resemblance to Spencer's list of life activities and to the Seven Cardinal Principles of the Commission on the Reorganization of Secondary Education. Bobbitt's categories were: (1) Language activities, (2) Health, (3) Citizenship, (4) General social contacts, (5) Mental health, (6) Leisure occupations, (7) Religious activities, (8) Parental responsibilities, (9) Unspecialized activities, such as the practical arts, and (10) Vocational activities.[13]

John Dewey and Progressivism. Life-activity analysis has taken a wide variety of forms during the course of the twentieth century. Some men like Bobbitt and others have devoted their time to the development of principles of curricular revision, while others spent time on the selection of subject matter and grade level content. Virtually all the curriculum reformers have been influenced by the philosophical and educational ideas of John Dewey (1859-1952).

It was Dewey's belief that the content of education should include all subjects required for shaping the young in the pattern of the parent society. He urged, however, that the subjects taught to each child should be determined in the light of the interests and needs of that child. He maintained that since there was no single kind of subject matter, such as the classical languages, that ought to be mastered by everyone, all subjects should be available, since any student might prove interested in and capable of learning any subject.

Dewey's recommendations that all subjects be taught gained wide acceptance, and his followers used it to introduce into the schools many subjects of a practical and enjoyable kind that were alien to the traditional curriculum. The concepts of the "child centered" school and "life adjustment" education were extrapolations from Dewey's opinions and represented the enthusiasm with which many accepted his recommendations.

Organization of the Modern Curriculum

The seeking of either a logical or psychological organization of the modern curriculum gave rise to a number of theories or schemes of curricular reorganization that enjoyed varying degrees of popularity from time to time.

Culture-Epoch and Recapitulation Theories. The recapitulation or culture-epoch theory is closely associated with the name of the great American educational psychologist, G. Stanley Hall

(1846-1924). Earlier, in the nineteenth century, the German psychologist-philosopher, Johann Friedrich Herbart (1776-1841) had formulated the hypothesis that the beginnings of knowledge in the individual had to be in accord with the course of the genesis of the knowledge of the race. The statement of Darwin's theory of biological evolution led many to see a parallel in man's cultural development.[14]

Hall theorized that mental and physical life were parallel. The child, he held, in his growth and development repeated each stage in the evolution of the race. In this "recapitulation" theory the stages were as follows: the prenatal, the primitive, the savage, and the civilized stage. In human development he saw the history of racial development. He assumed that curriculum makers would be guided by this culture-epoch, or recapitulation theory. The culture-epoch theory was popular in American curriculum construction for a number of years before and after the turn of the twentieth century.

Correlation. A different, though not entirely unrelated, approach to curriculum construction was represented by the theory of correlation. The fundamental idea in this approach was to so arrange the subjects in the curriculum that instruction in one would correlate with instruction in the others. Psychologically, the concept was an updating of the Herbartian doctrine of apperception—the idea that the child learns new knowledge in terms of the old. Correlation also meant that learning could be made richer in meaning as well as more interesting. Correlation outlasted the culture-epoch theory in popularity, and even today those who talk in terms of an integrated curriculum are, in fact, thinking of a concept not very different from Herbart's theory of correlation.[15]

Integration. The most radical approach to curriculum construction in the twentieth century was represented in attempts to work out a curriculum where the child's experience was the integrating factor. Curricula integrated in terms of child experience went by various names, such as "integrated," "experience," "activity," and "project" curricula. In each case, however, the curriculum originated in the immediate life activities of the pupils themselves. While such programs were too advanced for most American public school systems, school educators developed compromise variations of the integrated curriculum. Among these compromises were the "broad fields" and "core" curricula.

The broad fields curriculum sought to fuse related subject matters into a few major fields of learning, such as the physical and life sciences, the social sciences, the humanities, and the fine arts. Characteristic of the broadfields curriculum were such courses as: general science, social studies, communication arts, orientation and survey courses.

The core curriculum sought to link together two or more broad fields of learning. The core occupied a large block of time, perhaps as much as one-third to one-half of the school day, and the core subjects had to be taken by all pupils.

Conservative Reaction. After World War II, the conservative attack on the schools unleashed by the "cold war" placed greater emphasis on the basic structure of the respective traditional subject matter disciplines, and upon conventional wisdom. College academicians again resumed leadership in curriculum councils.

Conclusion

In this chapter the attempt has been made to trace the evolution of the secondary school curriculum from its beginnings in Grecian times down to the present. In this process it has been shown how the curriculum has changed from a subject-matter curriculum to an activity curriculum, from a logically organized to a psychologically organized curriculum, and back again. In the succeeding chapters investigation will be made of each of the broad curricular areas of the modern American secondary school.

Chapter XIII
Footnotes

[1] John S. Brubacher, *A History of the Problems of Education* (New York: McGraw-Hill Book Company, 1966), pp. 244-245.

[2] *Ibid.*, p. 247.

[3] W. H. Woodward, *Vittorino da Feltre and Other Humanist Educators* (London: Cambridge University Press, 1897), p. 177: as quoted by Brubacher, *op. cit.*, p. 249.

[4] G. P. Gooch, *History and Historians* (Boston: Beacon Press, 1959), pp. 40-41.

[5] Brubacher, *op. cit.*, p. 263.

[6] Gooch, *op. cit.*, p. 377.

[7] Brubacher, *op. cit.*, p. 265.
[8] *Ibid.*, p. 266.
[9] *Ibid.*, p. 267.
[10] *Ibid.*, pp. 270-271.
[11] *Ibid.*, p. 272.
[12] *Ibid.*, pp. 273-275.
[13] See: Franklin Bobbitt, *How to Make a Curriculum* (New York: Houghton Mifflin Company, 1924).
[14] Brubacher, *op. cit.*, p. 295.
[15] *Ibid.*, p. 298.

Selected References

Alcorn, Marvin D., and James M. Linney. *Issues in Curriculum Development.* New York: Harcourt, Brace and World, Inc., 1959.

Bobbitt, Franklin. *How To Make a Curriculum.* New York: Houghton Mifflin Company, 1924.

Brubacher, John S. *A History of the Problems of Education.* New York: McGraw-Hill Book Company, 1966.

Bruner, Jerome S. *The Process of Education.* Cambridge, Massachusetts: Harvard University Press, 1960.

Childs, John L. *American Progressivism and Education.* New York: Holt, Rinehart and Winston, Inc., 1956.

Clark, Leonard H., and others. *The American Secondary School Curriculum.* New York: Collier-Macmillan Limited, 1965.

Dewey, John. *Democracy and Education.* New York: The Macmillan Company, 1916.

Gwynn, J. M. *Curriculum Principles and Social Trends.* New York: The Macmillan Company, 1960.

Henry, Nelson B. (ed.). *The Integration of Educational Experiences.* Fifty-seventh Yearbook, National Society for the Study of Education. Chicago: University of Chicago Press, 1958.

Passow, A. Harry (ed.). *Curriculum Crossroads.* New York: Bureau of Publications, Columbia University, 1962.

Taba, H. *Curriculum Development: Theory and Practice.* New York: Harcourt, Brace and World, Inc., 1962.

Chapter XIV

THE PLACE OF THE HUMANITIES IN THE SECONDARY SCHOOL CURRICULUM

The English Language Arts

Language is a system of symbols by which one individual can share experiences, ideas, and feelings with another. The goals of teaching the language arts are as old as Western civilization itself. When the first English colonists came to America, they brought with them English traditions, practices, and institutions. The early colonists organized secondary education around Latin grammar schools in imitation of the grammar schools of England. In view of the great emphasis placed on learning classical languages, English as a school subject was excluded from any serious study, and was either taught at home or in a "dame school" held by a housewife in her home.

The establishment of Franklin's Philadelphia Academy in 1751 with three departments—Latin, English, and Mathematics— marked the introduction of English classics into the curricula of American secondary schools. The emphasis of English literature in Franklin's Academy also resulted in attention being given to English grammar as a prescriptive school subject. Interest in English grammar as a curricular subject increased as the nineteenth century ran its course. By mid-nineteenth century such prestigious institutions of higher learning as Harvard and Yale accepted English studies for college entrance purposes. In 1892 the Conference on English, organized by the Committee of Ten of the National Education Association, recommended that English be pursued for five hours a week during the four years of high school training.

The most troublesome problem facing curriculum makers at the beginning of the twentieth century was that of determining best ways of establishing uniform college entrance requirements. In the year 1900 the College Entrance Examination Board was established. Earlier in 1897 the National Conference on Uniform Requirements in English issued a list of recommendations that suggested ways to organize instruction. As summarized, these recommendations included:

1. That a list of prescribed books be regarded as a basis for English courses.
2. That a certain amount of outside reading in poetry, fiction, biography, and history be encouraged in English courses.
3. That each of the books prescribed for study be taught with reference to:
   a. The language of the work;
   b. The plan of the work;
   c. The place of the work in literary history.[1]

In the second and third decades of the twentieth century studies of reading interest did much to focus research on the factors affecting the interest, appreciation, and meaning students get from their study of literature. Perhaps the first effective effort to reform the English curriculum came with the publication of the "Hosic Report" issued jointly by the National Council of Teachers of English and the National Education Association in 1917. This report declared that the doctrine of preparation for college is fallacious and emphasized the relating of knowledge to the experience of adolescents. The report also stressed command of the art of communication in speech and in writing, and thoughtful reading leading to taste in the independent selection of books.

Influenced by the instrumentalist philosophy of John Dewey and others, the National Council of Teachers of English created in 1929 a Curriculum Commission, and in 1935 this commission issued its report entitled, *An Experience Curriculum in English*. Stressing individual and group reading of literature, and freedom of book selection for students at any grade level, the report concluded that experiences through literature are the ultimate objective, and that these experiences are the only valid reason for the reading of literature.

In 1939 the English Council published a follow-up study called *Conducting Experiences in English* in which were compiled accounts of 274 English teachers over the four-year period following publication of the earlier work. Through these accounts it can be seen how teachers tried to adjust their courses to the philosophy that literature is the written expression of the ideas and emotions caused by man's reaction to life. Grammar, which was taught to improve written expression by students, was given a minor role.[2]

The twenties and thirties also saw an awakening of interest in the study of the English language, *per se*. While scientific investigations of American English did not revolutionize the teaching of grammar and usage in the schools, they caused English teachers to become more aware of the importance of live scientific observation and description of the spoken language.

In 1940 Charles Fries published the book *American English Grammar,* a work commissioned by the National Council of Teachers of English. Fries recommended that teachers base their instruction on an accurate description of the actual practices of informal standard English. Throughout the 1940's and '50's language study underwent considerable change as influenced by the writings of such men as Fries, Jespersen, Leonard, Marckward, Roberts, Chomsky, and others. All efforts to develop new grammars were basically an attempt to intrigue students with language, and make them aware of its power, richness, versality, and cultural implications.[3]

Today the English language arts occupy the most favored position in the American secondary-school curriculum. Fully nine-tenths of all high school pupils are enrolled in courses in the English language arts. No other academic subject enjoys such an advantageous position. Basically, the subject consists of four areas: reading, writing, speaking, and listening.

The oldest format for English instruction, and perhaps the one that is still used the most widely, is the study of the elements of English, including the analysis of literature. This is a subject-centered curriculum. The most common divisions of English as a discipline are the grammar, or structure, of the English language, the mechanics of composition, such as punctuation and capitalization, the fundamentals of composition, both oral and written, spelling, reading as a skill, and literature.[4]

The second pattern is the block-of-work plan sometimes referred to as units of work. Under this arrangement, the various subject materials to be covered for the year are examined and divided into logical segments. The content is blocked out in such a manner as to give balance and variety to the year's work, and at the same time provide for continuity of ideas.

The third traditional pattern of organization is the division of content into a semester of literature and a semester of composition and grammar. In this arrangement the literature is usually taught by literary types or in chronological order. The composition and grammar are usually interspersed in the other semester.[5]

Today, according to the Commission on the English Curriculum of the National Council of Teachers of English, the essential characteristic of an adequate program in the English language arts for the junior high school comprises rich and purposeful experience with speaking and writing, reading and listening, in situations and for purposes that are important to boys and girls of this age.[6] For most students English suddenly becomes a distinct academic subject in grade 7, when for the first time they have a special period, room, and teacher set apart for the study of English. By the seventh grade, students from reasonably literate backgrounds have a fair command of language. The teacher's task is to increase the sophistication of their language practice. In composition students at this level are making the important shift from content-mindedness to form-mindedness. They should be able to think not only in terms of saying something, but also in terms of stating correctly ideas as a whole. The junior high school grades cover quite a spectrum of physical and mental development in the lives of pupils. A major problem at this level is how to break down the distinction many students make between what they like to read and enjoy and what is sanctioned "adult literature." The essential requirement in literary studies is to get pupils to read more and enjoy reading more.

The basic aspects of a good senior high school program, according to the English Curriculum Commission, are:

1. Broad units around centers of interest and concern to the pupil.
2. A close relating of the program to the life and activities of the school.
3. Provision of electives to meet special interests.
4. An individualized program for each student developed on the basis of diagnostic data.[7]

Within the limits permitted by the size of the school and the competencies of the faculty, senior high school students should be able to elect from as rich a selection as possible of courses which combine literature with composition and with the continuing study of the English language. Courses focusing on literature or language or composition which neglect or slight either or both of the other two components of English do disservice to students and neglect the opportunity of strengthening understanding and competency which comes from unified instruction. All courses should be designed to increase students' abilities to appreciate significant literary works, and to express themselves adequately as speakers or writers.

English instruction at the junior college level today is mainly differentiated from programs at higher levels by its responsibility for serving the needs of the whole student group rather than for the preparation of specialists.

Recently a number of English curricular projects have been federally funded, including those at the Universities of Oregon, Illinois, Minnesota, Nebraska, and the Carnegie Institute of Technology. The Oregon Curriculum Study Center at the University of Oregon is preparing a curriculum in English for grades 7-12 which, so far, has emphasized language instruction, literature, and rhetoric. At the University of Illinois a study has been made of English programs in selected high schools which consistently educate outstanding students in English. In this study the investigators have sought to identify characteristics of superior English programs which might be emulated in other schools. A study of an experimental senior high school curriculum in English for able college-bound students has been made by the Carnegie Institute of Technology. Student performance in a senior high school sequential cumulative curriculum in English for college-bound students was compared with the performance of similar students taking traditional courses of instruction. The study concluded that the new program, while in many ways superior to programs with which it was compared, was found to be weakest in its composition program.

In 1968 the National Council of Teachers of English (NCTE) and the University of Illinois published a study funded by the U.S. Office of Education pointing out severe shortcomings in the teaching of English in the nation's high schools.[8] The study of 158 high schools located in forty-five states discovered that two of the areas of greatest weakness are reading and writing—both special targets of public criticism in recent years. These conclusions were based on detailed investigation of 1,600 classrooms in schools with far-better-than-average English programs. The study observed that there is little direct instruction in writing in spite of the fact that 16 per cent of class time in the studied schools is devoted to composition. Reading programs, according to the report, are inadequate, uncoordinated, and almost non-existent. These conclusions are considered by the study to be essentially valid for most high schools.

According to Clark and others, at this moment in time it would seem that the following statements could be made about the current status of the English language arts program in secondary schools: (1) remedial and developmental reading programs are beginning to gain some acceptance; (2) fostering enjoyment and critical judgment is the purpose behind the teaching of literature; and (3) composition instruction is aimed at the development of clear communication skills.[9]

The Foreign Language Arts

The Classical Languages

The international language from the fall of the Roman empire through the period of the Renaissance was Latin. For centuries thereafter, however, the classical languages of Latin and Greek occupied a central position in the secondary school curriculum. The genesis of the modern secondary school is to be found in the Latin grammar school organized at the time of the Renaissance and brought to this country by the colonists who settled here. The secondary schools which came after the decline of the Latin grammar school still continued the practice of offering instruction in the classical languages. The three-year sequence in classical Greek was first to disappear from the curriculum. Until 1926, when the College Entrance Board dropped its prescribed Latin requirements, the typical four-year high school Latin sequence looked as follows:

Grade 9: Intense study of grammar and vocabulary in order to prepare the pupils to read Caesar.
Grade 10: Caesar's *Gallic Wars*, Book I-VI.
Grade 11: Cicero, *Against Cataline*
    On Behalf of Pompey
    On Behalf of Archias the Poet
Grade 12: Virgil, *Aeneid*, Book I-VI.

In the 1920's, new goals were set for the teaching of Latin, and the four-year Latin sequence was reduced to two. Today, possessing a good Latin style is no longer the mark of the cultured gentleman, and modern Latin courses do not emphasize Latin composition. Instead, they concentrate on teaching pupils to read Latin directly and to develop it into clear idiomatic English. A definite attempt is made to relate instruction in Latin grammar with English grammar, and to inculcate the Latin origins of English. There is also the movement to make Latin more functional by including much study of Roman history and institutions.[10]

Modern Languages

In addition to the classical languages, French, German, and Spanish played an important role in the early cultural development of the United States. In the southwestern and southeastern parts of the country, religious orders taught Spanish as early as 1606. William Penn, in 1682, requested Germans to teach their language in local parochial schools. Benjamin Franklin introduced both French and

German into his Academy at Philadelphia in 1751. Throughout the nineteenth century the disciplinary aim of teaching languages was paramount. It was believed that foreign language instruction helped to discipline the mind, strengthen the memory, and develop logical thinking.

The report of the Committee of Twelve of the Modern Language Association, in 1898, described and evaluated the status of foreign language instruction. It accepted the four-fold aim of speaking, writing, aural understanding, and reading. Reading, the Committee found, was the skill that would bring the greatest good to the greatest number of students. By 1913 89 per cent of the institutions of higher education in the United States required a modern foreign language for entrance.

In the year 1924 a fact-finding investigation was begun into the status of the teaching of modern foreign languages. Called the Modern Language Study, and financed with a grant from the Carnegie Corporation, a large committee was formed to cover the United States and Canada, and subcommittees were set up in every region of the country. The basic report of the whole investigation was written by Professor Algernon Coleman, of Harvard University, and called *The Teaching of Modern Foreign Languages in the United States*. Interpreting data from thousands of questionnaires and from extensive surveys of student abilities, Coleman's book had a far-reaching effect on the teaching of foreign languages in secondary schools. He found great variability regarding the period in school and the age of the student at which modern language study was begun; also, that 83 per cent of the high school students studied a modern language for a period of two years only. He found that 50 per cent of the two-year language students and 30 per cent of the three-year students could not use the language for reading and writing, and he also found that investigations of the cultural content in foreign language classes exposed a great lack of appropriate material. Coleman recommended that a single objective, the development of the ability to read easily with comprehension, be the goal of foreign language study in the United States.

The period of the 1920's and the 1930's witnessed the introduction of general-language courses into the junior high school where the pupil was given a sampling of Latin, French, German, Spanish, and sometimes Italian in order to whet his appetite for foreign language study in high school. The foreign-language program of the Stanford Language Arts Investigation, begun in 1936, was designed to enrich the general educational experiences of all students, and therefore offered courses in English on foreign cultures and literatures as well as unified programs which fused foreign languages, English, social studies, art, music, and dramatics. This study revealed that there was an increase of 300 per cent in the number of students who continued foreign-language classes beyond the usual two years, and that also among the students there was considerable gain in knowledge and information about the country and its people.[11]

When the report of the Eight Year Study of the Progressive Education Association was issued in 1942, it included the recommendation that foreign languages be made special interest subjects for college-bound students only.[12] Many language teachers, however, continued to believe that modern language study had a role to play in educating all students for international understanding.

In 1941 the Committee on the Language Program of the American Council of Learned Societies developed a plan devised by linguistic scientists called "The Intensive Language Program." This plan, designed for possible military and diplomatic use, presented a foreign language in practical situations; and the student, instead of learning rules of grammar, commits to memory phrases and sentences through drill and repetition. Hearing and imitating a native speaker helps the student understand and speak the language. In 1942 the Armed Forces established specialized language-training programs based on the aural-oral approach of the linguistic scientists.[13] Educators soon discovered in these programs important implications for the future of modern-language teaching in the schools.

The University of Chicago, in 1944, initiated an investigation of foreign language teaching under a grant from the Rockefeller Foundation. The purpose of the study was to compare conventional classes not stressing aural-oral objectives with experimental classes emphasizing these skills. Results from the investigation indicated that the experimental groups performed significantly better aurally; however, in reading skills they were usually significantly poorer. On speaking ability the experimental groups were superior to the conventional groups. What the study thus suggested was that aural-oral competence did not automatically create reading ability.[14]

In 1953 the Rockefeller Foundation also underwrote the six-year Foreign Language Program of the Modern Language Association. The purpose of this study was to survey the status of modern language instruction in this country and to produce means to improve it. Extensive surveys were made of high school certification requirements and foreign language enrollments. Over fifty conferences have been held on the problems of language instruction, and numerous teacher-guides and other materials have been produced.

In recent years the trend in foreign language instruction has definitely been toward the aural-oral approach. Because it seems that the proper use of good recorded material can improve the effectiveness of the audio-oral operations, many secondary schools are investing in language laboratories. How much schools should spend for complicated and expensive laboratories is still problematic. While a good teacher can teach well by the aural-oral method without them, the laboratories provide opportunities for reinforcement of the aural-oral approach. With the trend toward semi-intensive courses emphasizing speaking skills, the high schools in general offer a four-year program. Students take as much as their aptitude and interests permit with a minimum of two years required to obtain credit. There are, however, programs in the states of New York and California, and perhaps elsewhere, for six-year sequences for modern language study in the secondary school.

Despite the advances made in foreign-language instruction since the end of World War II, modern language teaching in the secondary school remained bleak until the passage of NDEA in 1958. A majority of all public high schools in the United States offered no modern language instruction. About 30 per cent of the public high schools enrolled fewer than 100 students in the modern language curriculum. Modern-language experience was almost negligible in the junior high school where the time is considered to be appropriate for exploration in all subject-matter areas. The National Defense Education Act of 1958 began to change that bleak picture by providing for federal funding of modern language programs in secondary schools.

Speech and Journalism

Speech Education

The classical tradition in speech education comes largely from such Graeco-Roman educators as Plato, Aristotle, Cicero, and Quintilian. This tradition was rediscovered at the time of the Renaissance, and was later carried on by the English rhetorician Edmund Wilson and others. Early American schools recognized the virtues of training in speech. Contributions to the subject were made by such eminent statesmen and educators as John Quincy Adams, who for a time held the Chair of Rhetoric and Oratory at Harvard, President John Witherspoon at Princeton, and Chauncy Allen Goodrich of Yale University. Declamation and debating were also among the more common subjects in the academies.

By the end of the nineteenth century, speech education consisted mainly of courses in elocution, debating, rhetoric, and public speaking. These courses were taught primarily at the university level. What speech education there was in the secondary school was of an elocutionary nature. As time went on, courses in the speech arts and speech sciences developed with increased emphasis on phonetics, speech pathology, and speech psychology. High schools throughout the nation began to expand their offerings in speech, especially in the area of public speaking and debating.

Today speech is taught as a subject-matter course, and in integrated programs of various kinds in secondary schools. Speech programs are included in special education for the retarded and handicapped, and in regular curricular and co-curricular activities for high achievers. However, recognition of speech education in the secondary school has been widely variable. Some schools have a rich and extensive program, whereas others have little or none. Only a few states have a program of substantial speech training in more than 60 per cent of the high schools.[15]

Journalism

Journalism is defined as the collecting and editing of material of current interest for presentation through the media of newspapers, magazines, radio, or television. The scope of the field and the vagueness of its limits are emphasized by the number of men in the United States who gained equal fame as journalists and statesmen: Benjamin Franklin, Alexander Hamilton, Theodore Roosevelt, John F. Kennedy; and in Europe, William Gladstone, Winston Churchill, Richelieu, and Clemenceau.

The first program in the preparation of young men for journalism was proposed by President Robert E. Lee of Washington College (later Washington and Lee University) at Lexington, Virginia, in 1869. It was not until 1879 at the University of Missouri that journalism became a university course. The Wharton School of Business in the University of Pennsylvania in 1893 offered the first curriculum in journalism in 1893. The first regularly organized school of journalism was established at the University of Missouri in 1908.

The secondary schools which offer instruction in journalism give it in one of three places: as a part of the regular English courses, as an extracurricular activity, or as a special course. Journalism is a special form of writing or composition. The typical publication is the school paper. Other publications of the school in which pupils may take an active part are a school magazine, the annual, and a handbook. The influence of the motion picture, TV, and radio on the pupil's life have caused and will continue to cause the expansion of the study of such courses as journalism on the secondary school level.

Conclusion

The term humanities comes from the philosophy of education common to the fourteenth, fifteenth, and sixteenth centuries called humanism. Humanism stresses the study of Roman and Greek languages, literatures, and civilization. It is the view that man is the measure of all things and that all being and truth are relative to man. Today, the term is used to designate such courses in the secondary-school curriculum as literature, language, speech, and journalism, and in this way thus distinguishing the humanities from the social sciences on the one hand, and the natural and physical sciences on the other. The purpose of this chapter has been to trace and to investigate the role which the humanities plays in the development of the curriculum of the American secondary school.

Chapter XIV
Footnotes

[1] William H. Evans, and Jerry L. Walker, *New Trends in the Teaching of English in Secondary Schools* (Chicago: Rand-McNally and Company, 1966), p. 8.

[2] *Ibid.*, p. 13.

[3] *Ibid.*, p. 25.

[4] Geneva Hanna Pilgrim, *Learning and Teaching Practices in English* (New York: The Center for Applied Research in Education, Inc., n.d.), pp. 17-18.

[5] *Ibid.*, pp. 18-19.

[6] The Commission on the English Curriculum, *The English Language Arts* (New York: Appleton-Century-Crofts, Inc., 1952), p. 128.

[7] *Ibid.*, p. 134.

[8] See The National Study of High School English Programs, *High School English Instruction Today* (New York: Appleton-Century-Crofts, 1968).

[9] Leonard H. Clark, and others, *The American Secondary School Curriculum* (New York: The Macmillan Company, 1965), pp. 210-211.

[10] *Ibid.*, p. 235.

[11] Emma M. Birknaier, "Modern Languages," *Encyclopedia of Educational Research* (3rd ed.), 684.

[12] See Wilford M. Aiken, *The Story of the Eight Year Study* (New York: McGraw-Hill, Inc., 1942), pp. 1-24.

[13] Emma M. Birknaier, "Modern Languages," *Encyclopedia of Educational Research* (3rd ed.), 684.

[14] *Ibid.*, p. 866.

[15] Franklin H. Knowes, "Speech," *Encyclopedia of Educational Research* (3rd ed.), 1935.

Selected References

California State Department of Education. *English Language Framework for California Public Schools.* Sacramento, California: The Department, 1968.

Christensen, Francis. *Notes Toward a New Rhetoric.* New York: Harper and Rowe Publishers, 1967.

Coleman, Algernon. *The Teaching of Modern Foreign Languages in the United States.* New York: The Macmillan Company, 1929.

DeBoer, John J., and others. *Teaching Secondary English.* New York: McGraw-Hill Book Company, 1951.

Evans, William H., and Jerry L. Walker. *New Trends in the Teaching of English in Secondary Schools.* Chicago: Rand McNally and Company, 1966.

Fries, Charles C. *Linguistics and Reading.* New York: Holt, Rinehart and Winston, Inc., 1963.

Gleason, H. A., Jr. *Linguistics and English Grammar.* New York: Holt, Rinehart and Winston, Inc., 1965.

Hatfield, Walter W. (Ed.) *An Experience Curriculum in English.* New York: Appleton-Century-Crofts, 1935.

Hook, Julius N. *The Teaching of High School English.* New York: The Ronald Press, 1950.

Hosic, James F. (Compiler). *Reorganization of English in Secondary Schools.* U.S. Bureau of Education Bulletin 1917, No. 2. Government Printing Office, 1917.

Johnston, Marjorie C. (Ed.) *Modern Foreign Languages in the High School.* Government Printing Office, 1958.

Loban, Walter D. *Language Ability: Grades Seven, Eight, and Nine.* Washington, D.C.: U.S. Department of Health, Education and Welfare, 1966.

National Council of Teachers of English, Commission on the English Curriculum. *The English Language Arts.* New York: Appleton-Century-Crofts, Inc., 1952.

National Council of Teachers of English, Commission on the English Curriculum. *The English Language Arts in the Secondary School.* New York: Appleton-Century-Crofts, 1956.

Pilgrim, Geneva Hanna. *Learning and Teaching Practices in English.* New York: The Center for Applied Research in Education, Inc., n.d.

Robinson, Karl F. *Teaching Speech in the Secondary School.* New York: Longmans, 1954.

Stockwell, Robert P., and J. Donald Bowen. *The Sounds of English and Spanish.* Also: Stockwell, Robert P., J. Donald Bowen, and John W. Martin. *The Grammatical Structures of English and Spanish.* Chicago: University of Chicago Press, 1965.

The National Study of High School English Programs. *High School English Instruction Today.* New York: Appleton-Century-Crofts, 1968.

Wallace, Karl R. (Ed.) *History of Speech Education in America.* New York: Appleton-Century-Crofts, 1954.

Weaver, Andrew T., and others. *The Teaching of Speech.* Englewood Cliffs, New Jersey: Prentice-Hall, 1952.

Chapter XV

THE PLACE OF HISTORY AND THE SOCIAL SCIENCES IN THE SECONDARY SCHOOL CURRICULUM

Introduction: The Social Sciences and the Social Studies

The social sciences are organized bodies of knowledge built up from the formal, scholarly, and advanced studies which deal with human beings and their interrelationships. They are concerned with the detailed, systematic, and theoretical study of human relationships. They provide a perspective within which human relationships may be described, classified, and explained. History, when considered a social science, is the oldest of the studies of human relationships and is the root from which all the others have grown. Briefly, history may be described as the study of past human experience organized in chronological sequence. Cultural anthropology is the study of the customs, folklore, social activities, and organizations resulting from man's reaction to his environment. Geography as a social science is a study to describe and explain man's environment, both natural and cultural. Economics deals with the material aspects of satisfying human desires. Political science is the study of the field of organized control of human society by means of government. And, finally, but by no means least, sociology is the study of the forms, institutions, and functions of human groups.

The social studies are the social science subjects taught in the elementary and secondary schools. They consist of those portions of the social sciences which are selected, simplified, and adapted for the purpose of instruction in the pre-collegiate grades. The difference between the social sciences and the social studies is one of purpose and degree of difficulty rather than in the nature of their content. Both deal with human relationships, but the social studies are simplified and presented so as to provide for the introductory study into the social sciences. The chief aim of the social studies is instructional utility.

History and the Social Studies Curriculum

Origins of History

History is one of the most widespread subjects taught in the pre-collegiate grades. Basically, history is the systematic written record of human events including a philosophical explanation of the cause and origin of such events.

Those ancient Athenian scholars, Herodotus and Thucydides, are considered to be the founders of history. The scientific spirit and artistic sense of these men enabled them to cast their material in the best of literary form. The Roman historians who also combined the conceptions of science and art in writing history include Sallust, Tacitus, and Livy. The Middle Ages produced a number of historical writers, but the essential conditions of modern historical study did not yet exist. Printing was unknown, books were scarce, and the critical treatment of documents had not begun.

A new spirit was reflected in the field of historical study with the coming of the Renaissance. Petrarch and Boccaccio were the fathers of modern historiography, and the Florentine scholar, Bruni, was the first historian to employ the principle of historical criticism. But it was the German scholar Barthold Georg Niebuhr (1776-1831) who raised history from its subordinate role as a branch of literature to the dignity of an independent science.[1]

In the nineteenth century the science of history came into its own. The techniques of research were perfected, and groups of scholars grew into national or international associations. Such men as Jared Sparks, George Bancroft, and Henry Adams are considered as founders of the American school of history.

Evolution of American History in the Secondary School Curriculum

American history is a required subject in the public school curriculum. U.S. history today is taught at two levels in the secondary school as well as offered in the junior college. Before reaching the secondary school the pupil has had work in American history materials at different levels in the elementary grades.

Phillips Exeter Academy in 1818 was perhaps the first school in the United States to include American history in the secondary school curriculum. In the years that followed increasing numbers of academies and high schools adopted the subject. Textbooks in history soon followed. John McCullock's *History of America* was published in 1787, and in 1820 the American Academy of Languages and Belles Lettres offered an award for the best textbook in American history for academies and schools. Public interest in American history was also shown by the fact that state laws required its teaching. The first such statutes were enacted in Massachusetts and Vermont in 1827, and by the time of the Civil War instruction in U.S. history was required by law in five states.

Educators and college academicians were also interested in the teaching of U.S. history in the public schools. American history was first required for college entrance by the University of California in 1868. In 1869, the National Teachers' Association, predecessor of the National Education Association, adopted a resolution urging more extensive teaching of the subject in the public schools. The Committee of Ten of the NEA in 1893 recommended U.S. history be taught in the eleventh grade, and there the subject has remainded ever since at the senior high school level.

The very influential Committee of Seven, of the American Historical Association, in 1899 recommended that the teaching of civil government be added to the high school American history course. This plan continued to be the standard offering in American high schools until well into the decade of the 1920's. The AHA established in 1926 a Commission on the Social Studies. This Commission produced an impressive series of reports in which numerous social scientists and educators summarized what they considered important concepts and attitudes which ought to be communicated to high school youth. Among the writers of the reports were Charles A. Beard, George S. Counts, Carleton Hayes, and Ernest Horn. Although the Commission made an exhaustive study of a curricular area, it did not issue a recommended curricular program.

The formal study of the history of the United States normally begins for the pupil in the elementary school in grade 5. The character of this study varies from school to school. It may encompass a biographical approach, a narrative approach, or it may be geographically oriented, or even a combination of approaches may be used. In most situations, however, it is the earlier periods of the history of the United States which are emphasized.

The second exposure of the student to the formal study of U.S. history usually occurs in grade 8. This course tends to be a comprehensive history. In order to make it somewhat more manageable, fewer topics are presently attempted, and in some cases a real effort is made to structure the course in terms of student interest at this grade level.

The senior high school U.S. history course is most often taught at grade 11. Every state in the Union requires this course for high school graduation. It is again a comprehensive history, and at the present time many schools are attempting to redefine the proper scope of the course. The junior college course in American history is usually also a broad comprehensive year's course.

In many secondary schools in the decades since the late 1920's, American history materials have often been correlated and integrated with materials from other social sciences, or even with broad fields of learning outside the social sciences. American history, geography, and civics are the social science subjects more commonly integrated. The junior high school has been the major citadel of core programs. The junior high school U.S. history course has been the level where socio-economic material is stressed. The senior high school course in U.S. history continues to be the one where political developments are most strongly emphasized.

The Development of the World History Course

The world history course which is normally taught in the grade 10 seems to have been a development which has occurred in the period between the two world wars of this century. The course has never been recommended by a committee of national scope on which there were any historians. It has always found its strongest supporters among school administrators who wanted to find a way to keep history other than American in the secondary school curriculum.

The Committee of Seven of the American Historical Association has recommended in 1899 a sequence of subjects designed to give the student an appreciation of the culture and civilization of Western Europe and America. The four courses proposed were: ancient history to the year 800 A.D., medieval and modern history, English history, and American history and civil government. Until the twenties this was the program of historical studies found in most high schools in the land.

The Report of the Commission on the Reorganization of Secondary Education issued in 1916 probably stimulated the world history movement.[2] This report recommended that ancient and medieval history be consolidated into a one-year course, and that a second history sequence ought to be a year's course in European history from the seventeenth century to the present. The new approach suggested by the Commission did not immediately replace the pattern of the old Committee of Seven. Gradually, however, the schools consolidated the recommended two-year sequence into a one-year world history course. A study of history courses in the junior college shows the world history course to be primarily a survey of Western civilization, or it is superseded by more specialized history offerings.

Most of the criticism of the high school world history course is based on the conviction that its scope is too great to be dealt with in any meaningful fashion in a one-year course. What began as a course in Western European history has been enlarged to include other culture areas. The result may be that the student, after a year's work, has acquired little more than hazy generalizations and scattered, and often isolated, information.

There is general agreement that a thorough revision is needed in the teaching of world history on the high school level. There is also general agreement that high school students ought to get a broad understanding of the world's main civilizations. Philosophers and historians have made numerous attempts to discover general patterns of development or general laws governing history. These attempts at macrohistory have not usually been well received by the history profession. Yet, in the face of the threat of world-wide atomic holocaust, ever increasing international pressures and tensions, and the revolutionary advances of mass communications, a new approach to the writing and teaching of world history is imperative.[3]

Anthropology in the Social Studies Curriculum

Anthropology is rarely taught as a separate subject in secondary schools. Among the established disciplines of the social sciences, anthropology is young. Much of the century of anthropological research has been devoted to the task of accumulating information about human customs and characteristics from which a mature theoretical system can be constructed. Since anthropology is a study of man, its affinity to history is obvious, and most anthropologists would consider human culture history to be a central concern of anthropology.

The anthropological concept of culture as the total way of life of a people can be of great value in teaching history and other social studies in secondary schools. Shortly after World War II social studies and history teachers began to be increasingly interested in anthropology. The war had brought Americans into much more intimate contact with non-Western societies and cultures. Both teachers and students felt the need to gain a better understanding of non-Western peoples. Existing social studies curricula provided few tools for this purpose. There was hope, however, that anthropology would shed light and help, and supply materials to accomplish this task. Many educators, including anthropologists, felt the principal contribution of anthropology was development of understanding of other cultures in their own terms.

The contribution of anthropology to the social studies has been largely the product of the interest of individual teachers, and in some instances of particular school systems. These efforts may be summarized as follows: (1) institution of courses in anthropology at the high school level, developed to a considerable degree in private schools; and (2) the application of certain anthropological concepts to the organization and analysis of traditional social studies materials at the secondary level. In 1954, a Stanford University conference identified four subject areas of anthropological knowledge of possible use in the schools. These were: cultural dynamics, the biological base of behavior, personality in culture, and cross-cultural education. Since then an increasing number of articles and books have dealt with various aspects of anthropology in relation to education.

In recent years concerted efforts have been made to introduce anthropological concepts and materials into the schools. The Anthropology Curriculum Study Project initiated in 1962 by the American Anthropological Association has as its principal tasks the definition of the role of anthropology in the high school curriculum, and the preparation of material to fulfill that role. The Project has prepared two units designed for World history courses either at grades 9 or 10. A sixteen-week course titled Patterns in *Human History: An Anthropological Perspective* is now also ready. A second major project is the Anthropology Curriculum Project at the University of Georgia that is engaged in preparing units for a sequential curriculum in anthropology for grades 1 through 7.

Geography and the Social Studies Curriculum

Geography as a social science has distinctive contributions to make to the secondary school social studies curriculum, whether it is offered separately or in an integrated part of the social studies. Geography is the study of man as an inhabitant of the earth, and of earth as the home of man. Geography uses data, concepts, and insights from the humanities, natural sciences, and the other social sciences. The geographer, although using different perspectives is, like the historian and anthropologist, interested in the total, integrated human experience.

Geography uses the methods of logical thought developed by the ancient Greeks, and also the concepts evolved by experimental science. The geographers of ancient Greece and Rome were concerned principally with three kinds of problems: (1) they sought to identify and describe those physical and human features that gave distinctive character to different countries; (2) they tried to find ways to fix the position of the earth accurately, and to measure the earth as a whole and also in its various details; and (3) they wanted to build theories regarding the origin of the things they observed. One of the great accomplishments of the Greeks was the calculation of the earth's circumference by Eratosthenes (c. 276-194 B.C.) working at the Museum at Alexandria. Making use of the principles of geometry and observations of the angle of the sun above the horizon on June 21, he reached a figure for the earth's circumference that was almost exact.[4]

Graeco-Roman knowledge of geography, almost lost during the early medieval period, was rediscovered during the Renaissance. The main stream of geographic scholarship was first given its modern direction by the German scholars Alexander von Humboldt (1769-1859) and Karl Ritter (1779-1859). During the twentieth century, geographic investigation has moved away from the type of encyclopedic descriptions characteristic of German scholarship during the nineteenth century, and is now organized more around problems of cause and effect relationships. Aerial photography and other technological developments, such as space explorations in the decade of the sixties, now make geographic studies almost as precise as statistics.

Geography was perhaps the first of the social studies to emerge as a separate subject in American schools. Jedediah Morse's *Geography Made Easy* was published in 1784. This book, as well as other geographies which followed, also included information about the history of the areas described. By the time of the Civil War geography was a popular offering in the elementary schools, and the textbooks published during the period suggest the emphasis was on physical geography. Around the turn of the century, geography enjoyed brief success in the high schools, but this effort was short-lived because the new general science courses absorbed much of what had been taught about physical geography.

At the present time students in grade 7 of the junior high school are most likely to study the geography of various countries or regions of the world together with a considerable amount of relevant history. Either the Eastern or Western Hemispheres may be stressed, depending on what has been taught in the preceding grade. A junior high course in world geography in which global concepts may be taught is found in some schools, particularly at grade 9. There is reason to believe that ninth grade world geography is displacing the traditional course in civics taught at this grade level. In the senior high school geography is an offering in the twelfth grade in some schools. The course may also be a multiple-grade elective in high school.

Curriculum revision in geography is presently being studied in two projects, both of which involve the National Council for Geographic Education. The first is an attempt to describe a geography curriculum for grades K-12 and will include recommendations for units, materials, and teaching procedures at each grade level. The High School Geography Project, of which the Association of American Geographers is a co-sponsor, has prepared and tested materials for secondary schools.

The High School Geography Project was initiated in 1961. The Project is designing a course which will present fundamental geographical ideas, leading the students by inductive methods to discover basic concepts for themselves. Two units, one on urban-geography and one in the geography of the fresh water resource, have been prepared. Eight more units are contemplated, and they will be accompanied by such teaching adis as films and filmstrips, teachers' manuals, tests, maps, overlays, supplementary readings, etc. Though the units are planned to fit into an integrated course, each unit is packaged separately to permit individual selection.

In the study of geography the social studies teacher has an exceptional opportunity to help youth deal with interrelationships, fit parts into wholes, and grasp larger conceptual relationships. Many understandings from other social studies can be illuminated through geographical insights.

Economics in the Social Studies Curriculum

The objective of economics in the social studies curriculum is the development of economic understanding necessary for responsible citizenship in today's world. Economic understanding serves many purposes both functional and cultural. In a democratic society concerned with issues of political economy, broad economic understanding may well become crucial to the life of that society.

Economics is the social science that studies how men employ productive resources to produce various commodities and distribute them for consumption. The purpose of the economist is to describe, analyse, explain, and correlate economic phenomena. Economics starts with the simple premise that man's material wants and desires are infinite, but his productive resources are clearly finite. The fact of scarce resources poses the over-all economic problem.

Economics began as a social science with the publication of Adam Smith's work, *The Wealth of Nations,* in the year of the American Revolution, 1776. Within a few years, scholars were studying political economy in British universities. During most of the eighteenth century the economic policy in Europe reflected the thinking of a group of theorists known as "mercantilists." These men advocated centralized control of the economy to promote the economic interests of the state.

Adam Smith, (1712-1790), not only denied mercantile theory, but argued for its opposite. He held that the economic well-being of the nation would be most advanced if government would deliberately refrain from economic policy-making and control. Smith's policy of minimum governmental interference in economic matters has been given the name, "laissez faire." At a time when political democracy was spreading, Smith voiced concern for the economic well-being of all members of society. What he called "national wealth" is very close to what is now called the "national income," or the gross production of goods and services. Smith hypothesized that, as capitalists save and invest these savings, they will hire more labor to expand their output and wages will rise. What he predicted was the harmonious development of all classes rising together with the welfare of the nation as a whole.[5]

The ideas of Smith were advanced and elaborated on by the prominent English financier David Ricardo (1772-1823). Ricardo was an advocate of free trade. Free trade, he said, would lead to expanded agricultural imports as the population grew and the economy developed. Ricardo's curate friend was the Reverend Thomas Malthus (1766-1834), who was the first English economist to treat the problem of depressions. Malthus was not convinced that the free-enterprise market economy would continue in a smoothly uninterrupted fashion. He foresaw that, as economic development continued, there was the possibility of general over-production which involved a flood of commodities without buyers.[6]

John Stuart Mill (1806-1873) was the leading British economist of the mid-nineteenth century. For Mill, economic systems were not fixed or mechanical, but could experience evolutionary growth. By

Mill's time the economic theory of laissez faire developed by Smith, Ricardo, and Malthus had become the policy of the nation-state. Mill, representing the end of the line of thinking about economic development which began with Smith, reached the conclusion that occasional intelligent intervention by the government in restricted areas of the economy was desirable, but he did not develop a formal analysis to explain where and how this governmental interference should take place.[7]

Whereas Mill took an evolutionary approach to economic reform the view of Karl Marx (1818-1883) was a revolutionary one. Adapting the dialectic of the German philosopher Hegel, Marx developed his tenet of the rise and fall of social systems. Marx saw the fundamental contradiction in capitalism as being the exploitation of labor. In an effort to protect their profits, Marx insisted that capitalists would introduce labor-saving machinery, throwing men out of work. Although the output of goods would continue to increase, the unemployed would have no income with which to buy these goods, and ultimately the system would be overthrown by a revolution.

From Adam Smith to Mill and Marx there was a common view of economic analysis in what is called the classical school of economics. These men believed that a relatively few simple principles would suffice to explain the workings of the economic system. In classical economics the problem was that of the ideal type of economic system and the role of government within it.[8]

Between 1870 and 1930 the leading West European and American economists developed what is now called the neoclassical school of economic thought. Drawing from the works of the classical economists, these scholars produced many improvements and refinements in economic concepts and analysis, and their work contributed much to the understanding of the way in which a free enterprise economic system functions.

During the depression decade of the 1930's the economic theories and policies advanced by the British economist John Maynard (Lord) Keynes (1883-1946) came to prominence. It was the view of the Keynesian school that in the event of a severe depression, if the capitalistic economy was not to stagnate and mass unemployment was not to become chronic, government must stimulate spending or create investments to assure full employment.

Since the 1930's, further important contributions have been made to the growing body of economic knowledge. This extension of knowledge has required a much greater degree of specialization within economics. In each of these areas of modern specialization, developments reflect attempts to increase understanding of particular aspects of economic behavior. Although starting from a common heritage, each specialty has developed knowledge and techniques appropriate to its own field.

The study of economics has traditionally received less attention than other social sciences in the secondary school curriculum. History and geography were recognized as fields of scholarship that might deserve a place in the secondary school curriculum by the Committee of Ten in 1892. Thus, these subjects had a head start on the younger, less well-established social science disciplines. Teachers were then trained to teach the subjects which were being taught. Even today, comparatively few teachers in high school social studies departments have the necessary training to introduce formal courses in economics in their schools.

Since the late 1940's, however, economics has become more widely offered in high schools. New political and economic ideologies once limited mostly to academic discussions have become threatening realities. Militant Communism, first adopted by the Soviet Union and later by China, posed a threat to the nation from without, and some Americans began to suspect a Communist danger from within. The greatly increased impact of government activity on the economy, and the increasing penetration of government into the affairs of citizens, have caused social studies teachers to emphasize the economic aspects of contemporary America in courses of history and government as well as in economics classes.

Courses in economics in high schools are generally offered at grade 12 where the offerings are frequently elective and run the gamut of the social studies field. The course in economics may be a rather simple how-to-do-it offering in consumer economics, or it may deal with economic problems, or it may be a more sophisticated course modeled after college courses in principles of economics.

While social studies teachers, unfortunately, have had little or no training in economics, several organizations have been trying to provide help. The most active of these is the Joint Council on Economic Education, founded in 1949 with private support. The Council has published such items as resource units and bibliographies, and has conducted a number of workshops and other programs in economics for teachers. Also, the Council for the Advancement of Secondary Education, founded in 1952, has made studies of needs in the field of economic education and has issued publications designed for high school students. More recently the American Economic Association created a Commission on Economic

Education which has cooperated with the Committee for Economic Development in formulating a statement regarding economics in the schools.

Political Science and the Social Studies Curriculum

Political science, or civics, as it is generally called in the pre-collegiate grades, has been a vital force in the social studies curriculum from the beginning. The study of political affairs is one of the oldest of all academic disciplines, although modern political science is a product of the twentieth century. More than two thousand years ago Plato's political treatise, called the *Republic,* proposed an ideal form of political organization.

Political science, as a social science, is concerned with the institutionalized forms of power functions in the body politic, and the behavior of people with respect to these institutions. The political scientist examines his subject from at least four perspectives:

1. He studies the processes, behavior, and institutions of political systems in order to make systematic generalizations and explanations about political phenomena.
2. He seeks generalizations about relations among political systems, especially the politics of nations in the international system.
3. He studies the end products, the public policies, of the political processes.
4. He studies the ideas and doctrines about government and the political system.[9]

The first professor of political science in this country was Francis Lieber (1800-1872), who came to Columbia University in the year 1858. Until the last quarter of the nineteenth century American scholars were trained in German universities, and the teaching of political science in American universities did not become common until the close of the century. Political science came of age in the United States with the founding of the American Political Science Association in 1903. Over its relative short history, American political science has been deeply influenced by a number of scholarly attitudes.

The first of these attitudes is reflected in the tradition of legalism. The concern here is with legal and constitutional frameworks, with formal legal institutions, with legal rights and powers. Another attitude is that of activism and reform. This school of thought arose when political scientists joined with reform groups to bring their wisdom to bear on the governmental problems of the day. The third of these major currents is the philosophical tradition. Political theorists, through an examination of the classics of political philosophy from Plato to the present, have sought to examine the question as to what is the good life and to identify the political arrangements which would best promote and insure it. Finally, there is the influence of science in political science. This approach is based on the belief that empirical observations of actual behavior and processes would yeild verifiable propositions about the political system. Despite their different orientations to political phenomena, these schools of thought have a common direction. They are all concerned with political and governmental institutions and processes.[10]

The traditional term for denoting the teaching of political science in the pre-collegiate grades is civics. Civics, when used in its broad sense, includes the study of the Constitution, the structure of American government on federal, state, and local levels, and citizenship education. Textbooks in government and civics were published in the United States before the close of the eighteenth century. These early works emphasized the Constitution and the national government, and were generally partisan in character. Up to the time of the Civil War, instruction continued to stress the Constitution and the federal government, and also tended to emphasize the Northern point of view. By 1900 the subject of civil government was generally taught in grades 7 or 8. In 1899 the American Historical Association's Committee of Seven had proposed that American history and civil government be taught as part of the four-year social studies sequence for high schools, and this proposal became the standard offering in American high schools for almost thirty years.[11]

An examination of the political science offerings in the secondary school today reveals that civics of some kind is the most widely offered course at grade 9. The content of this course varies widely from school to school, and ranges from a standard course in the structure and function of the United States, state, and local governments, to a course in community life, processes, and problems. Some type of vocational and educational guidance is usually included in this offering. At the high school, and in grade 12, the leading offering has been a course in the problems of democracy, although at the present time its position is strongly challenged by the course in American government, which incidentially is a required course in the senior year in many states. The course in problems of democracy was originally concerned with domestic problems, and was a more or less integrated offering in economics, sociology, and political science. The government course at the twelfth grade is usually a more formal offering than the civics taught at lower grade levels.[12]

Several projects in civic education have been undertaken recently, which may indicate new directions in the teaching of political science in secondary schools. One is the Lincoln Filene Center Citizenship Study at Tufts University. The aim of this project is to produce materials in different ideologies, world affairs, civil liberties, and practical politics for use in high schools. The second, sponsored by the Eagleton Institute of Politics and the Fund for the Advancement of Education, is concerned with the preparation of materials for the course in the problems of democracy. A third project is the publication series called *Judgment* issued by the National Council for the Social Studies. This publication is concerned with the preparation of case histories of democracy at work, as exemplified by decisions and opinions of the U.S. Supreme Court.

Finally, and not to be overlooked, is the aid to teachers of civics, and the definition of civics provided for in Title III of the National Defense Education Act of 1964. Civics is defined as including the teaching of the function as well as the structure of American government at all levels, including the impact on government of current developments at home and abroad. The law also lends support to interdisciplinary investigations, including the study of international affairs which have a direct influence in shaping American life, and the ferreting out of such information as will lead to greater understanding of the responsibilities of citizens in a democracy.

The direction of civic education in secondary schools today would seem to be the obtaining of information, the instilling of faith and loyalty, and the acquisition of skills. Campbell and Nichols summarize the objectives of training for citizenship into the following important behaviors:

1. To show concern for the welfare and dignity of others.
2. To support constitutional rights and liberties of all individuals.
3. To help maintain law and order.
4. To know the main structure and functions of our governments.
5. To seek school and community improvement through active democratic participation.
6. To understand problems of international relations.
7. To support rationality in communication, thought, and action on school and community problems.

8. To take responsibility for their own personal development and excellence.
9. To help and respect their own families.[13]

Sociology in the Social Studies Curriculum

Sociology is seldom taught as a separate course in the social studies curriculum of the secondary school, although much sociological information is spread throughout other social studies courses. Sociology, as a social science, may be defined as the scientific study of society. The sociologist studies the consistencies or patterns of behavior which humans manifest as they are oriented to each other and as they share common values. The sociologist studies social groupings, like the family, the tribe, or the nation, and why they persist over time, why they change or fall apart. And the sociologist studies the relationships among group members and among groups.

In seeking to find principles of social behavior, the sociologist seeks also to discover their causes. Since the end of the nineteenth century the sociologist has abandoned single-cause theories of social behavior, whether they be environmental, economic, or other theories of determinism. He finds that both the causes and effects of such behavior are very complex. He finds that any social event is the result of a multiplicity of causes. Similarly, he finds all institutions of society are interrelated over time. One intriguing question he faces is the following: will he be able to discover a sociological generalization that will delineate a theory of multiple causation and also explain the interrelationships of institutions? Such generalizations are, indeed, rare.

Sociology was given its name and directions by the nineteenth century social philosopher Auguste Comte (1798-1847). Sociology, however, could not be considered a social science until scholars in the field could devise the empirical methods to investigate it. Sociology as a social science did emerge almost simultaneously in Europe and the United States at the end of the nineteenth century.

Today, the international character of sociology is attested to by the fact that sociological investigation is going on in nearly all countries of Europe, in the middle-eastern nations of Israel, Turkey, and Egypt, in many of the newly formed nations of Africa, south of the Sahara, in India and Japan in the Far East, in Central and South America, and in Australia and New Zealand. Yet it is in the United States that sociology has developed more rapidly than elsewhere.

As a school subject in the pre-collegiate grades, sociology in the main consists of "social living," or of "social problems," or more rarely of sociological analysis.[14] Where sociology is taught in the high school, it generally appears in grade 12, or it is a multiple-grade elective. Sociologists are presently taking part in efforts to give the social studies new directions.

The American Sociological Association, in 1964, set up the Sociological Resources for Secondary Schools Project. This Project has two principal objectives: (1) to develop a body of sociological materials that can be used in a variety of secondary-school social studies courses, and (2) to develop a new course in sociology for secondary schools. In both these endeavors it is intended to incorporate the cumulative findings and the methodological approaches of contemporary sociology. The materials are in the form of self-contained "episodes," each examining a single topic from the sociological perspective and requiring between one and ten class periods. Most episodes include written material as well as charts, filmstrips, and other teaching aids. Emphasis is placed on involving students in the first-hand gathering or manipulating of data through laboratory experiments, field observations, or exercises in the classification or interpretation of information. Episodes have been prepared in the fields of communication, public opinion, conflict resolution, education, the family, large-scale organizations, population, race relations, and religion and science.

Conclusion

The social studies in the secondary school represent a reflection of the scholarly investigations pursued in the social sciences at a higher level. It is the assumption here that the social sciences have a common goal which is often overlooked amidst great concerns for academic jurisdictions and methodologies. This common goal is the attempt to formulate generalizations or principles concerning the nature of man and his society. The social studies is that segment of the secondary school curriculum that must concentrate on the improvement of the processes of citizenship education, particularly in the domain of political, economic, and social behavior. John S. Gibson, director of the Lincoln Filene Center for Citizenship and Public Affairs at Tufts University, defines the effective citizen as,

> ... a person who seeks to maximize all possibilities for intellectual growth, one who lives within the rules of the game of the governments under

which he lives but also participates, in an enlightened manner, in shaping or changing the rules of the game. He is one who believes in and enacts patterns of democratic intergroup relations, who accepts responsibility for most of his economic and social behavior, and who contributes wherever possible to the well-being of his fellow man.[15]

If the end of social studies teaching is to produce effective citizens who are knowledgeable about, and involved in the life of the social order, then it is the concern of the social sciences to produce the vital formulations upon which the social studies are based.

A large share of the growth of the social studies field during the past two centuries of the nation's history has come in relatively short periods of marked activity and energy, much of it in the first quarter of the present century. There have been some shifts and some changes in the last four decades, and presently, major reform is in its initial stages.

The possibilities of clarifying and giving greater meaning to social studies concepts have been enhanced in recent years as a result of the increased availability of materials of better quality and in greater variety. The scope and complexity of the social studies field, however, present a number of problems and issues which must be resolved by those who would undertake substantial changes. The amount of effort currently being expended in this direction augurs well for the future growth of the social studies.

Chapter XV

Footnotes

[1] G. P. Gooch, *History and Historians* (Boston: Beacon Press, 1962), p. 14.

[2] This was not the report of the Seven Cardinal Principles issued in the year 1918.

[3] Mark M. Krug, *History and the Social Sciences* (Waltham, Massachusetts: Blaisdell Publishing Company, 1967), pp. 270-271.

[4] Roy A. Price (ed.), *New Viewpoints in the Social Sciences* (Washington, D.C.: National Council for the Social Studies, 1958), pp. 40-41.

[5] Richard S. Martin, and Reuben G. Miller, *Economics and Its Significance* (Columbus, Ohio: Charles E. Merrill Books, Inc., 1965), p. 18.

[6] *Ibid.*, pp. 20-23.

[7] *Ibid.*, p. 24.

[8] *Ibid.*, pp. 25-27.

[9] Francis J. Sorauf, *Political Science: An Informal Overview* (Columbus, Ohio: Charles E. Merrill Books, Inc.), p. 7.

[10] *Ibid.*, pp. 12-13.

[11] Edwin R. Carr, *The Social Studies* (New York: The Center for Applied Research in Education, Inc., 1965), pp. 2-4.

[12] *Ibid.*, pp. 9-10.

[13] Vincent N. Campbell, and Daryl G. Nichols, "National Assessment of Citizenship," *Social Education*, XXXII (March, 1968), p. 280.

[14] Carr, *op. cit.*, p. 10.

[15] John S. Gibson, " 'Excellence' or Effective Citizens?", *Los Angeles Times*, April 2, 1968.

Selected References

American Council of Learned Societies, and the National Council for the Social Studies. *The Social Studies and the Social Sciences.* New York: Harcourt, Brace and World, Inc., 1962.

Broek, Jan O. M. Geography: *Its Scope and Spirit.* Social Science Seminar Series, eds. Raymond H. Muessig and Vincent R. Rogers. Columbus, Ohio: Charles E. Merrill Books, Inc., 1965.

Carr, Edwin R. *The Social Studies.* New York: The Center for Applied Research in Education, Inc., 1965.

Commager, Henry Steele. *The Nature and the Study of History.* Social Science Seminar Series, eds. Raymond H. Muessig and Vincent R. Rogers. Columbus, Ohio: Charles E. Merrill Books, Inc., 1965.

Engle, Shirley H. (ed.). *New Perspectives in World History.* Washington, D.C.: The National Council for the Social Studies, 1964.

High, James. *Teaching Secondary School Social Studies.* New York: John Wiley and Sons, Inc., 1962.

James, Preston E. (ed.). *New Viewpoints in Geography.* Washington, D.C.: The National Council for the Social Studies, 1959.

Johnson, Henry. *Teaching of History.* New York: The Macmillan Company, 1940.

Krug, Mark M. *History and the Social Sciences.* Waltham, Massachusetts: Blaisdell Publishing Company, 1967.

Martin, Richard S., and Reuben G. Miller. *Economics and Its Significance.* Social Science Seminar Series, eds. Raymond H. Muessig and Vincent R. Rogers. Columbus, Ohio: Charles E. Merrill Books, Inc., 1965.

Pelto, Pertti J. *The Study of Anthropology.* Social Science Seminar Series, eds. Raymond H. Muessig and Vincent R. Rogers. Columbus, Ohio: Charles E. Merrill Books, Inc., 1965.

Price, Roy A. (ed.) *New Viewpoints in the Social Sciences.* Washington, D.C.: The National Council for the Social Studies, 1958.

Riddle, Donald H., and Robert S. Cleary. *Political Science in the Social Studies.* Washington, D.C.: The National Council for the Social Studies, 1966.

Robinson, Donald W., and others. *Promising Practices in Civic Education.* Washington, D.C.: The National Council for the Social Studies, 1967.

Rose, Caroline B. *Sociology: The Study of Man in Society.* Social Science Seminar Series, eds. Raymond H. Muessig and Vincent R. Rogers. Columbus, Ohio: Charles E. Merrill Books, Inc., 1965.

Sorauf, Francis J. *Political Science: An Informal Overview.* Social Science Seminar Series, eds. Raymond H. Muessig and Vincent R. Rogers. Columbus, Ohio: Charles E. Merrill Books, Inc., 1965.

Thursfield, Richard E. (ed.). *The Study and Teaching of American History.* Washington, D.C.: The National Council for the Social Studies, 1947.

Wesely, Edgar B., and Stanley P. Wronski. *Teaching Social Studies in High Schools.* Boston: D. C. Heath and Company, 1964.

Chapter XVI

THE PLACE OF MATHEMATICS AND SCIENCE IN THE SECONDARY SCHOOL CURRICULUM

Mathematics

Mathematics may be the oldest subject in the secondary school curriculum. Stated simply, mathematics can be defined as the science that deals with the relationship of numbers and quantitative operations.

The origin of mathematics goes back to the ancient pre-Greek civilizations of Sumeria, Babylonia, and Egypt. The important distinction between pre-Greek and Greek mathematics is that the former was the empirical and pragmatic study of numbers, such as learning to count, while the theoretical study of mathematics began with the Greeks.

The early Greek philosopher and astronomer, Thales of Asia Minor, who lived in the second half of the sixth century B.C., made some geometrical discoveries. He and his contemporaries succeeded in developing what is now regarded as elementary mathematics. Pythagorus, who was born about 531 B.C., and his followers raised mathematics to the rank of a science, and many geometrical discoveries have been ascribed to Pythagorean disciples. Euclid, born around 300 B.C., brought geometry to such a state of perfection that no further advance was made until modern times.

Another aspect of the remote past on the study of mathematics is the Hindu-Moslem influence. It has left as its lasting credit the numeral system in use today, and a considerable development of symbolic algebra and trigonometry. The Arabic system of numeration was introduced into Europe about 1000 A.D.

Europe took the lead in mathematical knowledge, beginning with the Renaissance, and rapidly transformed the mathematical heritage from the Graeco-Roman world into what was to become the foundations of modern science. Algebraic equations were developed by Francois Viète (1540-1603) and elementary trigonometry was systematized by Johann Muller (1436-1476). During the course of the seventeenth century mathematics was shaped into its modern form. Innovations were made in analytic geometry by Pierre Fermat (1601-1665) and Rene Descartes (1596-1650). Sir Isaac Newton (1642-1727) and Baron Wilhelm von Leibnitz (1646-1716) developed differential and integral calculus. Finally, around 1830, Nikolai Lobachevsky (1793-1856) discovered non-Euclidean geometry.

The historical thread of the secondary school mathematics curriculum in America may be traced through the Latin grammar school, the academies, and the public high schools. Arithmetic from the beginning has been the basic program of mathematics through grade 8. Geometry, algebra, and trigonometry left the college level and entered the high school during the latter part of the nineteenth century.

During the course of the twentieth century, professional societies, national commissions, and committees have had great and widespread influence on mathematics education. The National Council of Teachers of Mathematics, founded in 1920, had exercised extensive leadership through its publications, meetings, and commissions. In the early part of the twentieth century, the general belief was held by educators that mathematical experience trained the mind better than any other curricular subject. It was claimed that this training gain could be transferred to other subjects, situations, and problems. Grave doubts were raised about the theory of automatic transfer in the 1920's by Thorndyke and other psychologists.

In the depression decade of the 1930's, teachers of mathematics were urged by progressive educators to show the practical value and social utility of their subject. Some of these attempts to make mathematics a practical problem-solving process were scorned by mathematics scholars.

In recent years the available data shows that the mathematics enrollments at both the junior and senior high school levels have been increasing. Practically all pupils in grades 7 and 8 are taking arithmetic. Where a junior high school has a two-track mathematics offering, pupils in grade 9 must choose between general mathematics or elementary algebra.[1] Frequently the criterion is whether the student has the preparation and the aptitude for algebra. General mathematics, which is generally the choice of the non-college-bound pupil, has two basic purposes: (1) to give the pupil a year of remedial arithmetic, and (2) to provide a review of arithmetic and exploratory work that will prepare for algebra by including informal geometry, arithmetic, and algebra.[2] Many large city high schools follow a fairly uniform pattern of sequential mathematics courses. Frequently the pattern is: elementary and intermediate algebra in grades 9 and 10; plane geometry in grade 11; advanced mathematics, including trigonometry, in grade 12.

In the 1950's steps were taken to enrich and accelerate the high school mathematics program. Faculty members from the Ivy League schools of Harvard, Princeton, and Yale called for the abandonment of solid geometry in grade 12, so that the time saved could be used for the learning of more important mathematics.

In 1955 the Committee on Advanced Placement of the College Entrance Examination Board assumed responsibility for the advanced standing programs for mathematics, as well as those for other high school subjects. The advanced placement program was supported by the Fund for the Advancement of Education. The program is a plan whereby high school students may take college subjects and receive college credit for them. The program has increased the opportunities for the student who is talented and interested in mathematics.

Also in 1955 the Commission on Mathematics of the College Entrance Board was appointed to make an intensive study of the secondary school mathematics curriculum, and to make recommendations for its modernization, modification, and improvement.[3] The program recommended by the Commission included the inclusion of courses offered in college within the framework of the high school such as calculus, analytic geometry, fundamental trigonometry, and elementary algebraic functions (polynomial, exponential, circular).[4]

The University of Maryland in 1957 initiated a project with four nearby public school systems—Washington, D.C., Arlington County (Virginia), Montgomery and Prince George Counties (Maryland). The project was supported by a grant from the Carnegie Corporation, and the goal of the endeavor was to find the maturity levels at which certain mathematical ideas can be learned.

The School Mathematics Study Group (SMSG) of the University of Illinois was organized in 1958 with substantial financial support contributed by the National Science Foundation and the U.S. Office of Education. The primary purpose of the SMSG is to foster research and development in the teaching of school mathematics. The Study Group has prepared text materials designed to illustrate the kind of curriculum which the members of the group feel is demanded by the increased use of science, technology, and mathematics in our society, and the preparation of materials designed to help teachers prepare themselves to teach such a curriculum. An integrated sequential mathematics curriculum for grades 7-12 is being planned by the

Group. Arrangements of topics will be chosen to maximize the efficiency of the program and to permit inclusion of the equivalent of a full year of calculus and some of the basic ideas of probability and numerical analysis. Text materials already prepared include the following: (1) junior high school texts which review and extend the mathematics of the elementary school in such a way as to provide a sound foundation for high school courses; (2) texts for slower students in grades 7-9; and (3) high school texts for average and above average students in a college preparatory program.

As is true with any extensive curricular revision, the recent innovations in mathematics have been subjected to considerable criticism. Yet the fact remains, the "queen of the sciences," which is usually an elective in the upper high school grades, attracts a large number of students. Today it is widely recognized that not only is mathematics education vocationally important, it is also vital to the defense of the nation.

The Biological and Physical Sciences

Origins

The biological and physical sciences are a vital part of the secondary school curriculum because science is deeply embedded in the life of man and is concerned with the practical activities of man as well as with his quest for knowledge. Basically, science may be defined as accumulated knowledge that has been systematized and formulated with reference to the discovery of general truths or the operation of general laws.

The beginnings of physical science grew out of the slow, unconscious observation by primitive man of natural occurences, such as the movements of the heavenly bodies, and similarly, the biological sciences must have begun with the observation of plants and animals useful to man. One of the earliest systematic advances in physical science was made by the early Greek philosopher, Anaximander, born about 610 B.C., who recognized the rotation of the heavens around the pole star. Simultaneously with the birth of the study of astronomy, the problem of matter came into attention. Empedocles (c. 493-433 B.C.) discovered what he thought were the four primary elements: earth, water, air, and fire. This hypothesis served to interpret natural phenomena for centuries. In the biological sciences, a similar course of development is to be noted. Aristotle, scion of a generation of Greek physicians, compiled a compendious account of the animals known in his day with many accurate details of their anatomical structure. Archimedes (287-212 B.C.), a century after Aristotle, formulated basic conceptions of hydrostatics and thus took the first step in the exact science of mechanics.

The ancient scientific learning survived only fragmentarily in accounts compiled just before the onslaught of the Dark Ages. At the time of the Renaissance, some men again began to observe nature and to experiment. Nicolaus Copernicus (1473-1543) discovered the heliocentric theory, Galileo (1564-1642) used the newly developed telescope to examine the stars and planets, Vesalius (1514-1564) again took up the study of anatomy. The philosophy of the new experimental methods was first studied by Francis Bacon (1561-1626). Besides the broad distinction into physical and biological science, minute subdivisions have arisen, and much emphasis has been laid on the results and applications of scientific knowledge on the life of man.

Chemistry

Chemistry is the traditional high school science offering at grade 11, although it is also offered in grade 10 to academically talented students. Chemistry is the science that deals with, or investigates, the composition, properties, and changes of properties of elementary forms of matter. The founder of modern chemistry was Antoine Laurent Lavoisier (1743-1794), who published *Elements of Chemistry* in 1789. Toward the end of the nineteenth century chemistry began to advance at a rapid pace, and the subject became divided into several branches.

Chemistry first entered the curriculum of American schools at the college level as early as 1800. In the early nineteenth century the subject flourished in the academies. During this period the practical value of chemistry in agriculture, medicine, and in other ways was increasingly recognized. In 1872 Harvard became the first college to require high school science courses for entrance. The Committee of Ten in 1893 helped to standardize the chemistry offering as a prerequisite to college entrance.

Throughout the first six decades of the twentieth century, the emphasis on chemistry as a college-preparatory course has continued, although some educators have felt that the subject had a general education value and objective as well. Most schools place chemistry at grade 11. In the 1930-1950 period the content of high school chemistry had a functional approach which emphasized the social implications of the subject matter. Most scholars in the field did not agree with this approach.

In recent years chemistry has seen two major curriculum-reform efforts. The first of these is the Chemical Bond Approach Project (CBA) which grew out of a 1957 conference at Reed College in Portland, Oregon, sponsored by the Division of Chemical Education of the American Chemical Society and the Crown-Zellerbach Foundation. The purpose of this project has been to develop a course for high school students. This course is presented through a textbook and laboratory guide designed to be used together. The course emphasizes logical schemes which permit students to investigate and interpret a variety of chemical systems. A major feature of the laboratory work is a scheme whereby groups of experiments are designed to fit together in such a way that students develop both technical facility and interpretive skill in moving from simple to complex investigations.

The second large scale chemistry curriculum project is the Chemical Education Materials Study (CHEMS), which was begun in 1960. The CHEM Study has been experimenting with means for making a first chemistry course as profitable as possible for all students who wish to take such a course. The text, laboratory manual, teachers guide, and motion pictures heavily emphasize an experimental approach to chemistry and the importance of laboratory work. The course seeks to present chemistry from the point of view of a person intimately involved in the profession of chemistry, but in terms both interesting and comprehensible to beginning students.

Both the CBA and CHEMS courses have been tested at length in high schools and revised on the basis of these tests. Both are now published commercially and are used in a substantial number of American high schools. The people involved in both projects maintain that they are not in competition with each other. Both point out there are many good ways to teach high school chemistry.

Physics

Physics has been considered the capstone course of the secondary school sciences because it has frequently been preceded by general science, biology, and chemistry in grades 9, 10, and 11, respectively. Physics is the science that deals with matter and energy in terms of motion and force. The founders of modern physics were probably Galilei Galileo (1564-1642) and Sir Isaac Newton (1642-1727).

Galileo was first to show, save for a small error due to resistance of the air, heavy and light bodies fall at the same rate. Newton proved mathematically that the observed motion of the planets around the sun could be explained by the supposition that the sun exerted a force on each planet proportional to the square of its distance from the planet.

The first important contributions to the fund of knowledge of the physical sciences in America were made by Benjamin Franklin (1706-1790), who founded the first notable scientific society in Philadelphia in 1743. The American Philosophical Society was a candid copy of the Royal Society of England. Time saw its members explore every imaginable realm of scientific knowledge. Toward the end of the nineteenth century the American physicist Albert Michelson (1852-1931) determined, with a high degree of accuracy, the speed at which light travels, thereby strengthening certain convictions which were soon to result in Einstein's celebrated relativity theory.

The content of physics was introduced early into American secondary schools as natural philosophy. The academies helped to popularize the subject during the closing decades of the eighteenth century. When the first public high school was opened in Boston in 1821, physics was included in its curriculum. In 1872 Harvard accepted the subject as a science credit for college entrance, and the Committee of Ten, in 1893, helped to standardize it as a college preparatory subject.

Physics, often the twelfth grade science offering, is classified by high school students as a tough course. First, by its nature physics is quantitative, and a knowledge of mathematics is presumed; and second, the subject requires mastery of a technical vocabulary. Also, the traditional physics course had no unifying theme. Each unit was self-sufficient unto itself, and that meant, in effect, there were generally six separate unrelated subjects: mechanics, heat, light, sound, electricity, and magnetism. Progressive educators of the 1930's and 1940's suggested that physics should be reorganized around problems, and that the social implications of physics instruction should be stressed. The emphasis on social implications in the 1930's, however, did not noticeably increase the popularity of physics courses in high schools.

Following World War II various individuals and groups became concerned with the quality of the high school physics course and began to initiate change. The culmination of these efforts came with the new program in high school physics developed by the Physical Science Study Committee, and funded in 1956 under a grant from the National Science Foundation. The PSSC group composed of scientific scholars and professional educators developed a new physics course with suitable materials and teaching aids. The PSSC physics course has four major sections: the first section is a general introduction to the fundamental physical notions of time, space, and matter; the second section is a study of light, both optics and waves; third is a study of motion from a dynamical point of view; and the fourth section is a study of electricity and the physics of the atom. The course concentrates on fewer facts than are usually included in an elementary physics course. The PSSC physics course program includes a textbook; a laboratory guide with new experiments; simplifed, low-cost apparatus in kit form; achievement tests; an extensive library of paper-bound books written by distinguished authors on scientific topics; and teachers' guides, which provide background material and make concrete suggestions for class and laboratory activities.

A second important physics undertaking is the Harvard Physics Project initiated in 1964. The purpose of Project Physics, as it is called, is to create a physics course that will be appealing and instructive to a wide variety of students, including those who may not go on to college. The new course will be centered on a solid introduction to physics, including some of its recent developments. A supplementary reader will stress the humanistic background of the sciences covering such matters as the following: how modern physical ideas have developed; who the men and women were who made key contributions; the effect which physics has had on other sciences; and how progress in physics contributes to contemporary technology and, in turn, is stimulated by it.

Biology

Biology is a fairly recent addition to the American secondary school curriculum, and it is pretty well stabilized as the tenth grade science offering, although it is also offered in grade 9 to the academically talented. Biology is the science of life or living matter in all its forms and phenomena. William Harvey (1578-1657) started the biological sciences on their modern course when he investigated the mechanism of circulation, respiration, digestion, and the other functions of living bodies. Both before and after the work of Charles Darwin (1809-1882) on the origin of living things, biologists have devoted their attention to the study of how useful variations of living things arise. Gregor Mendel (1822-1844) carried on a number of interesting experiments with plants, discovered Mendel's law of the inheritance of many characteristics in animals and plants. Another major contribution to biology was made by Thomas Hunt Morgan (1866-1945), who was awarded the Nobel Prize (1933) for discoveries relating to laws and the mechanism of heredity.

Biology as a school subject has replaced such separate offerings as botany, zoology, and physiology at grade 10. When the Committee of Ten met in 1893, it arranged for three conferences on the sciences, which included one on biology, zoology, botany, and physiology. The three science conferences in joint session resolved that at least one-fourth of the time of the high school student should be devoted to high school science courses, and that this amount of work should be required for admission to college. As a result of the work of the science conferences, biology became the standard science offering at grade 10.

Biology varies greatly in content from school to school. Earlier textbooks had a three-part organization of units around botany, zoology, and human physiology. Emphasis during the twentieth century has been on such central biological ideas as the following: evolution; relation of organisms to man (economic biology); organisms as users of, or competitors for, energy; physiological processes; and social and civic problems of a biological nature.

In 1958 the American Institute of Biological Sciences became interested in studying the teaching of biology in the high schools. With a grant from the National Science Foundation, the Biological Sciences Curriculum Study (BSCS) was organized. The developmental plan of the BSCS was generally similar to that originated by the physicists. The BSCS is a total program of curriculum improvement for secondary school biology including tests and laboratory materials for students of diverse abilities from below-average to gifted in grades 10-12. Three versions of a modern high school course in biology have now been developed for use in grade 10. Although approximately 70 per cent of the content is common to all three versions, each one approaches the study of biology from a distinctive point of view. These three programs, known as the Blue, Yellow, and Green versions were issued by three different publishers in 1963. The Blue Version uses a molecular-biochemical-evolutionary approach; the Green Version, an ecological-evolutionary approach; the Yellow Version, a cellular-biochemical-evolutionary approach. The three courses are equivalent in depth of content and designed for students of average and above-average ability.

A major problem in implementing a modern biology course is the sequence of high school science courses. The tenth grade biology course was established when biology was considered the "easy" science. Now biology has come to depend heavily upon the chemistry and physics which traditionally follow it. To date, the problem of providing a chemistry and physics background for biology students has been solved by building into a modern biology course enough training in physical science to allow the student to progress.[5]

General Science and Earth Science

The Science Conferences initiated by the Committee of Ten in 1893 accepted physical geography as the science offering for grade 9. In 1920, the U.S. Bureau of Education (now the U.S. Office of Education) recommended general science, including hygiene, as the ninth grade science. The junior high school movement, which gained momentum during the "twenties," helped to establish the general science offering. General science seemed to be a natural addition to the junior high school because its basic nature was exploratory. With the firm establishment of the junior high school, science educators sought to have general science topics taught at all grade levels in the junior high school, and frequently general science became a one-semester course at a given grade level.

The biological science portion of the general science course tends to be a preview of tenth-grade biology, and as such covers topics from botany, zoology, and health. The physical science portion of the program is, like the biological science segment, generally a survey of major topics.[6]

As a result of the recent activity in curriculum development by those in the scientific disciplines, the idea of a solid course in earth science has reappeared as a possible ninth grade offering. This proposal is an attempt to reintroduce a subject of considerable attention at the turn of the century.

In 1962 the American Geological Institute established the Earth Science Curriculum Project (ESCP) in an effort to produce an earth science course for ninth grade students. ESCP is an interdisciplinary, experience-centered course in which basic principles and concepts are applied to developing an understanding of the "how and why" of natural phenomena. Chemistry, mathematics, and physics are utilized in showing how the earth science disciplines of astronomy, geology, geophysics, meterology, oceanography, and physical geography contributed to an understanding of man's environment. Materials developed for use in the ESCP course include a text, laboratory manual, and teacher's guide. The text is organized into four major units: (1) Earth and Sun; (2) Earth Cycles; (3) The Earth's Past; and (4) Earth and the Universe.

Conclusion

This chapter has been an attempt to trace the place which mathematics and science play in the secondary school curriculum. In American education it is assumed that junior and senior high schools exist to serve the needs of all the children of all the people.

There is some indication that the new science programs are moving in the direction of the development of a multiple track system within the curricular area of science. The trend toward the development of a multiple track system in each of the curricular areas of the comprehensive high school is discussed in the final chapter.

Chapter XVI
Footnotes

[1] Leonard H. Clark, and others, *The American Secondary School Curriculum* (New York: The Macmillan Company, 1965), p. 262.

[2] *Ibid.,* p. 263.

[3] See: Commission on Mathematics, College Entrance Examination Board, *Program for College Preparatory Mathematics* (Princeton, New Jersey: Educational Testing Service, 1959).

[4] John J. Kinsella, *Secondary School Mathematics* (New York: The Center for Applied Research in Education, Inc., 1965), p. 31.

[5] J. Stanley Marshall, and Ernest Burkman, *Current Trends in Science Education* (New York: The Center for Applied Research in Education, Inc., 1966), p. 45.

[6] H. Seymour Fowler, *Secondary School Science Teaching Practices* (New York: The Center for Applied Research in Education, Inc., 1964), pp. 11-12.

Selected References

CBA *Newsletter. Chemical Bonds Approach Project.* Richmond, Indiana: Earlham College, February, 1961.

Commission on Mathematics, College Entrance Examination Board. *Program for College Preparatory Mathematics.* Princeton, New Jersey: Educational Testing Service, 1959.

ESCP *Newsletter,* NL-1 Earth Science Curriculum Project, Boulder, Colorado (October, 1963).

Fowler, H. Seymour. *Secondary School Science Teaching Practices.* New York: The Center for Applied Research in Education, Inc., 1964.

Hurd, Paul De Hart. *Biological Education in American High Schools 1890-1960.* Washington, D.C.: American Institute of Biological Science, 1961.

Isenburger, Katherine V. *A Half Century of Science and Mathematics Teaching.* Oak Park, Illinois: Central Association of Science and Mathematics Teachers, Inc. 1950.

Joint Commission of the Mathematical Association of America and the National Council of Teachers of Mathematics. *The Place of Mathematics in Secondary Education.* New York: Columbia University, 1940.

Kinsella, John J. *Secondary School Mathematics.* New York: The Center for Applied Research in Education, Inc., 1965.

Marshall, J. Stanley, and Ernest Burkman. *Current Trends in Science Education.* New York: The Center for Applied Research in Education, Inc., 1966.

National Committee on Mathematical Requirements, Mathematical Association of America. *The Reorganization of Mathematics in Secondary Education.* Department of the Interior, Bureau of Education Bulletin. 1921, No. 32. Washington D.C.: Government Printing Office, 1921.

National Society for the Study of Education. *Fifty-Ninth Yearbook, Part 1, Rethinking Science Education.* Chicago: University of Chicago Press, 1960.

New Developments in High School Science Teaching. Washington, D.C.: National Science Teachers Association, 1960.

School Mathematics Study Group. *Mathematics for Junior High School,* Vols. 1-2. New Haven: Yale University Press, 1962.

University of Illinois Committee on School Mathematics. *High School Mathematics.* Urbana, Illinois: University of Illinois Press, 1960.

Chapter XVII
THE PLACE OF THE FINE ARTS AND THE DRAMATIC ARTS IN THE SECONDARY SCHOOL CURRICULUM

The Fine Arts

Music and art have long been considered necessary components of a liberal education. Both music and art have a contribution to make to the general education of all youth, and a special contribution to the artistically talented.

Music Education

Music as one of the liberal arts has formed an integral part of the educational systems of Western civilization from Hellenic times to the present. In fact, since primitive times, music has modified human behavior. The power of music to incite joy, awe, contentment, sadness, or suspense was considered by the ancient Greeks as something magical and unintelligible. The term music is derived from the Greek word for the art of the Muses, referring to the nine Greek deities presiding over intellectual pursuits. In contrast with the Greek word for gymnastic, the Greek word for music implied the culture of the mind as distinguished from that of the body.

During the Dark Ages the Greek tonal systems were altered and preserved by the Church. Choir schools were instituted at Rome as early as the fourth century by Pope Silvester I (314-335 A.D.), and from 590 they were much emphasized by Gregory I (c. 540-604). By the eighth century the Church had given official sanction to a system of unison melody commonly known as "Gregorian," although apparently developed from Byzantine and Greek origins. Music education within the monasteries was conducted by the use of illustrated charts similar in size and purpose to modern day reading charts used in the primary grades. Outside the Church, gild schools and town musicians, such as the "meistersingers" at Nurenburg in Germany, contributed largely to the development of music education.

The Renaissance stimulated the further development of secular music, the invention of musical instruments, and new forms of composition, which evolved into the present system of harmony and measured time. During the seventeenth and eighteenth centuries spoken poetry grew into opera, the miracle play became the oratorio, and instrumental ensembles began to take the shape of the modern symphony orchestra.

The *Bay Psalm Book* (1640) was the first book published in the English colonies in North America. Only a decade after the establishment of the Massachusetts Bay Colony, it represents the first serious effort of Puritan culture in America. The book included only the texts to be sung at devotional services. Indeed, music received only slight attention in the days of the American colonists. Manuals of instruction in singing were prepared early in the eighteenth century to provide text material for reading music in "singing schools." Taught in most instances by itinerant singing masters, these public classes typically met once or twice a week for a month or two and ended with a performance at a public concert. The singing school movement grew in popularity during and after the Revolutionary period, but still reached only a few of the total population. The first teachers of music in the public schools were practically all singing-school teachers.

The first well-organized effort to provide a complete musical education in America was the Boston Academy of Music, founded by Lowell Mason (1792-1872) in 1833. Mason devised a system of musical instruction for children based on Pestalozzian methods, and he taught music in Boston schools. Emphasis was given almost solely to the reading of music rather than aesthetic expression. Music instruction was based mainly on the belief that music helped to train the mind. In 1837 the Boston School Committee adopted a resolution "to try the experiment of introducing vocal music, by public authority, as part of the system of public instruction, into the public schools of this city." Thus did music enter the public school curriculum as one of the formal studies.

From the time of the Civil War to World War I, Pestalozzian teaching methods were the dominant force in music education. Students were taught to sing intervals from tonal ladders, and such methods frequently became ends in themselves. The Music Educators National Conference was founded in 1907 by school music supervisors. Largely through this organization, with its affiliated regional, state, and local associations, publications, and activities, the teaching of music in schools has been advanced.

It is not seriously questioned that music belongs in general education. Three areas in which music makes contributions which are almost unique in that sense are: (1) aesthetic growth; (2) productive use of leisure time; and (3) emotional development. A common complaint of music educators is that many high school music programs are almost exclusively organized around selective performing groups. They believe that a general music course for young adolescents of junior high school age should include not only singing, but also listening, rhythmic expression, instrumental experiences, and reading and writing music—in fact, the whole range of musical experience.

General music courses are taught on the junior and senior high school levels throughout the nation. Usually, junior high school general music courses meet fewer than five days a week, and they may be offered in the seventh or eighth grades. Course emphasis is on providing exploratory experiences in music. Quite often the junior high course is the last formal musical experience a pupil has. On the senior high school level general music courses are likely to provide experiences in depth. Like the junior high school courses, the senior high school music courses emphasize the aesthetic quality of music and provide a variety of music activities.

Performing groups are popular in the secondary school, although recent years have seen a decline in both the number and quality of high school orchestras. School bands are more popular than school orchestras, and it would appear that the general public is more willing to support the flash, color, and sound of a marching band than attend formal concerts of a school orchestra. In the realm of vocal music, choruses and glee clubs in the secondary school provide an opportunity for additional numbers of pupils to participate in a musical activity.

Art Education

Art is one of those creative expressions of man which minister to his love of beauty. It was the ancient Greeks who raised art to a level of national expression and aspiration. Hellenic sculpture was humanity in being with the athlete as its model of manhood. During the Greek and Roman eras artists reached the highest levels of aesthetic significance. The eventual dissolution of the Roman empire became evident in the increasingly less significant and comparatively lifeless forms of painting, sculpture, and architecture produced by artists during the last century of that era.[1]

Art flourished again during the Gothic and Renaissance periods when countless numbers of magnificent works of architecture, painting, and sculpture were produced. Large segments of the public were involved in, and affected by, the arts created during these periods. But art became a plaything of the very wealthy and powerful during the seventeenth and eighteenth centuries, and as such it lost much of its vigor and integrity; its aesthetic significance was subordinate to its decorative qualities.[2] A high level of popular communication was again achieved by the late eighteenth and nineteenth century artists. Their portrayals of ordinary people and contemporary scenes have had a widespread effect upon the public at the time of the beginning of the era of the common man.

Creative art expression is believed to be a natural birthright of the child. If art were permitted to play its natural and essential role in human life, it would probably have pronounced effects upon improved individual welfare and upon nearly every element of the environment in which people live, study, work, and play.[3]

In the United States, prior to 1870, art instruction was considered an educational extravagance, and as a school subject it was usually taught in isolated situations by a volunteer teacher. During the fifteen year period between 1870 and 1885, some form of drawing instruction became part of the public school curriculum in a number of larger cities in the nation. Industrial drawing, consisting largely of copybook exercises, became popular in connection with the manual arts movement. By the turn of the century the child study movement of Herbartians emphasized concern for the place of cultural and aesthetic appreciations within the school curriculum. After 1900 the systematic theories of Dewey and others worked toward the conception of art as an integral part of general education.

Today, the emphasis in American secondary art education is placed upon the student's creative expression in drawing, sculpture, and various types of applied design. Many art educators view the secondary schools art program as one which should be basically oriented to general education rather than specialized education.

A good art program in the junior high school, according to art educators, should include two-dimensional and three-dimensional work with various media, such as clay, stone, wood, metal, cloth, and plastic. In practice, however, junior high school art programs vary considerably from school to school, depending on facilities and equipment made available, and the philosophy of the art teacher.

At the senior high school level art educators are agreed that the art program should be a part of the general education pattern of subjects that transmit our cultural heritage. Yet, few high schools require art for graduation. In the senior high school art experiences are offered in such courses as the following: (1) an exploratory course covering all aspects of art in which the emphasis is on developing an appreciation of art; (2) drawing, painting, and sculpture; (3) commercial design, a vocationally exploratory course emphasizing the development of techniques about materials and media for reproduction; and (4) courses which elaborate on, or specialize in, various aspects of the above listed courses.

While there is general agreement that every high school graduate should have at least some art experiences in his secondary education, it is difficult to see how art courses can be included in an already extremely crowded required curriculum. Perhaps the practice that holds the greatest promise is to have a basic art course in the ninth or tenth grade required of all students.

Dramatic Arts

The drama was one expression of Greek sensitivity which was the basis for their remarkable development of art, literature, and science. Choral singing and dancing, important elements in Greek drama, offered the most effective means of group instruction in ancient Athens. Dramatic competitions were also a part of the Panhellenic games and contests. Some of the greatest dramatists of Greece produced their plays at the great games. The rediscovery of the Greek culture and language at the time of the Renaissance reestablished the drama as a popular form of learning. During the Renaissance the Greek dramatists were approved for their moral effects.

Today, courses in dramatics, dramatic art, or play production are found in the curriculum of most large secondary schools. In some secondary schools extracurricular student groups are fostered to produce plays and pageants. Dramatics as an educational medium and activity are justified on many grounds, including personality development and the enhancement of artistic abilities.

Drama can also be a regular part of courses in English. Many excellent works of literature were written in the form of drama, and they were written, not to be read silently or orally, but to be enacted. The full benefit and pleasure from drama cannot be obtained unless it is enacted.

Conclusion

In this chapter the attempt has been made to trace the place and role of the fine arts and dramatic arts in the secondary school curriculum. Few content fields of study can offer the individual student more self-fulfillment than art, music, and drama. Yet it would seem that curriculum workers, while recognizing the importance of the arts on the one hand have, with the other, sold the program short. The fine arts and dramatic arts are essentials, not frills, despite the attacks of conservative educators and taxpayers.

Chapter XVII
Footnotes

[1] Howard Conant, *Art Education* (Washington, D.C.: The Center for Applied Research in Education, Inc., 1964), p. 27.

[2] *Ibid.*, p. 27.

[3] *Ibid.*, p. 29.

Selected References

Barkan, Manuel A. *A Foundation for Art Education.* New York: The Ronald Press Company, 1955.

Conant, Howard. *Art Education.* Washington, D.C.: The Center for Applied Research in Education, Inc., 1964.

―――――, and Arne Randall. *Art in Education.* Peoria, Illinois: Charles A. Bennett Company, Inc., 1963.

Gaitskell, C. D. *Art Education During Adolescence.* New York: Harcourt, Brace and World, Inc., 1954.

Kramer, M. E. *Dramatic Tournaments in the Secondary Schools.* New York: Teachers College, Bureau of Publications, 1936.

Munro, Thomas. *Art Education: Its Philosophy and Psychology.* New York: The Liberal Arts Press, Inc., 1956.

Chapter XVIII
THE PLACE OF PHYSICAL EDUCATION AND HEALTH AND SAFETY EDUCATION IN THE SECONDARY SCHOOL CURRICULUM

Physical Education

Physical education is an integral and vital phase of education. Physical education may be defined as that segment of the educative process that is concerned with the growth, development, and adjustment of youth by means of a systematic program of physical activities selected and organized according to social and hygienic standards.[1]

While physical education is one of the later subjects added to the curriculum of the American secondary school, it is also one of the oldest forms of education. Primitive people and prehistoric man used it to train their young people for various purposes according to their culture and needs. Gymnastics were considered a necessary part of education in ancient Greece. The Greeks, a highly civilized, reflective, and beauty-loving people, desired to train citizens both physically and mentally. In Sparta and Athens the training of youth, age seven through eighteen, consisted largely of games, sports, rhythms, music, and military training. The ancient Greek city-states held national festivals such as the one at Olympia, where winners were crowned with the sacred wild olive wreath, which was one of the highest Greek honors. In the Roman era, although Quintilian stressed the value of physical activity for the graceful use of the body in public speaking, the Romans were interested in physical activity primarily as it contributed to military training.

Physical education was slowly restored to the school curriculum at the time of the Renaissance under the leadership of Vittorino da Feltre, the Italian schoolmaster who combined physical and mental training. During the eighteenth and nineteenth centuries the prominent European leaders in physical education were: Johnn Bernhard Basedow (1723-1790); Christian Gottlief Salzmann (1744-1811); Johann Christoph Friedrich Guts-Muths (1759-1839); and Friedrich

Ludwig Jahn (1778-1853). The little Scandinavian country of Denmark was the first modern nation to make physical education a requirement in the schools.

In the United States school programs in physical education began first in the colleges, then entered the high schools. Early leaders in the physical education movement here were German immigrants. Swedish school gymnastics were introduced by Baron Nils Posse (1862-1895) at Boston, Massachusetts; and Diocletion Lewis (1823-1886) established the first physical education teacher-training school in Boston in 1861. Programs of physical education in the United States retained some good features of German and Swedish gymnastics, yet the U.S. program has been mainly a natural play activity program. Formal drills and group exercises of the European systems have had little appeal to U.S. students.

Physical education in U.S. secondary schools is a three-part program: instructional, intramural, and varsity athletics. General objectives for physical education may be set forth in the following inclusive statements:

1. Each physically educated person is physically fit.
2. A physically educated person has an optimum number of physical skills.
3. A physically educated person has healthy attitudes and habits.
4. A physically educated person has adequate recreational skills.
5. A physically educated person has a wide knowledge of games and sports.[2]

In the instructional aspect of the physical education program in U.S. secondary schools, the class, which all students are required to enroll in, is devoted primarily to instruction in which fundamentals, techniques, skills, attitudes are stressed. Activities included in the instructional program can be divided into the following categories: (1) adaptive activities; (2) games, sports, athletics, play and aquatics; (3) self-testing, combat, and self-defense activities; and (4) out-of-door activities.[3]

Adaptive activities are designed to correct physical defects and deficiencies such as, for example, poor posture. Games, sports, play, and aquatic activities are too numerous to list here. Self-testing, combat, and self-defense activities are important for meeting the physical fitness objective, and may include activities such as judo, boxing, and wrestling if proper equipment and supervision are available. Out-of-door activities include summer camp programs provided by a growing number of school districts. The carry-over value of camp programs in connection with science and social studies is stressed by proponents of these programs.

The intramural program supplements the instructional program, and each should motivate the other. Intramural activities consist of participation wholly within the particular school population in sports. Participation is voluntary and should be so. A properly organized sports program will provide opportunities for students to develop skills in sports and games they learned in the instructional physical education program. A difficulty in intramural athletics is the problem of providing time for the activities.

The varsity athletic program is designed to provide suitable competition in individual and team contests for the more highly skilled athletes. Interschool athletics are perhaps the most controversial activities of the secondary school. Critics of that program maintain that: (1) values engendered by present practices in some schools are bad for the players and other pupils; (2) participation in interscholastic athletics holds the highest esteem of all activities sponsored by the school despite the new emphasis on science, mathematics, and academic excellence; and (3) too great a drain is made on the financial and personnel resources of a school for the benefit of a few which results in a corresponding neglect of the many.

In the writer's opinion highly organized athletic leagues are not desirable for students of junior high school age. Physical education in the junior high school should stress a well-rounded program of instruction for all pupils, and an interesting, and widely varied program of intramural competition in team, dual, and individual sports.

Health and Safety Education

Health Education

Health is that phase of education in which factual, authentic material pertaining to health and health practices and attitudes is presented. Promotion of physical fitness began to permeate the schools in the years between 1830 and 1880. Calisthenics, gymnastics, and courses in physiology and hygiene were introduced into the schools. By 1890, as a result of powerful pressures exerted by the Women's Christian Temperance Union movement, every state had passed laws requiring schools to teach about the dangers of alcohol and narcotics. When the statistics concerning the physical unfitness of World War I draftees were publicized, compulsory health education programs were instituted in the schools. The depression of the

1930's temporarily arrested the expansion of school health programs, yet when World War II again focused the nation's attention on health, governmental and professional agencies sponsored national committees to prepare materials that would help schools promote physical fitness through health education. President Eisenhower, in 1956, created the President's Council on Youth Fitness, and both Presidents Kennedy and Johnson have taken steps to further the youth health program.

Today, health education in the secondary school is shared by various curricular areas, such as physical education, social studies, the sciences (especially biology and general science), and home economics. As a result of this sharing of responsibility, the health education curriculum is sometimes replete with duplication and repetition. Instruction in health education follows no set pattern, and the grade levels of the health education courses help to determine the content of the courses.

Safety Education

Safety education is that instruction relating to the sources of potential physical injury and health hazards as well as the necessary steps for their control or elimination. Safety education in the secondary school is primarily concerned with driver education. Like many other aspects of the curriculum, driver education is a controversial subject. Tens of thousands of people are killed each year on U.S. highways in what can only appear to be an American socially-condoned form of mass murder. To stop this carnage, insurance companies, safety groups, and state legislatures have appealed to the schools to institute programs of driver education and safety. It is during the years of secondary schooling that youths establish driving habits that protect or endanger their lives and those of other people.

The major reasons usually cited against including driver education in public secondary schools are:

1. Driver education is a very expensive program to conduct.
2. Driver instruction represents another invasion of the responsibilities and duties of the home and/or private enterprise.
3. Driver education is not basic academic instruction, and therefore should not be included in the curriculum of the secondary school.[4]

In a 1968 study made by Frederick McGuire and R. C. Kersh of the University of California at Irvine, the conclusion was reached that driver education courses in high schools that are costing 150 million dollars a year are not doing the job of preventing serious accidents. They found no difference in the accident rates of motorists who had had driver education courses in high school and those who had not. Family background, sex, age, emotional maturity and the degree of social conformity all affect the accident rate, they said. Driver education, however, does not.[5] Robert Terry, president of the California State Driver Education Association contests the findings of McGuire and Kersh. Terry claims thirty-three studies which emanated from at least twelve states show that driver education courses reduced accidents and traffic violators from twenty-five to seventy-five per cent.[6]

Safety groups have prepared publications, audio-visual materials, and provide services for secondary school teachers who are interested in, and concerned about, safety education. The National Commission on Safety Education of the National Education Association is one such organization. Another agency that does outstanding work is the National Safety Council, which publishes the magazine *Safety Education,* many teaching aids, and the annual statistical review, *Accident Facts.* The American Red Cross, the American Automobile Association, various auto and gun clubs, and many insurance companies also have useful materials.[7]

Conclusion

Physical education is a necessary part of general education. Physical exercise is vital for the body. There are no substitutes for a course in physical education. Even varsity athletics have purposes which do not supplement the values inherent in the class instruction program. A well-rounded physical education program should be offered by every secondary school. Activities should include body mechancis, team sports, individual and dual sports, and recreational games.

Health and safety education is a national concern. The secondary school has a function to perform in the expression of this concern. Health and safety educators need to establish clear-cut goals and objectives that will enable the secondary school adequately to tackle its responsibility in this area of the curriculum.

Chapter XVIII
Footnotes

[1] Karl W. Bookwalter, *Physical Education in the Secondary Schools.* (Washington, D.C.: The Center for Applied Research in Education, Inc., 1964), p. 1.

[2] Leonard H. Clark, and others, *The American Secondary School Curriculum* (New York: The Macmillan Company, 1965), pp. 355-356.

[3] Clark, *op. cit.,* p. 356.

[4] Clark, *op. cit.,* pp. 352-353.

[5] *Los Angeles Times,* October 30, 1968.

[6] *Ibid.,* October 31, 1968.

[7] Deobold B. Van Dalen, *Health and Safety Education* (Washington, D.C.: The Center for Applied Research in Education, Inc., 1963), p. 88.

Selected References

Anderson, Carl L. *School Health Practice.* St. Louis, Missouri: C. V. Mosby Company, 1960.

Bookwalter, Karl W. *Physical Education in Secondary Schools.* Washington, D.C.: The Center for Applied Research in Education, Inc., 1964.

Bucher, Charles A. *Foundations of Physical Education.* St. Louis, Missouri: The C. V. Mosby Company, 1968.

Clark, Leonard H., and others. *The American Secondary School Curriculum.* New York: The Macmillan Company, 1965.

Hetherington, Clark W. *School Program in Physical Education.* Tarrytown, New York: World Book Company, 1922.

La Porte, William Ralph. *The Physical Education Curriculum.* Los Angeles: College Book Store, 1955.

Van Dalen, Deobold B. *Health and Safety Education.* Washington, D.C.: The Center for Applied Research in Education, Inc., 1963.

Williams, Jesse Feiring. *The Principles of Physical Education.* Philadelphia: W. B. Saunders Company, 1959.

Chapter XIX
THE PLACE OF VOCATIONAL TRAINING AND THE PRACTICAL ARTS IN THE SECONDARY SCHOOL CURRICULUM

Introduction: Definition of Terms

Vocational training should not be confused with the practical arts. Vocational training as used here designates the specialized programs at the high school level that prepare pupils to work in specific vocations and consist of vocational courses dealing primarily with skills. The administration of vocational training starts at the federal level because there are federal funds to be allocated to the states. The U.S. Office of Education reviews and approves the state plans, and in general administers the federal program for vocational training. Each state has a State Director of Vocational and Technical Education, and in forty-two states, the State Board of Education is the policy-making body for vocational programs in secondary schools.

The practical arts are not federally financed. The practical arts is that area of the curriculum that places emphasis on the arts serving every day material needs and includes such programs as industrial arts and home economics. The practical arts are for the purpose of broadening the general education of youth.

The distinction between these two curricular areas oftentimes is one which is of intent more than of content. For instance, the term vocational may be used to designate the manner in which a course is supported. Thus, for example, an auto mechanics course offering that receives federal aid is called vocational auto mechanics as opposed to the designation of a nonfederally supported course which is called simply auto mechanics. In home economics, vocational home economics receives federal funds, whereas nonvocational home economics receives no federal assistance.

Vocational Training

Agricultural Education

Agricultural education in high schools is education for duties and responsibilities related in some way to agriculture. As a part of vocational training, agricultural education is provided for pupils who are expected to engage in farming and other agricultural occupations. In 1965 there were 517,000 secondary school students enrolled in federally aided vocational agricultural programs.[1]

Most Americans, in the beginning, wrung their living from the soil. The farming frontier has had a salient influence on the development of the American national character. It was only natural that agricultural education became one of the earliest forms of vocational training in this country.

The American Lyceum was among the early movements which affected the course of American education. Perhaps the first example of agricultural instruction of below-college level in the United States was the Gardiner Lyceum, founded in Maine in 1821.

The concern of the nation in the development of the science of agriculture was reflected in the passage of the Morrill Act of 1862, which set up the system of land-grant colleges and universities to establish a new type of liberal and practical education in agriculture and the mechanic arts. It was not, however, until 1888 that the first secondary school of agriculture was organized in connection with the University of Minnesota. Requirements for greater agricultural output per man at the time of World War I helped to stimulate Congressional leaders to press for enactment of vocational education legislation. With the passage of the Smith-Hughes Bill in 1917, most of the agricultural education in public schools became identified as vocational agriculture.

Several supplementary acts of Congress have extended and expanded the basic provisions of the Smith-Hughes Law, and added appropriations. The George-Barden Act of 1946 provided for further development of vocational education in the states and territories, and mentioned for the first time the Future Farmers of America Foundation, formed in the State of Virginia in 1944. The Vocational Education Act of 1963 provided that any amounts allocated under the vocational education acts for agriculture might be used for vocational education in any occupation involving knowledge and skills in agricultural subjects, whether or not such occupation involved work in the farm or of the home farm, and that such education might be provided without any directed or supervised practice on a farm.[2]

The principle that programs should be developed in accordance with needs and problems of individual communities has been a generally accepted principle in agricultural education. The major instructional areas in vocational agriculture are organized on the basis of groups of occupations requiring competence in specialized agricultural science subject fields, such as: (1) agricultural production (farming and ranching); (2) agricultural supplies; (3) agricultural mechanics (sales and service); (4) agricultural products (processing and marketing); (5) ornamental horticulture; (6) forestry; (7) agricultural resources; and (8) other agriculture. In most instances the subject field of agricultural production has been the single program offered in rural high schools under the provisions of vocational education acts of Congress. The other fields are mostly taught in technical institutes, junior colleges, or four-year colleges.[3]

Agricultural production may be defined as an organization of subject matter and learning activities concerned with principles and practices in the production of livestock, field crops, fruits and vegetables, fiber and other crops, on commercial and part-time farms. In addition to animal science, plant science, farm mechanics, and farm business management, instruction specific to each production enterprise is emphasized.[4] The course of study for a high school class that meets the equivalent of five times per week during the school year may be organized to include between six to twelve functional experience units. A unit may be an agricultural production enterprise, such as growing wheat, managing a sheep herd, or barley production. Only the specific crop and livestock enterprises of importance in the likely future employment of the students are taught in detail.

At the ninth grade level the subject matter in vocational agricultural courses is general in nature. Usually it is not until gardes 11 and 12 that students have the opportunity to specialize in agricultural courses. All-day high school courses of study are generally referred to and listed as Agriculture I, II, III, IV.

The Agricultural Education Service within the U.S. Office of Education reviews and approves the state plans, and in general administers the federal program for vocational agriculture. The kind of decreasing enrollment in agriculture courses probably reflects the gradual disappearance of the small farmer, the mechanization of agriculture, specialization, and corporate farming. The popularity of courses in agronomy and animal husbandry may also reflect the above-mentioned factors.

Trade and Industrial Education

Trade and industrial education may be defined as vocational education suitable to the needs of prospective and actual workers in the fields of manufacturing, industry, and trades. Trade and industrial education at the secondary school level includes education devoted to the preparation of youth for occupations in the crafts and trades at the skilled level, as well as for certain types of semiskilled and service occupations. In 1965 there were 253,000 secondary school students enrolled in federally-aided trade and industrial education programs.[5]

The traditional system of apprenticeship constituted the principle means for educating for trades and industries in America from colonial times until about the year 1830. The first organized schools for training craft workers appeared about 1830 in the form of mechanics institutes. These institutes generally housed libraries on vocational topics and cabinets of models and minerals. They were also the site of lectures for the advancement of ambitious young mechanics. Yet these and other programs designed to provide education for workers never really succeeded.

In the latter part of the nineteenth century the mechanics institute made way for the much superior technical institute based somewhat upon the model established by the Swiss nobleman and educator, Philipp Emanuel von Fellenberg (1771-1844). On his estate von Fellenberg had instituted a school where trades and agriculture were actually taught at first hand. After the American Civil War General Samuel Chapman Armstrong (1839-1893), who had been born in Hawaii, believed that what the American black man needed above all else after his emancipation was a practical and useful training. In 1868 the General organized and opened Hampton Institute where he emphasized instruction in farming, the manual arts and crafts, and in certain instances, the art and science of teaching. Hampton and Tuskegee Institutes were organized for the Afro-American, Haskell for Indians, Rensselaer, Cooper Union, Pratt, and Drexel were for primarily Caucasian working men. The technical institute not only helped to solve knotty problems created by the Industrial Revolution, but it also aided in racial adjustment in this nation.

On June 6, 1879, Calvin Milton Woodward (1837-1914) opened the St. Louis Manual Training School under sponsorship of Washington University. This pioneer in the manual training high school movement was convinced that the interests of young men required a system of education that fitted them for the specific duties of life in a more direct and positive manner than was found in the ordinary American high school at the time. The new type of secondary school was at once a popular success. By 1890 some fifty such schools were operating mostly along the Atlantic seaboard.

Another important event in the history of trade and industrial education occurred in the state of Massachusetts in 1905. In that year a Commission made recommendations which led to the establishment of industrial schools and classes in that state. In the rapid developments during the years that followed, leading to the passage of the Smith-Hughes Act of 1917, trade and industrial education continued to be a prominent part of the program of vocational education in the United States.

Despite the progress which had been made by trade and industrial education, when compared with the vigorous forward thrust of industry since the Civil War, it lagged sadly behind. To remedy this state of affairs, organized labor—with the cautious support and assistance from business, agricultural, and educational interests—set out to publicize the need for education. The result, after several years of toil, was the enactment in 1917 of the historic Smith-Hughes Law, which made provision for national grants to trade courses in the high schools, and which, in the years ahead, turned out to be the first of a long line of related acts.[6] The objective of the Smith-Hughes law and later legislation is pre-employment preparation. It is also the development of the student to the point where he can enter an occupation as an advanced learner or advanced apprenticeship.

The field of trade and industrial education offers a great variety of programs which, in secondary schools, may range from air conditioning and refrigeration to upholstering. Usually, instruction time in academic classes amounts to 25 clock hours, or thirty 50-minute periods per week. But because vocational classes seldom require extra preparation at home in addition to classwork, the norm for the total weekly instruction time in vocational high schools is set at 80 clock hours, or in terms of class periods, thirty-six 50-minute periods. According to the law, under federally supported vocational curricula, this time must be divided up among three areas. (1) shopwork, (2) related subjects, and (3) general education subjects. Fifty per cent of the instruction time, or 15 clock hours, is devoted to shopwork. One-half of the remaining time, or 7½ clock hours, is given to related subjects, which are generally science, mathematics, and technical subjects. These courses are structured to give students the background necessary for an understanding and appreciation of their vocational studies. The remaining 7½ clock hours are given to such general education subjects as English and social studies.[7]

Three patterns of administrative organization have emerged by which federally-aided trade and industrial education programs are conducted. One plan calls for this type of instruction to be conducted in technical high schools run by the state authorities, as, for example, in the state of Connecticut. In general, technical high schools have more freedom to vary the proportion of a pupil's time devoted to shopwork, related subjects, and general education. A second plan provides separate high schools, but as a part of the local school system. The third arrangement is to have the program offered under the local school authority, but housed as a department of the comprehensive local high school.

Business Education

Business education is that area of vocational training which develops skills, attitudes, and understandings essential to gainful employment in business. In the secondary school business education comprises the following: (1) job-preparatory education for initial office and selling positions, and for the management of individually owned, controlled, and operated business enterprises; and (2) general or basic knowledge and understanding of business. In 1965 there were 574,000 secondary school students enrolled in federally-aided business education programs.[8]

During the colonial period in American history an occasional Latin grammar school would include some "practical" subjects such as merchants' accounts and surveying. During the early colonial period the demand was for short intensive preparation in specific skills which would lead to immediate employment in a business office. Itinerant teachers who would remain only a fortnight or so in any one town would offer their instruction, frequently in the evening, and thus they became the forerunners of modern evening business schools.

Early in the eighteenth century, schools in such cities as Boston, New York City, Philadelphia, and Charleston offered instruction in such subjects as arithmetic, handwriting, and bookkeeping. Nearly all the early academies offered curricula, which included business arithmetic, bookkeeping, and other commercial subjects. The field of business education from about 1850 until shortly after 1890 was dominated by the private business college. The first few business colleges were probably in existence prior to 1830. The great success of the early business college attests to the great need and active demand for practical business education during those years.

Some business subjects, notably bookkeeping, were a part of the curriculum of the earliest American high schools. It was not, however, until late in the nineteenth century that the public high school offered any real competition to the private business college. The Business High School of Washington, D.C. was organized in 1890. In 1893 the National Business Education Association was formed as an affiliate to the National Education Association. In 1903 the Committee of Nine of the NEA recommended a rather broad list of elective business subjects for high school, which included the following: accounting, advertising, bookkeeping, banking and finance, commercial arithmetic, commercial law, commercial geography, history of commerce, penmanship, shorthand, typewriting, office practice, commercial English, and local industries.[9]

In 1915 another committee of the NEA presented proposals recommending two distinct high school commercial curricula, one in accounting and the other in stenography. Still another committee, in 1919, recommended a three-part business education curricula: (1) a general business and bookkeeping curriculum; (2) a stenographic and presecretarial curriculum; and (3) a retail selling and store service curriculum.

The Smith-Hughes Act, in 1917, provided the basis for assisting the development of business education through the use of federal funds. The Federal Board for Vocational Education set up by the Smith-Hughes legislation, issued a report in 1919 that provided for high school specialized programs in general clerical training, general business, accounting, stenographic and secretarial training, retail selling, and foreign trade and shipping.

In general today high school pupils in business education are prepared for four types of work: (1) stenography; (2) general office work, including typewriting; (3) bookkeeping; (4) selling. As much as thirty or more courses in business education may be found in the high school curriculum. Typewriting is perhaps the most popular of the business education courses. Typewriting may be offered in almost any grade of the junior or senior high school. Bookkeeping has the second highest enrollment in business education. It is commonly offered in grades 10-12.

General business and business arithmetic are usually taught in grade 9. Business law, salesmanship, and office practice courses are generally taught in grade 12. Other of the more common courses in business education include the following: economic geography, business English, consumer economics, record keeping, cooperative office and store training, key punch operation, and machine accounting.

Distributive education is concerned with providing work training for students planning to engage in distribution and services to the public. The occupations involved in distributive education are classified into three areas: retailing, wholesaling, and services. Although some schools may begin work for distributive education in grade 11, normally most school districts restrict the distributive education work program to high school seniors. Distributive education curriculum students are placed in the business establishment of a cooperating merchant where they usually work as paid employees for about 15 hours a week.

The majority of junior colleges offer at least one business subject. The general business curriculum in most junior colleges is a two-year terminal program and is designed to provide training over a wide spectrum of business activities.

The Practical Arts

Industrial Arts

Industrial arts is that phase of the educational program concerned with orienting secondary school students through study and experience to the technical-industrial side of society for the purposes of enabling them to deal more intelligently with consumers' goods, and to use leisure time more effectively. Briefly, industrial arts is that part of general education that includes a study of the materials, processes, and products of manufacturing.

Paleolithic man (c. 125,000 B.C.) probably made the first tool which was, without doubt, a piece of stone carved to fit the hand. Man's next industrial achievement was the more skillfully polished stone implements of Neolithic man. Jewelry dating back to 8,000 B.C. has been found in Mesopotamia. Even in these early times there were means of transmitting from one generation to the next the skills and crafts possessed by men. As time passed, more clearly organized systems came into being, leading finally to well established systems of apprenticeship.

The movement to make hand skills or manual arts a part of general school training dates from the Renaissance. The manual training movement was the precursor of present-day industrial arts. Men such as Leibnitz, Comenius, Descartes, and others developed theories of manual arts as a protest against the formalism of the classical-humanistic curriculum of that period. The early French encyclopedist and humorous François Rabelais (c. 1494-1533) maintained that industrial subjects were an integral part of a complete education.

The theory of Jean Bacques Rousseau concerning natural processes in the education of youth, and the French revolutionary philosopher's contention that agriculture was "the best and happiest of all occupations" was an important influence in Pestalozzi's decision to establish his industrial school on his estates at Neuhof in Switzerland in 1774. The prime purpose of the Swiss educational reformer, sometimes referred to as "the father of manual training," was to lessen the misery, poverty, and suffering of children of the poor by teaching them how to earn their bread, and also how to cultivate their intellectual and moral nature.

Another Swiss nobleman, educator, and agriculturalist, Philipp Emanuel von Fellenberg (1771-1844), organized and established schools of both academic and trade types. Through his efforts and those of men of similar mind, manual activities came to be seen as important elements in the education of children. It is in these experiments that one sees the beginnings of what would become industrial arts in the United States.

European school systems were first to include work-training programs in the curricula of the public schools. Uno Cygnaeus, a Finnish preacher and teacher, in 1858 outlined a plan of handiwork for primary schools, and in 1868 some form of manual work was made compulsory in all primary schools in that country for boys in rural districts. A well-organized scheme of educational tool work for boys between the ages of twelve and fifteen, aimed mainly at the production of domestic utensils, was developed into a recognized school work-system in Sweden. In 1877 this work system, called "Sloyd," was introduced into the Folk Schools as a voluntary subject, and government aid was granted in support of the instruction. A distinctive feature in French shopwork education in the upper elementary grades was that theoretical instruction was given by the classroom teacher while the practical instruction was given by artisan teachers.

One of the significant contributions to the development of manual education was made by the Russian technique of analyzing tool processes and construction methods. The "Russian System" first gained recognition in the United States through the exhibit of the Imperial Technical School of St. Petersburg (founded in 1828) at the Centennial Exhibition at Philadelphia in 1876. The central idea of this system of shop-work instruction is the analysis of a craft into its fundamental processes and typical constructions, and the presentation of these elements in an orderly and sequential scheme as separate exercises.

The modern industrial arts program in the United States has its roots in the manual training movement of the late nineteenth century. C. M. Woodward, often referred to as the father of manual training in the United States, founded the Manual Training School of Washington University at St. Louis on June 6, 1879. The school's motto, "The Cultured Mind—The Skillful Hand," reflects the Woodward philosophy that manual training held value for all boys. Many manual arts high schools were established during the 1880-1890 decade. The objective of the manual training high school was to offer, in addition to college preparatory work, programs which would give students a good foundation if they desired to enter a trade upon leaving high school.

At the turn of the century general high schools came to add some of the manual training courses to their curricula. The fact that the general high schools successfully introduced these courses was an important factor in the acceptance of manual training as an integral part of general education. In 1904 Charles R. Richards, director of the manual training department of Columbia University, suggested that the term industrial arts replace the term manual training. He and others thought the new term was more in keeping with, and descriptive of, the nature of this type of instruction.

Today, nearly all secondary schools offer some form of industrial arts instruction. In most secondary schools industrial arts curriculum offerings are organized around some or all of the following areas: (1) drafting; (2) woodworking; (3) metalworking; (4) power mechanics; (5) electricity and electronics; (6) graphic arts; and (7) crafts.

Industrial arts at the junior high school level has as its primary objective the provision of industrial experiences of an exploratory nature. Industrial arts offerings in junior high schools vary little from school to school. The typical junior high school pattern calls for a general shop course in the seventh and eighth grade, with some opportunity for elective courses in grade 9. The general shop course generally includes metal work, woodwork, plastics, leather, jewelry, and electrical work. Frequently, this pattern is split so that the student takes industrial arts for one semester in each of the seventh and eighth grades.

The senior high school industrial arts program is much more diverse than is the junior high school program. Industrial arts educators agree that the most appropriate function of industrial arts at the high school level is to provide opportunities for increasing competency and experience in industrial arts skills gained in the junior high school.[10] Some of the nonvocational industrial arts subjects offered in the senior high school are: general shop, woodworking, mechanical drawing, metal work, printing, electrical work, handicrafts, and automobile mechanics. These courses are commonly offered at multigrade levels.

It is possible to identify three types of programs of industrial arts in the senior high school. They are: (1) offerings for the terminal student who does not intend to pursue his education after graduation from high school; (2) offerings for the college-bound student; and (3) prevocational programs for those entering technical and vocational industrial programs.[11]

Home Economics

Home economics is the science and art of home living, including the areas of homemaking, family and social relationships, economic efficiency, and civic responsibility. Education for girls developed slowly in this country, and home economics, at first called domestic economy, was originally advocated by those concerned for the education of girls.

Home economics had its beginnings in 1798 when needlework was introduced in the elementary schools in Boston. During the early years of the nineteenth century some outstanding women pleaded the cause of education for girls. Feminists Mrs. Emma Hart Willard (1787-1870) and Catherine Beecher (1800-1878) operated private schools for girls in Vermont and Connecticut, respectively. Harriet Beecher Stowe (1811-1896), sister of Catherine, and also a leader promoting education for women, published in 1841 what perhaps may be considered the first textbook in home economics, called *A Treatise on Domestic Economy*. By 1885 sewing and cooking were often taught in public schools while boys were taking courses in manual training.

Pioneers in the field of home economics instruction met to exchange ideas and formulate plans in a series of conferences beginning in 1899. These meetings in the state of New York, known as the Lake Placid Conferences, resulted in the organization of the American Home Economics Association in 1909. It was this group which also suggested, in 1901, the name home economics, for this area of the curriculum devoted to the scientific, social, and economic study of the home.

Legislation played an important part in the development of school programs in home economics between the years 1905 and

1920. By 1914 nearly three-fourths of the states had authorized instruction in home economics. Most of this legislation also involved the promotion of manual training programs as well. Bills were introduced into the Congress of the United States as early as 1907 to provide aid for instruction in agriculture, mechanic arts, and home economics. Finally, in 1917, the Smith-Hughes Act was passed.

The Smith-Hughes Law had a great stimulus on the development of home economics education throughout the nation. The law provided federal assistance to fund agricultural, trade, home economics, and industrial education programs of less than college level to pupils fourteen years of age and over in public schools. An analysis of the job of homemaking made shortly after the federal law was passed furnished a basis for the kind of program which could be financed by vocational education funds. The George-Deen Law in 1936, and the George-Barden Act of 1946 further extended and expanded the original provisions of the Smith-Hughes Law.

Today, home economics as a separate subject of instruction appears in most school systems in the junior high school grades of 7, 8 or 9. The amount of time spent on home economics varies with the school. Many Boards of Education require a full year of home economics in both grades 7 and 8. Units in nursing and baby care are often included in home economics in grades 7 and 8. Federal subsidies for home economics do not begin until grade 9. In the ninth grade the home economics program is usually offered for the full year and provides an opportunity for pupils to study several aspects of home economics of interest to them as participating, responsible family members. Modern day home economics is rapidly losing its connotation of being "cooking and sewing" classes, and is becoming a family-oriented program.

The amount and kind of home economics offered at the senior high school level varies with the size of the school and with the types of pupils enrolled. Many tenth and eleventh grade courses are part of a sequence which begins in grade 9, and more of them are offered as part of a vocational program than as nonvocational courses. The course in grade 12 is more often than not called "Family Living." The sequential program, beginning with grade 9, is usually focused on preparation for home and family living. It is often presented as a vocational homemaking program. Many high schools are beginning also to offer a course, usually called "Family Living," for both boys and girls in grade 12. This is a course which attempts to deal directly with many of the present and future problems of the enrollees such as, for example, sex and finances.

Conclusion

The purpose of this chapter has been to trace and describe the place of vocational training and the practical arts in the American secondary school curriculum. Work is a fundamental element in the development and integration of human personality. If the nature of secondary education is essentially general or liberal arts education, and if the nature of the liberal arts is to develop the humanity of man, then, perhaps, a case can be made for the inclusions of some vocational training within the secondary school curriculum. The last chapter of this book will, among other matters, look at the question of whether secondary education ought to be liberal education or vocational education.

Chapter XIX
Footnotes

[1] U.S. Bureau of the Census, *Statistical Abstract of the United States, 1967,* as quoted by *Standard Education Almanac, 1968* (Los Angeles: Academic Media, Inc., 1968), p. 391.

[2] Public Law 88-210, 88th Cong., 1963.

[3] Glenn Z. Stevens, *Agricultural Education* (Washington, D.C.: The Center for Applied Research in Education, Inc., 1967), pp. 32-33.

[4] *Ibid.,* p. 33.

[5] U.S. Bureau of the Census, *op. cit.,* p. 391.

[6] Adolphe E. Meyer, *An Educational History of the American People* (New York: McGraw-Hill Book Company, 1967), p. 355.

[7] Leonard H. Clark, and others, *The American Secondary School Curriculum* (New York: The Macmillan Company, 1965), p. 326.

[8] U.S. Bureau of the Census, *op. cit.,* p. 391.

[9] Lloyd V. Douglas, *Business Education* (Washington, D.C.: The Center for Applied Research in Education, Inc., 1963), p. 12.

[10] John L. Feirer, and John R. Lindbeck, *Industrial Arts Education* (Washington, D.C.: The Center for Applied Research in Education, Inc., 1964), p. 39.

[11] *Ibid.,* pp. 40-41.

Selected References

American Council on Industrial Arts Education. *Research in Industrial Arts Education.* Ninth Yearbook. Bloomington, Illinois: McKnight and McKnight Publishing Company, 1960.

Clark, Leonard H., and others. *The American Secondary School Curriculum.* New York: The Macmillan Company, 1965.

Coon, Beulah I. *Home Economics Instruction in the Secondary Schools.* Washington, D.C.: The Center for Applied Research in Education, Inc., 1964.

Douglas, Lloyd V. *Business Education.* Washington, D.C.: The Center for Applied Research in Education, Inc., 1963.

―――, (ed.). *The Business Education Program in the Expanding Secondary School.* Washington, D.C.: United Business Education Association, 1957.

Feirer, John L., and John R. Lindbeck. *Industrial Arts Education.* Washington, D.C.: The Center for Applied Research in Education, Inc., 1964.

Graham, Jessie. *The Evolution of Business Education in the United States and Its Implications for Business-Teacher Education.* Los Angeles: University of Southern California Press, 1933.

Hamlin, H. M. *Public School Education in Agriculture.* Danville, Illinois: The Interstate Printers and Publishers, 1962.

Hammonds, Carsie, and Harold Binkley. *Farming Programs for Students in Vocational Agriculture.* Danville, Illinois: The Interstate Printers and Publishers, 1962.

Hatcher, Hazel M., and Mildred E. Andrews. *The Teaching of Home Economics.* Boston: Houghton Mifflin Company, 1963.

Mays, Arthur B. *Essentials of Industrial Education.* New York: McGraw-Hill Book Company, Inc., 1952.

Stevens, Glenn Z. *Agricultural Education.* New York: The Center for Applied Research in Education, Inc., 1967.

Williamson, Maude, and Mary Stewart Lyle. *Homemaking Education in the High School.* New York: Appleton-Century-Crofts, Inc., 1961.

Chapter XX

THE FUTURE OF SECONDARY EDUCATION

The Modern Industrial State and Education

Education may finally come into its own in the twenty-first century. Education seems predestined to become a principal preoccupation of the modern, industrial, nation-state. In a recent study measuring the costs of all types of education in the United States, the total cost for 1956-57 was computed to be $60 billion. This was 12.9 per cent of the adjusted gross national product for that year. Education has come to be regarded as a necessity to the state because it has seemed to be the path to prosperity and power. It does seem reasonable to conclude that the returns from educational expenditures are not only positive, but are at least of the same order of magnitude as the returns from other kinds of investment, both in terms of individual earnings and in contribution to the national income. The belief is widespread that the advance of industry and technology is intimately tied up with the expansion of education. Galbraith states in *The New Industrial State* that, "As compared with the pressures of the earlier industrialism, there can only be satisfaction at the influence which the industrial system exerts for improved primary and secondary education."[1]

Today, all states are growing more affluent in comparison with their former condition. Social class systems are breaking up. Universal, free, compulsory schooling is accepted as the goal in every nation. Traditionally, the American ethos has affirmed that the technological resources of modern society can and should be exploited to advance the excellence and significance of all, rather than an elite social class, and that education can significantly help to bring this about.

In the ancient world the relationship between the state and education was much discussed by such philosophers as Plato and Aristotle. During the latter phase of the Roman empire education did become a state monopoly. In medieval times education was the business of the church. The Christian Church was primarily concerned with the salvation of souls, and souls have no national characteristics.[2] It was not until the beginning of the nineteenth century when Napoleonic armies unleashed the forces of nationalism on the European continent, and the Prussian reformers such as Fichte and others proposed to use education for national purposes, that education truly became a national concern. Napoleon was content to train loyal citizens and efficient bureaucrats, whereas the Prussian leaders wanted to release and develop the abilities of the German people.

It is now taken for granted in every nation-state, with the possible exception of the United States, that education is a national responsibility. Even in the United States there is agreement that the obligation resting on government to promote the common welfare includes the duty to see to the education of the people. The only question is, which government—federal, state, or local. Many signs today point to increased centralization of national control of education in America. The cost of the education establishment is too heavy for local authorities, and only the nation-state can adequately finance such a vast enterprise.

Not only education, but production, health, religion, and recreation have become institutionalized into huge bureaucracies. American society today can be characterized as one in which change occurs rapidly, largely as a result of scientific and technological developments which are channeled through these vast highly centralized institutions. Increasingly, the problem in American society is how to fashion a way of life in which security, identity, and individuality can be retained at a time when the institutions basic to society become more and more centralized, concentrating more power into the hands of fewer leaders.

In the latter part of the twentieth century it would seem that the aim of educational systems in the United States and elsewhere is to process youth for the scientific, technical, industrial nation-state. Political, military, industrial, and business interests demand large numbers of scientists and technicians. They demand a search for and an exploitation of educated talent. The development of technology and automation with implications for changing labor requirements places new and substantial demands on the occupational mobility of the labor force. Changes in technology are proceeding rapidly. The new technology demands workers in new and more expanding occupations. This movement seems to threaten a reduction of education to the status of an instrument of military, economic, and political policy.

Galbraith states the industrial system has induced an enormous expansion in education, and he warns that unless its tendencies are clearly forseen and strongly resisted, it will place a preclusive emphasis on education that most serves the needs, but least questions the goals, of that system. Education, he writes:

> ... is among other things, an apparatus for affecting belief and inducing more critical belief. The industrial system, by making trained and educated manpower the decisive factor of production, requires a highly developed educational system. If the educational system serves generally the beliefs of the industrial system, the influence and monolithic character of the latter will be enhanced. By the same token, should it be superior to and independent of the industrial system, it can be the necessary force for skepticism, emancipation and pluralism.[3]

Today the sweep of Western science and technology is preparing the way for the formation of the world community of tomorrow. A world community is being formed by communication, by shared knowledge, by economic ties, by travel, and by a developing sense of common destiny. At the same time the world is being united by technology, it is being divided by post-colonial nationalism into a larger and larger number of nation-states, and each sovereignty will direct its educational system toward the preservation and expansion of national power.[4]

The status of education in the emerging world community is not unlike the situation in the United States. Here in this country education has been the responsibility of the individual states. The remnants of this arrangement can be perceived in the emphasis the schools place on local history and government. Yet nobody today thinks it sensible for a state to educate its pupils as though they were going to live and die there.[5]

Educational systems are the work of the nation-states or are approved and supervised by them. An educational system must reflect what the political community wants it to do. The aims of educational institutions are determined by the culture in which they are situated. What an education should do, ideally, for the individual is to prepare him to understand his experience and reflect upon it in such a way as to be wiser than he would otherwise be.

In a democracy a government can maintain justice and order, peace and freedom, only by the exercise of intelligent decision-making. Consent of the governed should mean that every act of assent on the part of the governed is a product of learning. Political freedom cannot endure unless it is accompanied by the provision for the unlimited acquisition of knowledge. Unless everybody can be educated, democracy is a fraud and an illusion.

Liberal Education Versus Vocational Education

What is Education?

Thomas Henry Huxley, the great nineteenth century British biologist, once defined education as the instruction of the intellect in the laws of nature in which he included, not merely things and their forces, but men and their ways; he included also in his definition the fashioning of the affections and of the will into an earnest and loving desire to move in harmony with those laws of nature. Webster's Third International Dictionary defines education as the act of providing with knowledge, skill, competence, or desirable qualities of behavior or character; a conditioning, strengthening, or disciplining of the mind or faculties. An educator might define education as the aggregate of all those processes by means of which a person develops abilities, attitudes, and other forms of behavior of positive value in the society in which he lives. Jean Piaget, the Swiss psychologist-biologist-philosopher, concludes that education exists to create men who are capable of doing new things, not simply repeating what other generations have done, producing men who are creative, inventive and discoverers. Hutchins merely defines education as the deliberate, organized attempt to help people become intelligent.

Every person who has not sustained brain damage can learn. Everybody has a mind and everybody has the ability, aptitude, and need to learn to use it. Learning does not stop as long as a person lives. The pivot of educational strategy is the secondary school because it is the high school in America—and its counterpart for the education of adolescents elsewhere—that mediates between the potentialities of childhood and the actualities of adulthood. What is vitally needed is a comprehensive and systematic view of the secondary school curriculum. Secondary education and training, be it vocational, technical, or academic, must be constantly reevaluated. There is an abiding need also for a reassessment of what the outcomes and uses of secondary schooling actually are in the society of the modern industrial state and emerging world community.

Education, it has been pointed out, is a basic responsibility and need of the nation-state. Each nation has its trained manpower requirements. Each nation must educate for citizenship and indoctrinate for loyalty to the state. The twentieth century has witnessed the gradual democratization of secondary education. In America, the most advanced industrial country, the notion of an elite secondary school supported by taxes has never taken hold. The United States has undertaken to get everybody into school and keep him there as long as possible. In Europe school entrance examinations are being eliminated or made less deadly. Upper educational units are being deprived of their control over the admission of students from lower units. Progress through the educational system is being made easier for students who do not have a natural aptitude for the standard academic subjects.

A fundamental educational question to be answered in the closing decades of the twentieth century is this: is the problem of providing secondary education for all children fundamentally different from that of providing a particular kind of secondary education for a few selected pupils? Traditionally, the secondary school has provided a nonvocational education generally referred to as liberal or general education. This education was thought to be suitable for a freeman as distinguished from that training suitable for a slave; in other words, a broad academic education as opposed to a strictly vocational education. The purpose of secondary education was to free the mind and enable the possessor to assume the positions of leadership in his society. It is a fact much overlooked, however, that almost all liberal arts education given at the secondary level is, in a broad sense, vocational in function. It represents a program necessary for modes of employment which require university-level training.

The modern nation-state, including the post-colonial underdeveloped nations, are seeking to become industrialized as rapidly as possible because along that road lies the goals of national wealth and power. These goals require increasingly complex and sophisticated manpower training needs for which longer periods of schooling are mandatory. It is therefore necessary that all nations provide some form of schooling for all their adolescents. Should secondary education for all adolescents consist of the education previously available for the few, or is it to consist of a variety of curricula so as to ensure that different aptitudes, abilities, and interests will be provided for? Should secondary education be a liberal education, or should it be a vocational education?

The case for Vocational Education

In the twentieth century education has come to be regarded as a sound investment in national wealth and power. The belief is widely held that the larger the pool of literate, schooled citizens, the greater will be the industrial, technological, and scientific progress of the nation-state. Education promotes the wealth of individuals as well as nations: it reduces unemployment, increases earnings, augments productivity, encourages occupational and geographic mobility, and provides more employment opportunities. The fact that the most advanced industrial nations of the world have the most extensive educational systems has given considerable credence to this belief in education.

Totalitarian regimes have particularly emphasized the vocational aspect of education. The educational system in the Soviet Union is directed to producing manpower. Soviet schooling strongly emphasizes vocational, technical, and scientific training. It is the author's belief that the leaders of the Soviet Union strongly hold the conviction that scientific, technical, and industrial development is the path to national power and prosperity.

Many of the post-World War II nations on the continents of Africa and Asia also have sought to develop school systems around nation-building curricula. While most administrators and teachers in these new nation-states are products of colonial-area training, many are beginning to turn against the elite school systems of which they are products. President Julius Nyerere of Tanzania in Africa is a former teacher who is trying to revolutionize education in his country. Recently, one Tanzanian education official stated, "We must rethink the value of education. We may eventually find that mass liberal education is detrimental to the goals of our country."[6]

The reorganization of the French school system caused the French premier to say in 1965 that it was the object of the schools to sort out the different kinds of people and fit them into their careers. In Britain, the traditional grammar school is disappearing in the changeover to neighborhood comprehensive schools. Business studies have been introduced to 14 and 15-year-olds in levels of secondary schools. The inclusion of business studies as a subject in the examinations for the General Certificate of Education is regarded as a forward step by some British educators. In the United States, where the democratization of secondary education was begun, the comprehensive high school with its college-preparatory curriculum, vocational curriculum, and commercial curriculum was devised to serve the diverse needs and interests of American youth.

As secondary education has become possible and even legally required for large groups of adolescents who previously would not have sought it, there has been the effort to adjust school programs in order to make them relevant to the diversity of the new school population. This effort, in fact, has been largely to orient the curriculum more and more in terms of the vocational needs of the individual and of the society.

Along with land, labor, and capital, education may be added as the fourth factor of production. The current economic value of education stems in large measure from the growing demand for people with specialized skills and knowledge and a corresponding decline in the demand for people lacking such a background. This shift in labor demand is a result of the increasing rate of change in science and technology, as exemplified by automation and computer science. Technology has created a new relationship between man and his work, and only through more and better education and training can this gap be bridged. For most of the occupations of this new technological world, job entry and upgrading become increasingly a matter of education. Education has become the critical ladder and barrier in the world of work.

In the United States in recent years, the education of the disadvantaged and of minority group youths has received considerable attention. The dropouts from secondary education of whom slum youth, and especially Negro slum youth, constitute a significant number, are said to need vocational education in the secondary school which will fit them for immediate employment. It is said, also, that a general education of liberal arts, and especially a sophisticated, intellectual program of studies is irrelevant to their capacities, concerns, and circumstances.

Today, for young workers entering an occupation, a high school diploma is a virtual necessity to obtain entry into a production-oriented job. The position of those who favor vocational education as the road which the secondary school should follow have two basic points to make. First, they are convinced that vocational education is necessary for the preservation and expansion of national wealth, power, and prestige. Second, they believe that vocational education is much more relevant to the needs, interests, and abilities of the adolescent youth now attending the secondary school than the traditional, highly academic liberal arts program of the rapidly disappearing elitist secondary schools of the past.

The Case for Liberal Education

The liberal educator believes that liberal education, which is non-specialized, non-vocational, general education, will have to be provided by the secondary school. With specialization and differentiation increasingly emphasized at the post-secondary and higher education levels, the secondary school is the last refuge of general education.

A liberal education is designed to develop students as personalities rather than as trained specialists, and to transmit a common cultural heritage. It is a broad type of education aimed at developing attitudes, abilities, and behavior considered desirable by society, but not necessarily preparing the learner for specific types of vocational pursuit.

A liberal education at the secondary school level is a common education for all educable adolescents in all their great diversity. The cultivation of diversity in education is essential for the growth and survival of society. It is human diversity, Hutchins states, that enables society to adapt itself to changing situations, and it is the teacher in the classroom who can recognize and cultivate diversity among human beings.[7] But how will a common program of liberal arts studies provide for diversity of abilities and interests among adolescents? How will a liberal education meet the needs of the slum and the suburb, the gifted and the dull?

The liberal educator would answer that variability for different ability levels can be obtained by adjusting the sophistication and detail of what is taught. He would deny that a liberal education is a survey of generally everything. He would maintain that what is taught should consist of those central skills, ideas, and understandings which can be most significantly and widely used in order to deal with life in our times. To the liberal educator it seems clear there is need for grounding in general studies as a foundation for vocational preparation, with specialization waiting for post-secondary training. If there is to be a maximum of choice and mobility to the student in his life, and if early technological unemployment is to be avoided, then says the liberal educator, specificity in vocational training must await post-secondary training.

The liberal educator must, perhaps reluctantly, agree that the concern for preparing youth to meet narrow and specific role expectations probably cannot be avoided in the modern industrial nation-state. Yet he feels that as long as the ideals of citizenship and the cultivation of intelligence are valid for secondary education, any curriculum which limits students' role conceptions merely to the character of job openings at a given time is contrary to those ideals.

The nation-state which tries to ration education according to the predicted demand for specialists five, ten, or fifteen years ahead, will fail. Frequent changes in Soviet educational policy have largely resulted from the failure of the system reliably to forecast the manpower requirements of the state. Chairman Khrushchev is reported to have remarked in 1965, "We do not have any scientifically reliable method of estimating how many and what kind of specialists we need in different branches of the national economy, what future demand will be for a certain kind of specialist, and when such a demand will arise."[8]

Hutchins maintains that the rapidity of change in today's technological world, the superiority of training on the job, and the prospect of increasing leisure time to which vocational training can have no relevance, all tend to move vocational education away from the center of educational interest. Furthermore, he states, the amount of training required for most jobs is so slight that extended preparation for them in schools is a waste of time.[9] Galbraith says that education that accords with the needs of the industrial system does not have a natural aspect of interest, plausibility, or importance. Much of it, he declares, is dull.[10]

Present vocational educational programs may well be preparing a wave of school graduates for technological unemployment ten or fifteen years hence. The type of educational program that can assure immediate employment for the dropout may, in fact, be only a temporary stopgap in a rapidly changing labor market. In vocational training programs, the fundamental elements which are basic to understanding, anticipating, and preparing for scientific and technological change are almost entirely missing. The dropout who gets a job immediately is going to be a social problem by the time he is in his late twenties or early thirties because he will not have the base in knowledge and skills needed for the job mobility and quick retraining in a labor market which is demanding greater intellectual acuity.

What, then, are the advantages of a liberal education for all youth? The liberal educator answers that a liberal education prepares youth for anything that may happen. It fits today's young people to be tomorrow's citizens of the nation-state and world community. It prepares them for a life of learning. It frees their mind of prejudice. It lays the basis of practical wisdom. It implies the habit of thinking about the most important matters. It implies the capacity to distinguish the significant from the inconsequential. It develops critical standards of thought and action.[11] It teaches them to reason reflectively and humanely upon man, his world, and his problems. It teaches them to become effective decision-makers.

Trends in Secondary Education

The point of view of the liberal educator seems most likely to prevail in the secondary school. Secondary education will be a common program of liberal art studies for all youth. The comprehensive school seems likely to be the characteristic secondary school of the future. Sudden-death examinations in European school systems are being eliminated or made less lethal. Upper educational units are being deprived of their control over the admission of students from lower units. Progress through the system is being made easier for students who do not take readily to the academic subjects.

The philosophy of the comprehensive secondary school offering a common program of liberal arts studies is based on the assumption that it is possible to teach an essential set of key concepts, skills, and logical operations to all adolescents in the normal range of intelligence. The Harvard psychologist Bruner states in *The Process of Education:*

> *We begin with the hypothesis that any subject can be taught effectively in some intellectually honest form to any child at any stage of development. It is a bold hypothesis and an essential one in thinking about the nature of the curriculum. No evidence exists to contradict it; considerable evidence is being amassed that supports it.* [12]

The pupil in the secondary school of the future will study a subject at a level corresponding to his scholastic achievement in that subject. All students will be tested carefully upon entry into the secondary school for placement in one of the levels of each of the curricular areas. Evaluated criteria to be used for placement purposes will include standardized group and individual IQ tests, reading comprehension tests, achievement tests in the respective curricula or subject-matter areas, review of past records of students in the curricular areas, consideration of job and home demands upon students, and the assessment of the physical health and emotional maturity of the pupils.

To adept instruction to differences in ability, the variable element is not the content, but the way it is taught, the rate at which it is taught, and the level at which it is taught. In the advanced level of any subject the increase in complexity, abstractness, and sophistication of the material will offset the superior rate with which the brighter student works, and so the length of time needed for each course on the various levels will be equalized.

It is possible to foresee a four track program for each curricular level in a large high school. Track One will be an honors course for the academically gifted students. Track Two will be for the normal or average academic students. Track Three will provide a program for the slow, nonacademically oriented pupils. A fourth track might be established for the under-achieving, reluctant or special problem pupils.

Special attention will be focused on the educational problems of the culturally deprived slum child. The child from a poor family and a bad neighborhood is confronted in school with an alien culture. If he is also a member of a minority race, the situation is even worse. Can one expect him to master relatively high-level skills, knowledge, and arts, when it seems evident that his interest is solely in getting a job in the current labor market? His family and his neighborhood decisively mold the slum child before the school has a chance.

Slum schools are the educational problems they are primarily because they are first of all economic, political, and social problems. While serious attention and considerable expenditures have been made on improving the schools in depressed and impoverished areas, unless these efforts are accompanied by equally extensive efforts to improve the conditions under which the pupils live, they are bound to have slight effects.

The slum child must be removed from the environment of the slum. Boarding schools, formerly restricted to the privileged classes are now being considered for those who are culturally deprived. Time will be required to solve the educational problems of the slum child. But the answer must be found unless the curriculum is to remain, in effect, an institutionalized apologist for social neglect.

The technology of the twentieth century will invade the sacred precincts of education in the twenty-first century. The process of educating will become the dialectical method called maieutics. Maieutics is the learning process ascribed to Socrates by which he sought to elicit and clarify the ideas of others by interrogation and insistence on close and logical reasoning. This form of intellectual midwifery, as the derivation of the word suggests, most certainly should comprise the heart of the program of common liberal art studies of the comprehensive secondary school.

The new technology of education will speed up or end the teacher's time spent on cramming students with information. Where information is required, teaching machines can impart knowledge more effectively than by any means previously known to man. Whether teachers will then utilize the maieutic function depends on the convictions and resolutions of teachers, administrators, and laymen alike.

Technology as defined is the systematic application of scientific or other organized knowledge to practical tasks. In education it is now possible to select, admit, teach, examine, and graduate students by machine. Methods of examination can be computerized. Classes can be scheduled by computers. Courses of all kinds can be taught by mechanical means: films, closed and open circuit television, and programmed learning. Technology has freed the educational system from limitations of space, staff, and time. The new educational technology will extend training, rote learning, and the transmission of information because these are the objects it can most easily accomplish.

Programmed learning is the technique in which the material to be learned is organized and presented in a format permitting self-instruction and self-testing, and enables the student to learn at his own pace with a minimum of formal instruction. Programmed learning is commonly associated with the use of teaching machines, but it doesn't require one. A teaching machine is any device employed for the purpose of presenting a self-instructional program to a student. It may be an elaborate electronic device, or it may be a textbook in which control of the sequential learning steps is achieved through the physical arrangement of the materials on the printed page.

Several techniques of programming have been developed. First, there is the linear, or straight-line program. In linear programming, what a student should learn from a program is set up as the goal. The student is given an item of information and he is required to answer a question and then he is provided with the correct response for comparison with his own. He then proceeds to the next frame where the process is repeated. The subject is presented one step at a time, building from the simple to the complex.

The second technique is called branching programming. The branching program presents the student with an item of information, provides him also with alternate answers, and on the basis of his decision, instructs him to advance to another frame. At the subsequent frame he is informed whether his choice was correct and, if not, is told why his choice was incorrect. The student either returns to the original frame or is routed through a sub-program designed to remedy the deficiency indicated by his choice of the incorrect response. When he selects the correct alternative, he moves to the next frame in the program. This process is repeated at each step throughout the program.

Audio-visual media, such as films and tapes, are designed to improve learning. Investigators have found that the use of audio-visual materials, together with textbooks and other devices, makes an improvement in students' performance that is statistically measurable. Educational theorists since Comenius have pointed out that perception is largely visual experience, reinforced by auditory and other senses. Motion pictures and television can present the lectures of good teachers in place of the lectures of the poor ones. Reproductions of any process, artistic or scientific, can be brought into the classroom on film. Information, when it is required, can be more effectively communicated by the new technology in education than by any previously known to man.

The secondary school of the future will produce men and women who are human beings in the fullest sense. They will not be robots or automatons or narrowly specialized technicians, but human beings in full possession of their educated faculties, and obsessed with the desire to live and enjoy the good life.

Conclusion

In 1818 Thomas Jefferson wrote, "If the condition of man is to be progressively ameliorated . . . education is to be the chief instrument in effecting it." The twenty-first century should realize the vision of the third President of the United States. The secondary school in the third millenium A.D. should be a truly comprehensive institution of education. Secondary schooling, required of all, ought to be a common program of liberal art studies. Education, said Thomas Henry Huxley, "is the instruction of the intellect in the laws of Nature under which name I include not merely things and their forces, but men and their ways; and the fashioning of the affections and of the will into an earnest and loving desire to move in harmony with those laws."

The theory of the comprehensive secondary school is based on the idea that it is possible to teach essential concepts and skills to all adolescents within the normal range of intelligence. To adapt instruction to differences in ability, the variable element is not content, but the way it is taught, the rate at which it is taught, and the level at which it is taught.

In the twenty-first century, teaching machines and programmed instruction will free the secondary teacher from the onerous task of being, simply, a transmission belt to convey knowledge to students. The maieutic function of education never fully realized and implemented since the time Socrates will become the major strategy of teaching. Students will be taught how to reason reflectively in terms of humanitarian interests and goals. Conceptual-inquiry processes of reasoning will consist of: (1) the analytic mode of reasoning, (2) the integrative mode of reasoning, and (3) the decision-making or policy mode of reasoning.

A democratic society in a world community can maintain justice and order, peace and freedom only by the exercise of intelligence. Consent of the governed should mean that every act of assent on the part of the governed is a product of learning. Progressive amelioration of the human condition, the dream of Jefferson, requires the new education.

Chapter XX

Footnotes

[1] John Kenneth Galbraith, *The New Industrial State* (Boston: Houghton Mifflin Company, 1967), p. 377.

[2] Robert M. Hutchins, "The Learning Society," *Britannica Perspectives*, II, (Chicago: Encyclopaedia Britannica, Inc., 1968), p. 695.

[3] Galbraith, *op. cit.*, p. 370.

[4] Hutchins, *op. cit.*, p. 695.

[5] *Ibid.*, p. 698.

[6] *Time Magazine,* July 26, 1968.

[7] Hutchins, *op. cit.*, p. 705.

[8] Nicholas DeWitt, *Educational and Professional Employment in the USSR* (Washington, D.C.: National Science Foundation, 1961), p. 517.

[9] Hutchins, *op. cit.*, p. 702.

[10] Galbraith, *op. cit.*, p. 374.

[11] Hutchins, *op. cit.*, p. 713.

[12] Jerome C. Bruner, *The Process of Education* (Cambridge, Massachusetts: Harvard University Press, 1960), p. 33.

Selected References

Bloom, Benjamin S., and others. *Taxonomy of Educational Objectives.* New York: Longmans, Green, 1956.

Broudy, Harry S., and others. *Democracy and Excellence in American Secondary Education.* Chicago: Rand McNally and Company, 1964.

Bruner, Jerome C. *The Process of Education.* Cambridge, Massachusetts: Harvard University Press, 1960.

Bush, Robert N., and Dwight W. Allen. *A New Design for High School Education.* New York: McGraw-Hill Book Company, 1964.

Conant, James B. *Slums and Suburbs.* New York: McGraw-Hill, 1961.

DeWitt, Nicholas. *Education and Professional Employment in the USSR.* Washington, D.C.: National Science Foundation, 1961.

Hutchins, Robert M. *The Learning Society.* New York: Frederick A. Praeger, Publishers, 1968.

Scott, C. Winfield, and others (eds.). *The Great Debate—Our Schools in Crisis.* Englewood Cliffs, New Jersey: Prentice-Hall, 1959.

NAME INDEX

Abelard, Peter, 31
Adams, Henry, 239
Alcuin, 26, 29
Alexander I, 74
Alexander VI, 51
Alexander the Great, 9, 12
Anaximander, 260
Antoninus, 18
Aquinas, Saint Thomas, 37
Archimedes, 261
Aristippus, 10
Aristotle, 5, 9-10, 13, 233, 260, 295
Armstrong, General Samuel Chapman, 284
Arnold, Thomas, 79
Athalaric, 25
Augustus, 19-20

Bacon, Francis, 55-56, 65, 75, 217, 261
Baker, James H., 142
Bancroft, George, 218, 239
Barnard, Henry, 143-145, 194
Basedow, Johann Bernhard, 275
Beard, Charles A., 240
Beecher, Catherine, 291
Benedict of Nursia, 27
Berthoin, J., 92
Bismarck, Otto von, 104, 107
Bobbitt, Franklin, 220
Boethius, 25
Borgia, Francisco, 51
Brimm, R. P., 151-152
Bruner, Jerome, 304
Bruni, Leonardo, 239
Burckhardt, Jacob, 38
Butler, Nicholas Murray, 173

Cabot, John, 124
Caesar, Julius, 19
Calvin, John, 48, 49, 52
Capella, Martianus, 25
Cassiodorus, Flavius, 25-26, 27
Catherine the Great, 74
Charles the Great (Charlemagne), 26, 28
Cheever, Ezekiel, 125
Cicero, Marcus, 16, 19, 37, 39, 47, 233
Clement III, 31
Coleman, Algernon, 231

Colet, John, 49
Columbus, Christopher, 124
Comenius, Johann Amos, 56-58, 65, 75, 217, 288
Comte, Auguste, 252
Conant, James Bryant, 152, 178-181
Condorcet, Marquis Marie Jean Antoine Nicholas de Caritat de, 69
Constantine, 32
Copernicus, Nicolaus, 55, 261
Counts, George S., 240
Cousin, Victor, 70
Crosland, Anthony, 84
Cygnaeus, Uno, 289

da Feltre, Vittorino, 39-40, 43, 275
Dante (Alighieri), 37
Darwin, Charles, 264
Descartes, Rene, 55, 56, 65, 75, 288
Dewey, John, 112, 143, 146-148, 173, 226, 272
Douglass, Harl R., 160

Eichhorn, Karl Friedrich, 218
Eliot, Charles W., 142, 172, 178
Elyot, Thomas, 49
Empedocles, 260
Ennius, Quintus, 16
Epicurus, 11
Erasmus, Desiderius, 42-43, 49
Eratosthenes, 244
Euclid, 257

Fellenberg, Philipp Emanual von, 219, 284, 289
Fermat, Pierre, 258
Fichte, Johann Gottlieb, 72, 296
Finch, Robert, 192
Franklin, Benjamin, 127, 129-130, 131, 134, 230, 263
Frederick II, 32
Frederick the Great, 71
Frederick William I, 71
Frederick William II, 71
Frederick William III, 71-72
Fries, Charles, 227

Name Index

Galbraith, John Kenneth, 295, 297, 303
Galen, 13, 20
Galileo, Galilei, 55, 261, 262
Gardner, John W., 166
Gibson, John S., 253
Gorgias, 6-7
Gratian, 19
Groote, Gerhart, 41
Guarino of Verona, 40, 43, 216
Gutenberg, Johann, 43
Guts-Muths, Johann Christoph, 275

Hadrian, 18
Hall, G. Stanley, 143, 145-146, 221-222
Harper, William Rainey, 152, 173
Harvey, William, 264
Hayes, Carleton, 240
Hecker, Julius, 72, 217
Herbart, Johann Friedrich, 64-65, 75, 218, 222
Herodotus, 13, 239
Hippias, 6
Hippocrates, 13, 20, 32
Hitler, Adolph, 105
Hoffman, Julius J., 163
Homer, 3
Horn, Ernest, 240
Howe, Harold, 167
Humboldt, Alexander von, 244
Humboldt, Baron Wilhelm von, 72, 73
Hutchins, Robert, 298, 302
Huxley, Thomas Henry, 217, 298, 307

Isidore, Saint, 26

Jahn, Friedrich Ludwig, 219, 275-276
Jefferson, Thomas 130-131, 134, 307
Jesus, 24
Julian, 18-19
Justinian, 19

Kepler, Johann, 55
Kersh, R. C., 278-279
Keynes, John Maynard, 247
Khrushchev, Nikita, 302
Kingsley, Clarence, 155

La Salle, Jean Baptiste de, 69
Lavoisier, Antoine Laurent, 261
Leibnitz, Baron Wilhelm von, 258, 288
Lenin, Nikolai, 74, 112
Leo X, 45
Lewis, Diocletion, 219, 276
Lieber, Francis, 249
Livius, Andronicus, 15
Lobachevsky, Nikolai Ivanovich, 258
Locke, John, 58-61, 65, 75, 130, 217, 219

Louis VII, 31
Louis Philippe, 70
Loyola, Ignatius, 50-51
Luther, Martin, 42, 44-46, 47, 48, 49, 124

Makarenko, A. S., 119
Malthus, Thomas, 246
Mann, Horace, 131-133, 134, 137
Markushevich, A. I., 116-117
Marx, Karl, 247
Mason, Lowell, 270
McCullock, John, 239
McGuire, Frederick, 278, 279
Melanchthon, Philipp, 46-47, 49, 52, 70
Mendel, Gregor, 264
Michelson, Albert, 263
Mill, John Stuart, 246-247
Morgan, Thomas Hunt, 264
Morot-Sir, M. Edouard, 96
Morse, Jedediah, 244
Muller, Johann, 258

Napoleon, 70, 72, 98, 218, 295-296
Newton, Sir Isaac, 262
Niebuhr, Barthold Georg, 239
Nightengale, A. F., 143
Nyerere, Julius, 300

Panetta, Leon E., 163
Paul III, 50
Peter the Great, 74
Petrarch, 38, 216, 239
Philip of Macedon, 11
Piaget, Jean, 298
Pius II, see Aneas Silvius
Plato, 5, 7-9, 13, 233, 249, 295
Plutarch, 17, 37
Posse, Baron Nils, 276
Prodicus, 6
Prosser, Charles A., 160
Protagorus, 6
Pythagorus, 257

Quintilian, Marcus, 17-18, 37, 38, 39, 43, 233, 275

Rabelais, Francois, 289
Rafferty, Max, 160-161
Ricardo, David, 246
Richards, Charles R., 290
Ritter, Karl, 244
Roberts, Benjamin, 161
Rousseau, Jean Jacques, 61-64, 65, 75, 130, 289

Salzmann, Christian Gottlief, 275
Silvius, Aeneas, 40-41

Name Index

Smith, Adam, 246
Snedden, David, 155
Socrates, 7, 37
Sparks, Jared, 239
Spencer, Herbert, 154-155, 156, 217, 220
Stalin, Joseph, 112, 113
Stowe, Harriet Beecher, 291
Studebaker, John W., 160
Sturm, Johann, 42, 47, 49, 52, 70

Terry, Robert, 279
Thales, 257
Theodoric, 25
Theodosius, 19
Thorndike, Edward Lee, 258
Thucydides, 13

Trajan, 18

Varro, Marcus, 16
Vergerius, Paulus, 39, 43
Vesalius, Andreas, 261
Vespasian, 18
Viete, Francois, 257
Vitruvius, 17

Wilhelm I, 72-73
Willard, Emma Hart, 291
Wilson, Edmund, 233
Woodward, Calvin Milton, 284-285, 290

Zeno, 11
Zwingli, Ulrich, 47-48

SUBJECT INDEX

Abitur, 109, 110
Academic freedom, 98
Academies (American), 127-129, 134, 136, 140, 171, 231, 263, 286
Academies (French), 70, 79
Academy of Pedagogical Sciences, 118
Accreditation, 175-178
Adult education, 71, 97
Agréges, 98
American Anthropological Association, 243
American Council of Learned Societies, 232
American Economic Association, 248-249
American Geological Institute, 266
American Historical Association, 240, 241, 250
American Home Economics Association, 291
American Institute of Biological Sciences, 265
American Political Science Association, 249
American Sociological Association, 253
Anthropology Curriculum Project, 243
Association of American Geographers, 245
Athenian education, 5-6
Audio-visual media, 305-306
Aufbauschulen, 105, 108

Baccalaureat, 95
Berufsfachschulen, 107
Biological Sciences Curriculum Study, 265
Board of education, (local), 208-209
Boston Academy of Music, 270
Boston English High School, 136-137, 171, 263
Boston Latin Grammar School, 124-125
Brethren of the Common Life, 41-42, 44, 47, 52
Brevet, 95
British education, 67-69, 79-90
Brothers of the Christian School, 69
Brown vs. Board of Education, 161, 168 197-198
Bryce Commission, 79-80
Burgerschule, 73
Burgher schools, 33, 34, 70, 124
Burnham Committees, 89-90

Calisthenics, 219, 277
Carnegie Corporation, 143, 157, 259
Carnegie unit rule, 143, 178
Catechetical schools, 27
Catechumenal schools, 27
Cathedral schools, 28, 31, 49, 66, 70
Certificate of Secondary Education, 87
Chantry schools, 33, 34
Chemical Bond Approach Project, 262
Chemical Education Materials Study, 262
Chivalry, 29-30
Church education, see private education
Civil Rights Act of 1964, 162-163
Classes d' orientation, 91
Classes nouvelles, 91
Classical-humanistic curriculum, 66, 67, 71, 125, 127, 288
Coeducation, 113, 137, 140
College Entrance Examination Board, 230, 259
Colleges, 19, 50-52, 70, 91, 92, 93, 94, 95
Collegiate schools, 28
Commissioner of education, (State), 203-204
Commission de l' Ecole Unique, 91
Commission for the Creation of Public Schools, 74
Commission on Economic Education, 248-249
Commission on Life Adjustment Education, 160-161
Commission on Social Studies, 240
Commission on the Reorganization of Secondary Education, 141, 154-156, 168, 241
Committee for Economic Development, 249
Committee of Fifteen, 172
Committee of Nine, 154, 155, 287
Committee of Privy Council on Education, 68
Committee of Seven, 240, 241, 250
Committee of Ten, 141-142, 151, 172 178, 240, 248, 261, 263, 265, 266
Committee on College Entrance Requirements, 141, 143, 151

- 314 -

Subject Index

Committee on Economy of Time in Education, 141, 154, 173
Committee on Six Year Courses, 141, 173
Committee on the Articulation of High School and College, 141
Common Entrance Examination, 80, 86
Common school district, 207
Comprehensive secondary school, (British), 82, 83
Compulsory education, 68, 70, 71, 72, 81, 89, 92-93, 95, 97, 105, 106, 113
Cooperative Study of Secondary School Standards, 177-178
Core curriculum, 222, 241
Council for the Advancement of Secondary Education, 248
Council of Trent, 49-50, 52
Counter-Reformation education, 49-50, 50-52
County school district, 208
County superintendent of schools, 210-211
Court schools, 28-29, 34, 39, 66, 124
Cultural education, (French), 96, 97
Cycle de determination, 91
Cycle d' orientation, 91

Desegregation, 161-163, 197-198
Deutsche Oberschulen, 105, 108
Direct-grant schools, (British), 81, 82
Dramatic arts education, 273
Driver education, 278, 279

Eagleton Institute of Politics, 251
Earth Science Curriculum Project, 266
Ecoles moyennes, 92
Education Act of 1870, (British), 67, 68-69
Education Act of 1902, (British), 69, 80
Education Act of 1944, (British), 80, 89, 90
Educational Policies Commission, 158-159, 168, 178
Eight year School, (Soviet), 114-115
Eight year Study, 157-158, 168, 232
Elementary-Secondary Education Act, 166, 167, 168, 191-192, 194
"Eleven Plus," See Common Entrance Examination
English Curriculum Commission, 226, 227-228
English language arts, 225-229
English Public Schools, 49, 52, 67, 79-80, 83-84, 86
Epicureanism, 11, 20
Everson Case Decision, 196

Fachschulen, 108
Factor Act, 67
Federal aid, 184-194

Feinberg law, 196-197
Fine arts education, 220, 269-273
Foreign language arts, 230-233
Franklin's Academy, 127, 129, 231
Freeman's Bureau, 185
French education, 69-70, 91-99
Fund for the Advancement of Education, 259
Furstenschulen, 29

General Certificate of Education, 86-87
General education, 83, 91, 92, 95, 116, 298
G. I. Bill of Rights, see Servicemen's Readjustment Act
Grammar school, (British), 80, 81, 82, 87
Grammar school, (German), 109
Grammaticus, 15
Greek education, 3-11, 215-216
Grundschule, 105, 107, 108
Guilds, 30, 33-34
Guild schools, 33-34
Gymnasium, 47, 52, 70, 73, 74, 104, 105, 108-109, 112, 153
Gymnastics, 219, 275, 276, 277

Handicapped children, see special education
Harvard, 125, 263
Harvard Physics Project, 264
Hatch Act of 1887, 186
Health education, 219, 277-278
Hedonism, 10-11, 20
Hellenistic education, 11-14, 15, 216
Herbartians, 65, 272
Higher Education Act, 190, 192
High School Geography Project, 245
High schools, 136-148
Home Economics, 281, 291-293
Hosic Report, 226
Humanism, 37-38, 216-217
Humanistic education, 38-39, 49
Humanities, 216-217, 225-235

Impacted areas school aid, 187-188
Imperative Educational Needs of Youth, 159
Industrial Arts, 215, 281, 288-291
Initiation rite, see puberty rites

Jesuit schools, see Society of Jesus
Job Corps, 190
Joint Council on Economic Education, 248
Journalism, 234-235
Junior college, 152-153, 167, 175
Junior college district, 175, 208
Junior high school, 151-152, 167, 172-174, 228, 231, 233, 241, 244-245, 258, 271, 272, 290, 292

Kalamazoo Decision, 139-140

Langevin Commission, 91
Latin grammar school, 14, 34, 48, 49, 52, 58, 66-67, 124-125, 126, 127, 128, 130, 131, 134, 225, 230
Lantham Act, 187
Law of 1833, (French), 70
Liberal arts, 25, 26-27, 28, 30, 32, 45-46, 58, 95, 123, 215
Liberal education, 38, 39, 41, 42, 185, 298-299, 300-303
Life adjustment education, 160-161, 168
Lincoln-Filene Center Citizenship Study, 251
Local Education Authorities, 69, 80, 81, 87, 88, 89
Long programs, (French), 95-96
Loyalty oaths, 197
Ludus litterarius, 15
Lycees, 70, 91, 92, 93, 94, 95, 98, 153

Maieutics, 304, 306
Massachusetts Law of 1642, 125
Massachusetts Law of 1647, 125-126
Massachusetts Law of 1827, 137-138
Massachusetts School Law of 1852, 138
Mathematics education, 257-260
Medieval education, 24-34, 216
Middle States Association of Colleges and Secondary Schools, 176
Mittleschulen, 106, 107
Modern Language Association, 231, 232
Modern Language Study, 231
Modern secondary school, (British), 80, 82, 85, 89
Monastic schools, 27-28, 66
Morrill Act, 185, 282
Museum, 13
Music Educators National Conference, 270

Napoleonic laws of 1802 and 1808, 69-70
National Business Education Association, 287
National Commission on Safety Education, 279
National Conference on Uniform Requirements in English, 225-226
National Council for Geographic Education, 245
National Council for the Social Studies, 251
National Council of Teachers of English, 226, 227, 229
National Council of Teachers of Mathematics, 258

National Defense Education Act, 157, 168, 188-190, 194, 251
National Education Association, 141, 142, 143, 155, 158, 172, 226, 240, 279, 287
National Education League, (England), 68
National Science Foundation, 188, 263, 265
National Teachers' Association, see National Education Association
National Teachers Corps, 190
Newcastle Commission, 68
New England Association of Colleges and Secondary Schools, 176
North Central Association of Colleges and Secondary Schools, 176
Northwest Ordinance, 169, 184

Oberrealschule, 73, 104, 105, 108
Oregon Case Decision, 195-196

Paedagogus, 5, 12, 15
Palaestra, 5
Parochial schools, see private education
Phillips Academy, 127
Physical education, 38, 40, 52, 97, 215, 216, 218-219, 275-277
Physical Science Study Committee, 263-264
Plessy vs. Ferguson, 161-162, 198
Practical arts education, 281, 288-293
Premier cycle, 93-94, 96
President's Council on Youth Fitness, 278
Primitive education, 1-2
Private education, 79-80, 93, 106
Programmed learning, 305, 306
Progressive education, 147-148, 221
Progressive Education Association, 157, 232
Progymnasium, 73, 104, 108
Project Head Start, 190
Prorealgymnasien, 104, 108
Prussian education, 71-73
Puberty rites, 2
Public Prayer Decision of 1962, 165-166, 168
Public Schools Commission, (British, 1861), 79
Public Schools Commission, (British, 1965), 84

Quadrivium, 25, 26, 27, 28, 215, 216
Quincy Grammar School, 171

Rahmenplan, 109
Ratio Studiorium, 51-52
Realgymnasium, 73, 104, 105, 108, 112

Subject Index

Realprogymnasium, 73
Realschule, 72, 73, 104, 108, 217
Reason, Age of, 55-56
Reformagymnasien, 105
Reformation education, 43-48, 217
Religious instruction, 72, 81-82, 84, 85, 93, 107, 113, 196
Rennaissance education, 37-43, 216
Rhetor, school of, 15, 19
Roman education, 14-20, 216
Russian education, 73-75; also, see Soviet education

Safety education, 278-279
School Mathematics Study Group, 259-260
School principal, 209-210
Schools Inquiry Commission, (British), 79
Science education, 217-218, 260-267
Scriptorium, 27
Secondary School Code of 1864, (Russian), 112
Secondary school, (Soviet), 115
Second cycle, (French), 94-96, 96-97
Senior high school, 228, 229, 240, 241, 245, 258-259, 271, 272-273, 290-291, 292
Servicemen's Readjustment Act, 187, 190
Seven Cardinal Principles, 154, 155, 156, 158, 168
Short programs, (French), 95
Six-year High School, 174-175
"Sloyd," 289
Smith-Hughes Act, 156-157, 168, 186, 282, 285, 287, 292
Social sciences, 238-254
Social studies, 238-254
Society for the Propagation of the Gospel in Foreign Parts, 126
Society of Jesus, 69
Sociological Resources for Secondary Schools Project, 253
Sophists, 6-7
Soviet education, 112-118
Spartan education, 4-5
Special education, 90
Specialized schools, (Soviet), 115-116
Speech education, 233-234

Stanford Language Arts Investigation, 231-232
State board of education, 202-203
State commissioner of education, 202, 203-204
State department of education, 202-206
Stoicism, 10, 11; 20
Superintendent of public instruction, 202, 203-204
Superintendent of schools, (local), 209

Teacher education, 89, 98, 110, 117, 140
Technical education, 74, 92, 95-96, 116
Technical school, (British), 80, 82-83, 85-86
The Northwest Association of Secondary and Higher Schools, 177
The Southern Association of Colleges and Secondary Schools, 176-177
Township district, 207
Trivium, 25, 26, 32, 215, 216

U.S. Bureau of Education, see U.S. Office of Education
U.S. Commissioner of Education, 160, 186
U.S. Department of Health, Education, and Welfare, 186, 193
U.S. Office of Education, 144, 157, 160, 162, 173, 185-186, 193-194, 205, 229, 259, 281, 283

VISTA, 190
Vocational education, 48, 67, 95, 97, 107-108, 115, 116, 156-157, 168, 190, 215, 219-220, 281, 282-288, 298, 299-300
Vocational training, see vocational education
Volkschule, 107, 108, 171
Vorschule, 105

Western Association of Schools and Colleges, 177
West German education, 104-112
White House Conferences on Education, 164, 166
Work-training programs, 190
Writing and reading schools, 33

Youth Employment Service, (British), 90